To Na-Ma

The *The* PHOTOJOURNALISM *of* DEL HALL

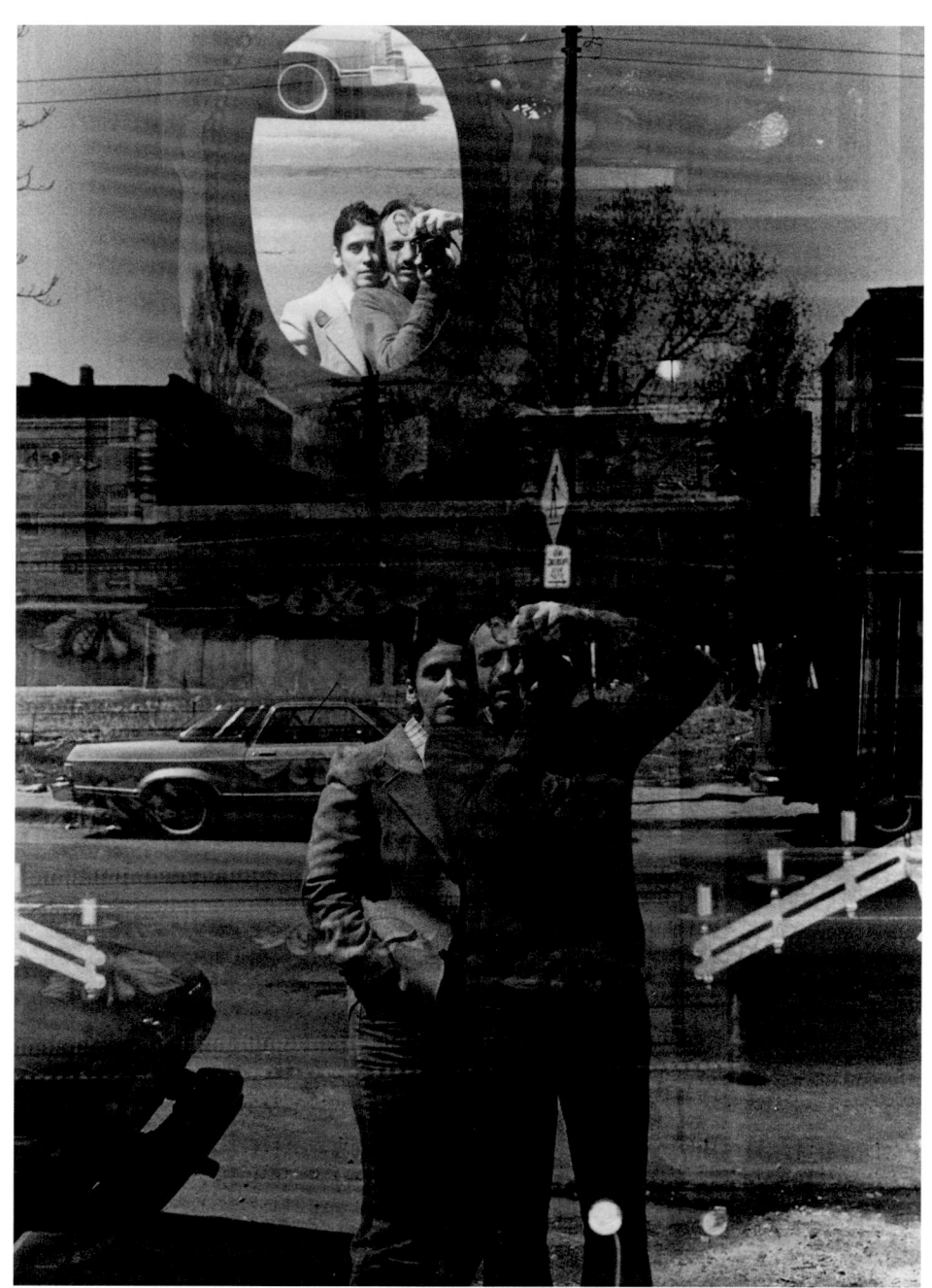

The PHOTOJOURNALISM *of* DEL HALL

NEW ORLEANS AND BEYOND, 1950s–2000s

RICHARD CAMPANELLA

LOUISIANA STATE UNIVERSITY PRESS

BATON ROUGE

Published with the assistance of the V. Ray Cardozier Fund

Published by Louisiana State University Press
Copyright © 2015 by Louisiana State University Press

Manufactured in Canada
First printing

Frontispiece: Double selfie, 1970s-style, Del and Ginger Hall

DESIGNER: *Mandy McDonald Scallan*
TYPEFACE: *Calluna*
PRINTER AND BINDER: *Friesens Corporation*

Library of Congress Cataloging-in-Publication Data
Campanella, Richard.
  The photojournalism of Del Hall : New Orleans and beyond, 1950s–2000s / Richard Campanella.
     pages cm
  Includes bibliographical references.
  ISBN 978-0-8071-6066-4 (cloth : alk. paper) — ISBN 978-0-8071-6067-1 (pdf) — ISBN 978-0-8071-6068-8 (epub) — ISBN 978-0-8071-6069-5 (mobi) 1. Hall, Del, 1935– 2. Photojournalists—United States—Biography. 3. New Orleans (La.) —Biography. I. Title.
  TR140.H257C36 2016
  770.9763'35—dc23

                                                        2014049785

CONTENTS

PREFACE

ONE DAY IN 2008, I received a phone call from a stranger on an unusual mission. He had a collection of aerial photographs of New Orleans he had captured fifty-one years earlier, stowed away ever since, and hoped to place them in appreciative hands. A local archivist suggested he call me, a Tulane University geographer who relishes historical aerial imagery of New Orleans. "You found the right guy," I said ten seconds into the conversation.

What I didn't realize at the time was that the caller, a Chicago resident named Del Hall who had been born in New Orleans in 1935, had a much bigger story to tell. In subsequent meetings at French Quarter coffee shops, I learned how this son of a Mexican immigrant, born during the Depression and raised in segregated public housing, had witnessed and filmed a thrilling sweep of world history, and in the process helped invent modern television news. He documented key moments in Louisiana's civil rights struggle, got arrested at a sit-in, single-handedly covered Vatican II for a first-of-its-kind color news documentary, kissed Pope John XXIII's ring and sat at Ringo Starr's drums, got chased by the Ku Klux Klan and shot at by the Viet Cong, became the first journalist beaten by police at the 1968 Democratic Convention, served as a witness for the Chicago Seven, covered President Richard Nixon in Moscow, worked regularly with CBS's Walter Cronkite and *60 Minutes,* won an Emmy for his camerawork on Charles Kuralt's *On the Road* and an Emmy nomination for his Vietnam work, was nearly killed in a helicopter crash at the America's Cup, and had before his camera everyone from Martin Luther King to Juan Perón, from Earl K. Long to John F. Kennedy, from a rude Bette Davis to a jovial Dalai Lama. From the 1950s to the 2000s, Del Hall was at the forefront of every major media revolution—the transformation from print to televised news, still photography to film, film to videotape, magnetic to digital video, messenger boys to the Internet for data delivery, and linear editing of both film and video to computer-based nonlinear editing of digital video.

I found Del's story compelling on a number of grounds. His memories of growing up in midcentury New Orleans abounded in the sort of gritty local detail and personal intimacy that, to an empirical researcher like me, evade and enrich the reams of municipal records and census data I usually analyze. His job as a television news cameraman starting in 1959 enabled him to pioneer a new profession and, as he says, "invent it as we went along." His eyewitness accounts of a dizzying itinerary of world events add to the historical record, and his awareness of the power of the camera elevates the oft-overlooked and uncredited role of the cameraman to a position equal to that of any other in journalism.

Perhaps that's what I found most inspiring about Del's story: it demonstrated that the quiet observer in the corner, with a keen eye for what's truly important and the skill to capture it, can help make history, and in the process, rise personally from the most humble of circumstances to the top of his profession. That the man in question was a native-born New Orleanian "from the Projects" only added to my wish to tell this story. That he had a vast collection of amazing photographs—most never published, including those aerials—cinched my conviction.

When I first broached with Del and his wife Ginger (who is also his professional partner) my interest in writing a book on their experiences, they seemed surprised—delighted, in fact—and offered to match my commitment. We agreed that I, as researcher and author, would maintain control over the content and interpretation; this would not be an authorized biography, and no money would change hands. I proceeded to interview Del and Ginger for twenty-three hours in the summer of 2013 and followed up with hundreds of email communications with them, their colleagues, and other informants. Del and Ginger provided me stacks of personal records, which, along with the interview content, I cross-checked against primary and reliable secondary sources. That autumn, the three of us inspected Del's thousands of still photographs and newsreels, some untouched in fifty years, and culled from them the best and most important.

One evening after a marathon interview session, we decamped to a Fourth of July picnic hosted graciously by Gigi Pritzker at her family farm outside Chicago. There I met, among others, the Halls' longtime friend and colleague Bill Kurtis, of A&E *Investigative Reports* and *American Justice,* whose career also dates to the early days of television news. I listened intently as the old friends compared notes on specific historic moments they had witnessed and documented for the world to see. "We always had the best seat in the house," Bill mused.

Indeed—and my hope is that readers will gain a comparable seat to the exciting world of news cameramen through one of the most tumultuous eras in American history.

The *The* PHOTOJOURNALISM *of* DEL HALL

TAKE ONE

South Rampart Street Blues, 1935–1959

NEW ORLEANS IN the 1930s was a world that still bore the patina of the 1800s. Most of the city's building stock dated from that century, or the prior one, and antebellum times remained living memories for elder citizens, many of whom were either former Confederates or former slaves. One could still occasionally hear in the streets vestiges of the French language— or, more commonly, Sicilian, Spanish, German, and other tongues, in this, the most cosmopolitan city of the South.

It was also the largest and most important, a mercantilist port for the financing and transshipping of commodities between vast hinterlands and forelands. Splendid opulence could be found in places like the Garden District and St. Charles Avenue, and plutocrats wielded great power from the boardrooms of shipping lines, banks, law offices—and firms like the United Fruit Company, which controlled much of the tropical fruit industry, and Central America, from its downtown office.

For every patrician, however, there were many more indigents, usually of African ancestry, and for every indigent there was roughly an equal number in the laborer and middle classes, usually with bloodlines traceable to all corners of the Gallic, Gaelic, Anglo, Saxon, Latin, and Slavic worlds. On gritty streets such as South Rampart lived New Orleanians of these varied classes and castes, in striking residential propinquity.

Into this world was born, in 1935, one Delos Frederick Hall. He derived from plebeian stock nearly as diverse and idiosyncratic as the city itself; indeed, his family tree generally resembles a map of the city's demographic pathways. His father José had been born in Tabasco, Mexico, the son of a beautiful *doña* named Delfina Ruiz and a dashing southerner named Delos Lamar Hall, an Atlantan who somehow found himself practicing dentistry in the middle of revolutionary Mexico. Ella, his mother, had been born in New Orleans of deep-rooted French and German blood that blended later with Anglo-Saxon lineages from Illinois and New York. That northern contingent had arrived in Louisiana "following the races"—that is, betting on horses, until they found themselves broke and stuck in New Orleans. A comparable financial fate was in store for the Mexican side of the family, which had immigrated to New Orleans and invested in a boardinghouse—a fine idea for the Roaring Twenties, but a bust during the Depression. Delfina and Delos did, however, manage to put their young son (who, like so many immigrant children, preferred an Americanized "Joe," and later "Mike," over his baptismal "José") into Holy Cross Boarding School in the Lower Ninth Ward.

Joe Hall met and married Ella in 1934, and a year later came infant Del, courtesy of the old Touro Hospital. Twenty-one and lacking an identifiable profession, Joe managed to provide for his family by selling wooden floorboards and working other odd jobs. Perhaps to hide his humble position, Joe, or "Pops" as his children would call him, was something of a dandy. He prided himself on his attire, as most Americans did in this era, donning immaculate white shirts and having his pants pressed midday to keep the crease. He also had a penchant for booze—a connoisseur of scotch, he fancied himself, the type who would send back a bottle—and an archetypal New Orleans *laissez faire* disposition, neither of which were good survival strategies for the Depression.

Inevitably, Pops's meager income fell short of the going rent for a decent home. So he had to swallow his pride and submit to the quiet humiliation dreaded by all young husbands: moving in with the in-laws. Fortunately, "Na-Ma," as Del would call his maternal grandmother, was a warm and gregarious soul, with an eye that twinkled mischievously, a mouth that cussed like a sailor (and smoked like a chimney), and a face that blossomed easily into a loving smile. Her husband, "Grandpa Fred," despite his predilection for the bottle, kept productively employed as an amateur radio repairman and a projectionist in good standing with the International Alliance of Theatrical Stage Employees. His employer was the "C-theater" people—the Lazarus family, which ran the Center, the Coliseum, the Circle, the Crown, the Carver, and the Cinema—and he worked every day of the year except Good Friday. This was, after all, a thoroughly Catholic town.

It was that professional connection that landed Na-Ma and Grandpa Fred a good deal on a convenient if not tranquil apartment at 129 South Rampart, on the "uptown side" of Canal Street, the bustling Broadway of New Orleans. Sharing a rear wall with the grand Loew's State Theatre, the building was controlled by the local IATSE chapter, and because the union held meetings on the second floor, it gave member-in-good-standing Fred a break on the rent in exchange for his watchful eye.

To reach their third-floor apartment in the stout circa-1850s Greek Revival storehouse, the three generations of family members had to brave theater crowds and patrons of the adjacent Joe's Bar and Grand Hotel, ascend an extraordinarily steep switchback staircase above the Busy Bee Shoe Repair, proceed down a shadowy hall past the battered wooden chairs and judge's desk where the unionists met, and climb another twin staircase to arrive finally at Na-Ma's door. The high ceilings and transoms inside, typical of antebellum architecture, towered incongruously over the family's painfully modest domesticity. To Del's young eyes, however, it was all the world, and what particularly fascinated him—when he wasn't piddling about in his little metal toy car—was the forbidden terrain of Grandpa Fred's radio room, replete with the delicately intricate machinery of mass communications. It suggested there was a larger and more interesting world out there, the likes of which stoke a little boy's imagination.

Na-Ma's apartment, which would become Del's home for his first six years, could not have been better positioned as a locus of local society. Two blocks away was the First Precinct Police Station, an intimidating fortress rimmed with medieval-looking towers built in the 1890s for constabulary, courts, and incarceration. A few blocks upriver was the malodorous "Jahncke Basin," where barges on the circa-1830s New Basin Canal unloaded raw materials at the docks by the Jahncke warehouse. Closer to Na-Ma's, steps past Pierre's French Pastries, was the heart of the South's biggest Chinatown, where since the 1870s merchants operated a colorful enclave of notions shops and groceries—and where jazz legend Jelly Roll Morton would buy opium to deliver to the madams in the red-light district three blocks downriver. That den of iniquity was the infamous Storyville—opened in 1897, closed in 1917 by order of the Department of the Navy, and by now a slum. Storyville's business had since shifted to the so-called Tango Belt at the edge of the French Quarter, and, by the 1930s, to an up-and-coming nightclub district on a street named Bourbon. All of this lay within five minutes of Na-Ma's.[1]

Despite its grit, South Rampart at Canal also prided itself as a theater district—tops in the South, boosters said—and if first-rate shows and A-list entertainers ever came to New Orleans, it was to the Saenger, Loew's, and Orpheum they came. *Gone with the Wind* and *The Wizard of Oz* both premiered locally within steps of Del's bed, along with hundreds of live shows featuring a litany of famous names.

Geographical proximity in New Orleans neighborhoods, however, never had much to do with social proximity. Elegance and eminence in the Canal Street theater district hardly spilled over into neighboring blocks, and citywide, whites and blacks may have shared the same shotgun-doubles, but otherwise occupied different strata in the social hierarchy. The Loew's State Theatre had the most influence on Del because it was literally next door—the "colored" door, that is, with its modest marquee both separate and unequal to the main Canal entrance for whites. Black folks would line up outside 129 South Rampart, buy their tickets from a constantly primping older white woman encased in a tiny glass booth, and head up to the "colored" balcony. Later, they might cross South Rampart for a drink at the Elite Lounge—or rather, its "colored" side, which was separated from the white side by the kind of lattice you would put in your garden. In this peculiar manner, each race fulfilled the mandate of segregation while otherwise being able to see, hear, and interact with the other.

Same for the streetcars rolling past the Halls' apartment. Black and white passengers were separated by a movable screen pegged into the seatbacks, and anyone of any race could relocate it depending on the racial distribution of the ridership. When the streetcar reached the end of the line, the conductor would flip the varnished wooden seatbacks, shift the screen to where he estimated the racial line might form, and seat himself at the opposite controls for the return trip.

Taxis were more strictly segregated; different companies served different races. Blacks would be picked up by Night Hawk and other outfits; whites, by Checker, Yellow, and White Fleet cabs (still active). Hacks had to make snap racial judgments—not the easiest thing, given this famously miscegenated population—on prospective riders as they braved downtown traffic. "[Segregation] was perfectly normal; everyone seemed happy," reflects Del seventy years later, channeling his childhood perspectives. Pausing, he adds, "I could be wrong about that." When asked if a standing white passenger could eject an already seated black patron on a streetcar or bus, he recoils. "Oh *no;* that would just be unfair."

Dance halls, vaudeville venues, social aid and pleasure clubs (benevolent societies and fraternal organizations), saloons, "nighteries" (night clubs), illicit gambling dens, brothels, hotels ranging from sleazy to swanky, and eateries from the everyday to the epicurean could all be found within minutes of Na-Ma's apartment. At one end, for example, was the Roosevelt Hotel, where dignitaries and divas stayed, and where bluebloods wined and dined at the trendiest clubs. And just a couple of blocks away was madam Norma Wallace's brothel, where it was (correctly) rumored that just about any sexual desire could be satisfied for the right price. Equidistant in the opposite direction was 1019 Gravier Street, a bordello so sinister that mere mention of its address made eyebrows rise.

Along South Rampart proper, particularly after Common Street, ran a long line of black-owned businesses, Jewish-owned pawn shops and tailors, and Italian-owned butchers and bakeries serving the predominantly black clientele who lived in the wards "behind" South Rampart. Louis Armstrong, who had been born here in 1901, called this neighborhood the "back o' town," a term that spoke to its physical position with respect to the Mississippi riverfront as well as its déclassé social position. Del Hall was not quite born in the back-of-town, nor in the front-of-town, but rather along the margin, between rich and poor, neighbor to white and black, privy to elegance and decadence and everything in between. It was a perfect place, one may surmise, to observe and bear witness.

South Rampart did not divide as much as connect. Everything was connected in this biggest little city in America, or the Americas. New Orleans seemed, at least to outsiders, marvelously exotic, with a hint of the Caribbean and a dash of the Mediterranean, an air of aristocracy and a scent of Bohemia. But it was also down-home southern, particularly to natives, and whatever mystique the rest of the world saw into this ostensibly foreign city, those who lived on South Rampart suffered no such delusions of grandeur. Folks in those sorts of neighborhoods dressed the best they could afford, and "sir" and "ma'am" accompanied every salutation. But they also spoke a port-city brogue that turned "ask" to "ax," "first" to "foist," and "oysters" to "ersters," and everyone there seemed to know each other's "momma-n-'em." Mule-drawn carts were still a common sight, as were newsboys in knickers, messengers with satchels, and little black boys toting handmade wooden stands, asking *"Shine, Mista? Shine, Mista?"* Many back-of-town streets were all but unpaved, and people still called the uneven sidewalks *banquettes,* a throwback to old French times. Overhead, utility wires dangling from leaning poles cluttered the airspace, and smokestacks of food-processing plants broke the skyline—big breweries on Bourbon and on Decatur, a macaroni manufacturer on Chartres, a huge sugar-processing plant on North Peters, even Dickey's potato chip maker directly downstairs from Na-Ma's—all of which spewed into the air gastronomic odors fair and foul, and entailed constant visits from noisy fuming trucks. As if that weren't enough, downtowners would occasionally find their neighborhoods blanketed in greasy black soot as captains thoughtlessly blew out their ships' boiler tubes after a period of inactivity. Exhaust and other pollutants bonded with the humidity and enveloped the city in omnipresent insalubrious miasma. And then there was the heat, relentless, from May through September, climaxing with an occasional hurricane. Five people crammed into a tiny flat under such conditions made for a frazzled household.

With all due deference to their elders, Joe and Ella Hall longed for a place of their own. High rent stood in their way, and in that regard they were not alone. Politicians knew that the cost of urban housing beleaguered families during the Depression, and in 1934 and 1937 Congress passed two acts that got Washington into the business of landlording. Partnered with federal agencies, the Housing Authority of New Orleans (HANO) surveyed neighborhoods for what they considered to be unsightly and dangerous slums, to be replaced by the latest in modern progressive housing design. Topping its list was that dilapidated district formerly known as Storyville. In 1940 workers bulldozed the old bordellos and cribs and erected in their place the Iberville Housing Development, a superblock of brick garden apartments with airy verandahs and green space, designed to bring architectural order to social disorder through utopian urban planning.

Racial order, however, remained paramount, and like nearly everything else in this city, "the Projects" were strictly segregated. The Iberville was one of two whites-only public housing developments in the front-of-town, while another one (the Lafitte, although Del never knew it by this name) a few blocks down and behind North Claiborne was for "colored," along with other housing projects farther back. The Halls' race and income level qualified them for residency in Iberville, and while a certain stigma was attached to the locale, it was nonetheless, finally, a place of their own. It was also brand new, with amenities unknown on South Rampart, like a fenced garden, a porch, a clothesline, kerosene heating instead of dirty coal, wood parquet floors, and best of all, playmates next door. A generally happy childhood ensued for Del at 1507 Bienville at Marais. The toponym "Bienville," it's worth pointing out, saluted the French colonial who established New Orleans in 1718 on the edge of a marshy swamp—*marais* in French—while his brother, Iberville, had founded Louisiana nineteen years earlier. Names like these circulated in the deep social memory of this past-oriented society, and they came from a history that still lived and breathed.

One chilly gray afternoon shortly after the Halls moved into Iberville, Na-Ma came running over from South Rampart. This was unusual: while the Halls went to Na-Ma's every Friday for dinner, rarely did she come to the Projects. Her distraught look told six-year-old Del that something was amiss. He and everyone else soon learned that the Japanese had attacked a place called Pearl Harbor, and that this surely meant a two-front war. New Orleans, the nation's principal southern port, would play a heroic role in the ensuing global conflict, as an embarkation point, a nexus of the southern military training circuit, and most importantly, as home to Andrew Jackson Higgins's seven gargantuan ship plants and their thirty thousand workers.

Back in the Projects, children could only dream, and dread, what was going on out there. The only terrors locally were little Jackie and Albie Demen, the source of most neighborhood mayhem. One time, when a bullet hole appeared on Miss Gene's front door, police ascertained that the trajectory pointed straight to Albie's lair. Del nonetheless befriended Jackie and managed to redirect the Demens' marksmanship away from Miss Gene's door and toward the Nazis. Together they would sit in the courtyard and draw pictures of P-47s shooting down Messerschmitts and B-17's leveling German factories. (Many years later, Del happened to photograph Albie—in a police lineup.)

Everyone did their part for the war effort. Neighbors attended the Parade of Stars bond-buying rallies at City Park, and tried to follow all the rationing rules and mobilizations. Del himself dutifully gathered coins for Roosevelt's March of Dimes ("for as long as I lived in the Projects," he recounts, "it seemed like Joe Louis was the heavyweight champ and Franklin D. Roosevelt was president"), volunteered for the paper drive at his St. Joseph School on South Roman, and went with his New Orleans Athletic Club wrestling and boxing team to entertain veterans convalescing at local hospitals. There he would see up close the consequences of the far-off violence: paralysis, missing limbs, bodies wrapped in gauze, as well as Axis prisoners behind barbed wire by the air station on Elysian Fields Avenue.

Pops, meanwhile, served as an air raid warden, a duty that he took with the utmost gravity. He marched solemnly around the Projects, unarmed but armored by a dented World War I helmet, and berated eye-rolling neighbors who violated however briefly the frequent black-out drills. Mother wore hinged wooden-sole shoes (leather was rationed) and dutifully saved her kitchen grease in metal cans. She negotiated the family food rations as well, but being a mother first, and a friend of the butcher over at the Canal-Villere, she managed to come home with more than her share of fresh-killed chickens, run through the plucking machine, and high-grade beef, always ground twice.

There was now another mouth to feed: a baby sister named Sharon, born in 1943, who was as adorable to her parents as she was a nuisance to her brother. For extra food Mother expanded her shopping radius to include the French Market, which at the time was "a live, real marketplace . . .

not a tourism attraction," and Central Grocery across Decatur, where she would buy dry garbanzo beans right out of the bag. Del would inhale deeply the store's rich aroma, still discernible today. When times were flush, fancier foods could be found at Solari's on Royal, which felt like an emporium in Paris or delicatessen in Manhattan. Otherwise, basic staples could be had at any one of a dozen open-stall public markets or Italian corner stores.

Mother, Del, and infant Sharon shared the streets with thousands of troops in transit, who took their leave from southern boot camps to sightsee in the French Quarter or debauch on Bourbon Street. Rarely were uniforms seen in the Projects, unless servicemen had relatives there, like Uncle Richie, an artilleryman on the Western front.

War was adults' business; children had their own world, one of work and play, preferably the latter. Work meant obeying the diligent Sisters of Charity at St. Joseph School who, in their starched wimples and stern but kindly manner, taught one particular adage that would ring in Del's ears for the rest of his life:

> Good, better, best.
> Never let it rest.
> 'Til your good is better
> And your better's best.

Work also meant, a few years later, a paper route. This was Del's first job, for which he had to acquire a "Louisiana Street Trades Permit for Boys 12 to 15." Before dawn he would pick up his papers at a depot on Bourbon Street, where he would see, amid flickering neon, the last of the previous night's revelers tumbling into taxis. Mounting his bike, he glided through the predawn streets across North Rampart, amid houses that were at least a century old, tracking addresses and remembering when to toss or hold. His most dreaded spot?—the old warehouses on Marais, from which would swarm a thousand bats, the terror of local children. His favorite?—Sunrise Bakery at Orleans and North Claiborne, where he would succumb to the wafting scent and treat himself to an entire French loaf as dawn broke over

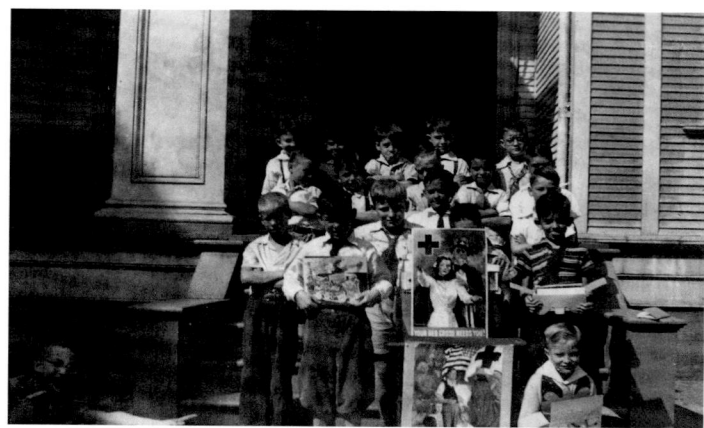

Del (second row from top, second from left) with St. Joseph School classmates during World War II. *Hall Family Collection.*

the splendid Claiborne oaks. "That smell would get you every time," he savors. "*Every* time."

But enough of work. Playtime was happy time, and for Iberville kids there were myriad options. They relished the delectable spookiness of the above-ground St. Louis cemeteries, playing make-believe at the crumbling tombs of old Creoles, long-dead masters and slaves, voodoo queens like Marie Laveau, and pirates like Dominique You, whose crypt Del can identify to this day. They would scramble upon the last remnants of Storyville—a few old cribs that had not yet fallen for the expanding Iberville, as well as the remains of Mahogany Hall and the sporting house of madam Lulu White. Project kids also gathered around "The Circle," a green space with a ringed concrete walkway, where, in summer, the superintendent would turn on the sprinklers for children to frolic in the cooling mist and, on Christmas mornings, kids would raise a screeching racket trying out their new metal-wheeled roller skates.

The streets around the Projects were full of amusing characters, some pushing picturesque carts or guiding mule-drawn wagons. There was the Fruit Man ("*I gotta gotta gotta peaches, lay-dees; I gotta gotta gotta melons*"); the Rag Man, who bought and sold old clothes at a time when paper towels were scarce; the Bottling Company Man, who delivered root beer crates up two floors; the Cleaning Man and the

Milk Man, who Del swears got around in an electric truck with no doors and a stand-up steering wheel; the Knife Sharpener, with his cringe-inducing grinding wheel; the Kerosene Man, who carried five-gallon cans up the back stairs to the heater; and "the Mad Russian," a crusty old comrade who sold five-cent ice cream while children giggled behind his back. Relatives visited regularly, and Del and Sharon were always particularly happy to see Grandma Minnie, who would prepare foods from her native Mexico—specialties like Tabasco-style mole sauce over chicken, a reprieve from the standard southern cooking of Mother and Na-Ma.

The Projects abounded in resident characters as well. Across the way, for example, was Jackie and Albie's dad, who shouted loud enough for the whole neighborhood to hear. In adjacent units were Miss Bernice the gardener and her husband Mr. Bill, a gruff cab driver better avoided, and Bobby Hiver the magician, whose bag of tricks piqued Del's growing interest in observation and spectacle. Next door was a father who dressed in a tuxedo to wait tables at Antoine's, a job so desirable that it was rumored *you* had to pay *them* to work. Little Jules Johnson, a budding opera singer (or so he thought), lived around the corner, near a young boy who once set himself on fire playing with matches. Aside from some of the peddlers, the only black faces in Iberville were Lafitte residents who would cut through to get to Canal Street. No problems arose from this racial-spatial transgression because it was clear those black bodies were on the move. Who knows what the response might have been had they stopped and loitered. None ever did.

Diversion could also be found beyond the Projects. Lunch counters and cafeterias were everywhere—they were the fast food of the era—and the Halls would go to those at the various downtown department stores, or the Holsum's in the Masonic Temple, or Morrison's on Gravier, where waiters in white jackets and silver badges would carry your tray to your table. Christmastime meant a trip to see the animated window displays at the elegant Maison Blanche ("I remember the elevator doors opening like a curtain," Del says, "unveiling the toy department on the third floor"), and the Santa Claus waving outside the century-old D. H. Holmes ("I asked him, 'what happens when you stop believing in Santa Claus?' He answered, 'You stop getting presents.' I never mentioned it again.").

Mardi Gras, of course, was the greatest of all living spectacles. Del and Sharon would dress up in Grandma Minnie's lovingly handmade costumes—he usually ended up in Distinguished Gentleman/Crazy Old Codger get-ups, she in Baby Doll/Little Gypsy outfits—and the whole family would brave the crowds on Canal to see Proteus, Rex, and the mysterious nocturnal Krewe of Comus, its splendid floats manned by masked aristocracy and illuminated by black *flambeaux* carriers.

Del loved to travel "The Belt," a ten-mile circumnavigation of the St. Charles, Carrollton, and Canal streetcar lines, which provided, for all of seven cents, pretty sights and fresh breezes, particularly if you got to sit up front. He participated in the New Orleans Athletic Club's boys' program, which offered wrestling classes and a groundwater-fed pool. NOAC was, of course, segregated by race (only the masseuses were black) as well as gender (men only), but not by age, and everyone—boys, men, elders—swam naked in the salty water. The ferry ride to Algiers and swimming trips to Pontchartrain Beach or West End also provided cheap delights, as did Audubon Park, in that rarefied place called "uptown," where folks talked different and looked different, if they looked at you at all. At the park's zoo, Del and Sharon enjoyed visiting Monkey Island, the simian atoll that never quite gained the fame of Monkey Hill, and the beloved geriatric pachyderm Itema, named for the local *States-Item* newspaper that Del delivered.

Back downtown, Del took in magic shows whenever possible, an interest he acquired from his neighbor in the Projects. The tricks pitted his creativity against his rationality—*was that really magic? Nahhh, see, here's how he's doin' it*—while the exotic costumes and Mideastern music ("In a Persian Market" was the standard) appealed to his sense of adventure. So enthralled was Del that he'd volunteer whenever the magician called for audience participation—like when Harry Blackstone placed Del's hand atop a shrouded cage and caused a dove to disappear, or when Dr. Neff lay

Del on a guillotine and proceeded to chop off his "head"—of cabbage—to the gasps, and later cheers, of the audience. (The doves, Del points out, were not so lucky: a new one was needed for every show.)

At the magic shop on St. Charles, where performers furtively purchased their tricks, Del treated himself to a $5 green-and-yellow parakeet he named Peachy. Inspired by folktales of swashbuckling Louisiana pirates, Del trained Peachy to perch on his shoulder as he wandered about centuries-old streets—down Bienville, to the Southern Railway Station on Canal where he'd read the funny books at the newsstand, across the tracks on Basin and past Norma Wallace's bordello into "the Quarters," New Orleans's oldest neighborhood. His destination, every Saturday, was the Cabildo, the 1799 Spanish governing house, now a museum, where he would spy Napoleon's death mask and the creepy cramped prison in the courtyard, trusty Peachy on his shoulder. (Na-Ma had a more frank take on Del's feathered friend. "All that bird does is sit and shit!," she chortled.)

One September, as the semester got underway at St. Joseph, Del and classmates got an exciting break from childhood routines. A tropical storm was bearing down on New Orleans, the first big one in years. Time off from school! The unnamed Hurricane of 1947 wreaked the most havoc on the city since the Great Storm of 1915, but what twelve-year-old Del remembers most was the strange meteorological tranquility of the storm's vortex, whose edge sideswiped downtown. During that moment, "my dad took me down Marais Street to Canal, to survey [while] the eye passed over. The sky was perfectly clear, [calm] like a church, [and] there was very little damage to the Projects." Fifty-eight years later, a comparable storm named Katrina would put Del's childhood home under four feet of sea water.

Del's favorite pastime was "the show," as everyone called the movies. Every few days, sometimes twice a day, he would march to kitschy palaces with names like the Tudor, the Globe, and his favorite, the Liberty. Best to go alone: his kid sister hated the movies, Mother was indifferent, and Pops would laugh a bit too loud at goofy shorts like "The Three Stooges." Plunking down nine cents for a ticket, he'd watch,

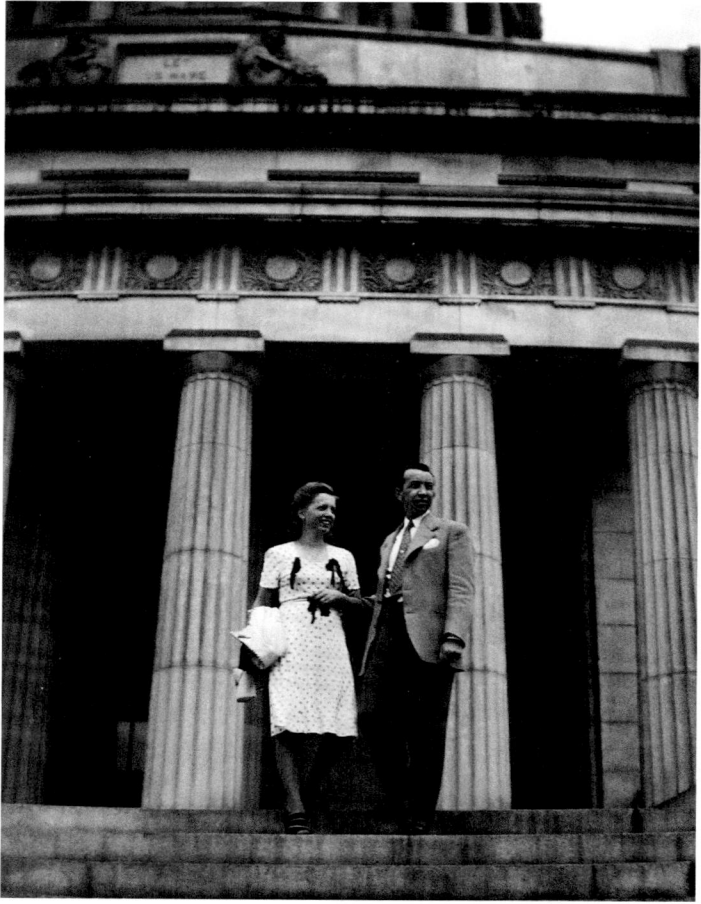

Del's first photograph, of parents Ella and Joe on the steps of Grant's Tomb in Manhattan, 1949. *Photo by Del Hall.*

across very differently, if at all. Between all the technical radio and film paraphernalia in Grandpa Fred's den, and the dazzling final products playing at the movie houses, Del's future began to take form.

Making movies was a pipe dream, but taking pictures fell within reach. Del had long admired the photos and photographers of *Life* magazine, many of whom were quite famous. If filming lion wrestling in Africa was the world's greatest job, *Life* photographer ranked a close second. He also loved the stately gear of the cameraman, the almost sacred aura that freshly exposed film exuded as it came out of the camera, and the excitement as the imagery emerged from the chemistry.

That joy first came in 1949, when the Halls took a train trip to New York City, a pretty big deal for a kid from the Projects. Del got to see Manhattan's famous sights, ride Coney Island's landmark parachute jump, and see a show at Radio City Music Hall, where for the first time in their lives, the Halls sat next to black people. It was at Grant's Tomb that Del got to take his first photograph using the family's bulky box camera. After returning home and developing the film, he thrilled to see that the photograph, of his parents on the monument's steps, came out perfectly. He was smitten.

One day coming home from high school, Del noticed in Reiner's Pawn Shop window a Kodak Retina 35 mm camera, which, unlike a box camera, allowed for photographic experimentation. "I lusted after that Retina," he remembers. How to get it? Pops, who now worked as a bilingual clerk for United Fruit, didn't make enough for such a whim; besides, if Mother didn't intercept Pops's Friday paychecks, he'd probably drink them away at Earl's Lounge or go "on the boat," as disapproving kin would euphemistically call his dalliances. Could Mother buy the camera for him? She had a hard-enough time stretching Pops's pittance; besides, they together often indulged in more merriment than either could afford, what with their forays to the Blue Room and the Fountain Lounge, stargazing the likes of Desi Arnaz and Sophie Tucker.

Then he thought of Na-Ma, who just happened to live directly across the street from Reiner's. Na-Ma was the *best* about stuff like this.

A visit to Na-Ma's had a certain ritual to it. Del would

wide-eyed, decade-old flicks of animal-collector-turned-movie-star Frank Buck and his adventures (*Bring 'Em Back Alive, Wild Cargo, Killer of the Amazon*) capturing feral beasts for American zoos. "That's what got me interested in camera work," he explains. "I thought, what a great job, to go to Africa and film these adventures." He also gained a view of the wider world through newsreels of the conflicts in Europe and Asia and the subsequent Cold War. He made the connection that everything appearing on screen had been witnessed firsthand and up close by a cameraman, and that without that camera and that man, the story would come approach 129 South Rampart, wait for a lull in the traffic din, and issue a four-note birdsong whistle toward the third floor: wee-oh-WEE-OOHH! wee-oh-WEE-OOHH! Eventually Na-Ma would hear it—windows were usually open in those days before air-conditioning—and, upon spotting the caller, would drop the key out the window into Del's hands. (Why didn't the family simply make a copy of the key? Because they had such a great system!) The teenager unlocked the door, sprinted up the world's steepest staircases, and on this particular day in 1951, found a patron for what would become his career. Twenty dollars in hand, he slid gleefully down the banister, paid a visit to Reiner's, and bought his future.

That was lucky for Del, because, scholastically, nothing much seemed to stick. True, he mustered up enough ambition to want to go to Jesuit, the city's most competitive Catholic boys' high school, but only because he spied a darkroom in its promotional brochure. True, he gained admission, but barely, and hardly did he identify with any one subject, much less excel. He didn't even receive report cards, because his parents couldn't keep up with the tuition. One lesson he did learn during his Jesuit years stung more than it uplifted. A trip had been planned to Washington, D.C., the prospect of which absolutely thrilled him. Having visited New York a few years earlier, Del fancied himself something of an authority on exotic travel, and he anticipated photographing the landmarks of the nation's capital. Maybe he would meet President Truman! Then, for reasons unremembered, the trip fell through. The seemingly mundane letdown taught Del a lesson of surprising incisiveness, one that would steel him against life's vicissitudes: never again would he raise his hopes for something beyond his control, or get overly excited about something that might slip away. This attitude might seem unduly pessimistic for a teenager, more impediment than empowerment, and to be sure, Del Hall never did develop the strategic qualities of a man with his eyes on the prize and a road map of how to get there. Yet, paradoxically, that lack of laser focus helped him develop keen prescience and peripheral vision—that is, an ability to assess context, understand the lay of the land, and foresee what things would look like over the next ridge, while remaining as deft

and flexible as possible to meet them head on. It also made him comfortable as an invisible observer of events, rather than the decisive catalyst in the limelight.

Between Pops's halfway-decent job calculating bills of lading at "the Fruit Company," and Mother's clerking position at the Sears on Baronne, the Halls gradually rose into the middle class. The family indulged in new conveniences and amenities: Na-Ma got her first television and Uncle Johnny purchased a car, both firsts for the extended family. One day in March 1950 when Mother went to file some paperwork at the Iberville office, she came home with an unpleasant surprise. Their income, as revealed by the tax returns required by HANO, no longer qualified them for residency in the Projects. That Mother took this news as heartbreaking speaks to just how cohesive and pleasant a community this was at the time, a stark contrast to the reputation Iberville would later gain. Del had a more conflicted view of his home. While he loved it there, he was all too aware that others held it in disdain. At Jesuit he brushed shoulders daily with wealthy uptown boys, some of whom had hardly ever been downtown, yet knew enough to sneer at the stigma of the Projects.

Classism of this subtle sort did not necessarily beleaguer Del, but hardly was it uplifting, and his level of achievement during his high school years could be fairly well characterized as mediocre. He did okay in Spanish, probably because Pops and Grandma Minnie spoke it, and he won a letter for wrestling. But he struggled with math, science, and the four mandatory years of Latin. He tried to improve himself by hanging out with his tutoring buddy, Tommy Schoen, who had the advantage of a nice quiet place to study: his family's funeral home. But instead of physics and chemistry, Tommy surreptitiously taught Del how to drive Mrs. Schoen's '49 Chevy—much to the surprise of Del's mom, who caught the two of them at a red light. If the St. Joseph nuns' *Good-better-best* mantra resonated with the teenager, he excelled at hiding it.

Culturally he differed from the Jesuit crowd as well. Those uptowners mostly listened to the latest hits on pre–rock and roll radio, whereas Del preferred the down-

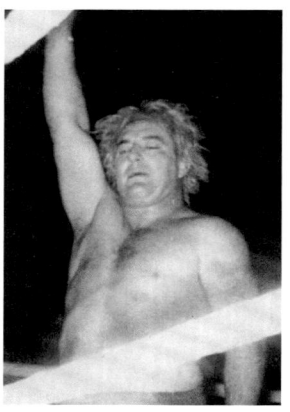

Gorgeous George at the Coliseum Arena. *Photo by Del Hall.*

town sound, from the likes of Johnny Ace or Fats Domino. After their exile from Iberville, the family moved to a rather forgettable upstairs rental on Dublin Street in Carrollton, and later to an equally humdrum shotgun double at 2726½ Onzaga in the predominantly Creole Seventh Ward, yet another point of estrangement from Jesuit. It probably also didn't help that Del's dad was Mexican born and not properly documented, a situation that forced Pops to return to Mexico and reenter the U.S. legally. This was not your typical Jesuit dad, and Del wasn't your typical Jesuit student, and his performance showed it. Decades later, at reunions, his classmates would joke that Del turned out to be not "Most Successful," but rather "Most Surprising Success."

Del's hobbies and part-time jobs were his salvation. He'd take that Kodak Retina over to the Fairgrounds near Onzaga and try again and again to snap the perfect racehorse shot. That didn't happen, but he did photograph famed jockey Willie Shoemaker being led to the gate, which he sold to the starter for 75 cents, the beginning of his entrepreneurial camera work. He also photographed wrestler Gorgeous George preening his bobby-pinned blond mane at the Coliseum Arena across North Claiborne—the same night he met a stylish young black fellow outside, foot perched jauntily against the wall, who turned out to be Fats Domino. It was at the Coliseum that Del first saw massive new tripod-mounted television cameras, labeled with the letters WDSU, and watched with admiration their specialized handlers.

Processing all this film was what made photography an expensive hobby. To the rescue came Arthur Kingsmill, a buddy from Jesuit, who was one of the few kids in the city who had his own darkroom. What Art didn't have, however, was a particularly good memory. He popped Del's film in his shirt pocket, promptly forgot it, and sheepishly retrieved the congealed mass after his mom washed the laundry. So went Del's photographs of early-1950s New Orleans.

To deflect costs and help with family finances, Del became a soda jerk at Waldoff's Pharmacy at Broad and St. Bernard—one of those archetypal 1950s teenager hangouts, where he mastered the art of flipping hamburgers and making malts. He also became popular for treating his friends and himself to free eats, a little *lagniappe* to his fifty-cent-an-hour wage. "I learned a valuable lesson at Waldoff's," he chuckles. "You have to make more than you spend. An epiphany!" Another job, at the Matus Machine Shop on Washington at Broad, came his way courtesy the Spanish-speaking owner, who happened to be pals with Pops. Better yet, he had a daughter, Raquel, who, despite her unbecoming nickname "Rocky," was cute as a button, and a swell dancer to boot. Del and Rocky had been playmates since the 1930s, when their parents would push them on swings in Coliseum Square. Now as teenagers Del took Rocky out to dances on the *President* steamboat, to swims at City Park, and to sanctioned shindigs at Jesuit, where school officials had warned a rebellious young classmate named Mac Rebennack against playing that newfangled "rock and roll." To the delight of all the kids, that's exactly what Mac played. Transgressions like that eventually got Rebennack kicked out of Jesuit—and toward a musical career that, under the stage name Dr. John, would sell millions of records, win six Grammy awards, and earn him induction into the Rock and Roll Hall of Fame.

Things with Rocky lasted about as long as a New Orleans summer rain, after which Del went back to work. His night-shift stint at Higgins, the shipyard known for its amphibious landing craft that helped win World War II, did not last long, in part because he succumbed to the temptation to watch movies visible on the drive-in screen across the Industrial Canal. No problem; better opportunities could be found downtown anyway, running errands. In those days, errand boys or messengers coordinated any business dealings that could not be transacted in person or by phone or mail. The streets proliferated with teenaged boys hustling packages to offices, or, just as commonly, "numbers" lists to bar backrooms running illicit lotteries. Del found a messenger job for an importer/exporter firm running bills of lading to the U.S. Customs House at the foot of Canal Street. In 1952, he got a better position with Western Union in the arcade of the St. Charles, third in a lineage of grand old nineteenth-century hotels at 201 St. Charles Avenue. Mr. Ray, his boss, would type the telegram on a ticker, fold it into a distinctive company envelope and address it, and with a "Here, Boy!" send Del on his way to every corner of the Central Business District—into the Cotton Exchange, up the Hibernia Bank tower, into the Whitney and National banks, and in and out of all the classy hotels with their important guests. Once he had to deliver a telegram to the Jax Brewery, and found the chief toiling amid the metallic jungle of malty, steamy apparatus. "Hey son," intoned the man, grinning mischievously, "wanna try some fresh brew?" That was Del's first taste of beer—a big cool swill on a hot summer day, in the heart of the French Quarter, overlooking the Mississippi River.

Another time, Del was dispatched to intercept Senator Estes Kefauver as the candidate made his way to address an audience of skeptical New Orleanians in his bid for the 1952 presidential election. Del sneaked a peak at the telegram: NEW ORLEANS DOES NOT RHYME WITH BEANS, it read. "I quote that line to this day," he says, whenever an uninformed soul makes the mistake of saying "New Or-LEANS." Whether Senator Kefauver heeded the oratorical counsel is unknown, but history records he lost the election.

On another errand, Del biked up Tulane Avenue to deliver a telegram to the Criminal Courthouse at Broad. Making his way around a lumbering bus, his eye fell upon a particularly comely lass waiting at the stop. Moments later, Del found himself knocked to the ground. Pedestrians ran to his aid, and he soaked up their sympathy as they lambasted the bus driver for nearly killing the poor lad. Del knew better—ogling the girl, he actually hit the bus—but kept it to himself, chuckling through his pain. He never did get that girl, but he did get a sympathetic mention in the newspaper, plus $75 for his injuries. Now finding himself in need of new wheels, he bought a beat-up 1938 Chevy Coupe with a missing fender. "Not bad for a kid from the Projects," he gloated as he fired up the engine for his first drive. Two seconds later, he crashed into the car behind him, causing it to lose its fender.

After graduating Jesuit in June 1953, Del landed a position at the Volkart Brothers Cotton Company. His job was to assist the "classifier," who judged the quality of cotton lint by extracting a square core sample four inches into each bale and grading its length and color on a qualitative ranking system. "Fair and middling," for example, meant a generally white fiber of medium length that would yield an average price. The classifier, bending over a big table covered with samples, would analyze the core and holler his judgment over to Del, who would scribble it down on a ledger along with the bale number. It was a scene right out of *A Cotton Office in New Orleans,* which French impressionist Edgar Degas had painted in the 1870s just a few blocks from Volkart's office. When complete, Del would run the ledger over to a "computing" firm, which transferred the data to a punch card and analyzed them on a mechanical adding machine. "I thought to myself," he says sixty years later, I-Pad on his lap, "there had to be a better way."

Cotton ranked at the very top of New Orleans's commodities trade, and right behind it was coffee. Del had his hand in that industry as well, packing imported beans roasted by the Reily Company under the Luzianne brand. Ten years later, another drifting local youth, his name Lee Harvey Oswald, would work at the same South Peters Street facility. Though the two never met, their paths would cross in a number of ways over the next decade.

Teenagers can get away with aimlessness because society does the aiming for them. After high school, however, that task shifts to the individual, and the dearth of a plan can lead to a failure-to-launch.

Del couldn't quite figure out how to parlay his interest in photography into a paying job, and found little inspiration from Pops's and Mother's clerking, or from Grandpa Fred's go-nowhere unionized projectionist position. (Gramps, sadly, had worked himself to a fatal stroke, and was buried wearing his union pin—not the way Del wanted to end up.) It didn't help that many adults in his family harbored drinking problems, particularly the men. Seeking mentorship elsewhere, he noted that his most admired buddies all wanted to be pilots, so he applied for Tulane University's ROTC Navy pilot training exam—and passed, only to be rejected by the psychiatrist because he bit his fingernails. With private universities too expensive and no public university available locally, his only other option was Southeastern Louisiana College in Hammond, an hour north of New Orleans. Living in a Quonset hut dormitory in this era of G.I.-bill campus overcrowding, Del made the mistake of choosing an utterly inappropriate major (mathematics, never his strong suit) and getting involved in the zany antics of the 1950s college scene—initiations, beanie hats, and pantie raids, the last of which got him thrown off campus and back to New Orleans, collecting rent for a real estate firm. Worse yet, his '38 Coupe, parts falling off left and right, was now overheating from a radiator leak. Knowing no better, he cooled it off with water—Lake Pontchartrain sea water. The engine blew up, and now not only did Del have nowhere to go, he had no way to get there. *Good-better-best?* Fair and middling would be putting it kindly.

True, he did have a new sweetheart by this time, a girl named Greta Malone, whom he met on a blind date in 1952. Greta, adopted, had a troubled past but a promising future, and her folks were fairly well off, with fancy digs on pricey Palmer Avenue. Professionally, however, Del's options were diminishing. "The only thing left," he explains today, "was to join the Air Force." He swore in on August 26, 1955, in the century-old Customs House on Canal Street, and by nightfall found himself aboard a Constellation four-prop bound for Texas. It was his first flight.

"Ya never had it so good!" jeered an acerbic mess-hall goon as the new recruits filed in for their first meal at Lackland Air Force Base in San Antonio. He was right: Del's eleven subsequent weeks of boot camp made that lousy grub seem like dinner at Antoine's by comparison. Even worse were his initial assignments—which were so intolerable that instead of waiting for a slot in Russian language training, he lunged for an unexpected opening in Aerial Photo Interpretation.

The opportunity got Del back into photography, and to Shaw Air Force Base in South Carolina for training, where he would spend the next four years with the 363d Tactical Reconnaissance Wing (of later fame for its role in the Cuban missile crisis) working with specialized cameras mounted in the bays of Douglas RB-66 Destroyers. His task was to train pilots to plot the target on a map; calculate air speed, altitude, and focal length; and photograph the site at nadir while getting 60 percent frame-to-frame overlap for the purposes of stereo interpretation. All this required practice, for which Del arranged missions over downtown Charleston, or the state capitol building in Columbia, or rural nighttime targets, for which gigantic flash bombs were dropped to illuminate the countryside. One time in late 1957, Del, on a whim, submitted a request for a flight over his hometown of New Orleans. To his surprise, it was accepted. Today Del has in his possession unique detailed aerial coverage of the city of New Orleans as it stood during the height of its postwar infrastructure boom. You can even see the Greater New Orleans Mississippi River Bridge under construction.

Big changes were in store for Del as well. Things had gotten serious with Greta, and they married in 1956. A year later their son was born, Delos M. Hall, delivered in an Air Force hospital for a fee of seven dollars. The new responsibility and his upcoming military discharge forced Del to ponder his future. He knew he wanted to work in photography, and he cherished a sense of adventure and purpose. But all such jobs had scores of seekers for every opening. Was there a niche left open?

One day, while lying on a cot at North Field, he was struck by a rare moment of strategic clarity. "It hit me a like a bolt of lightning," he recalled. "TELEVISION! Everyone with a camera wanted to be a photographer. But I didn't know anyone in television. That's the job I wanted."

It really helped to have that goal. Things started to fall in place after the North Field epiphany. Del found a photographer position with the base newspaper, the *Recon Record,* and won an award for a dramatic shot of an RB-66 de-icing on a frigid Alaskan dawn. He got his first movie camera while on leave in New Orleans, a Bolex 16 mm purchased from the Sears where Mother worked, using funds once again generously gifted by Na-Ma. Using the Bolex, he sold his first footage, of the Miss South Carolina beauty pageant, for $7.50, to a Columbia television station. (Alas, the Bolex turned out to be the last of Na-Ma's influential gifts, as her blissfully unhealthy lifestyle, plus those treacherous staircases at 129 South Rampart, finally landed her in Charity Hospital with a heart attack, where she eventually died.)

Del next answered an ad placed by one Leo Willette of Asheville, who billed himself as WLOS's "new aggressive News Director." Willette, who would play an influential role later in Del's career, offered freelance cameramen "top dollar for top film." Del, armed with his Bolex, jumped at the opportunity. As a "stringer" for WLOS, he filmed a young Billy Graham evangelizing at Fort Jackson in South Carolina ("I was so close I could see his makeup") and covered a local candidate who ran his political campaign on leave from his jail cell ("he treated me to a pheasant lunch")—good practice for Del's future career covering Louisiana politicians.

In fact, while on leave back home in June 1959, that prac-tice came in handy. The budding entrepreneur took his trusty Bolex to WDSU-TV, the first and biggest New Orleans television station, and convinced news director John Corporon to hire him as a one-day stringer covering the only-in-Louisiana story of a kicking, cussing Gov. Earl K. Long getting released from a mental hospital in Mandeville to be taken to a hearing in Covington. Del made his way across Lake Pontchartrain to the scene of the story, which was getting national atten-tion. As journalists surrounded the courthouse, commotion flurried at the main entrance, suggesting that the governor was about to arrive. Everyone scurried in that direction to get the best shot—everyone, that is, except Del, whose instincts told him to stay put and cover the suspiciously quiet back door. Moments later, there arrived a defiant Governor Long, grizzled and grousing, straight into Del's rolling camera. The footage aired that evening. It was magical.[2]

Shortly thereafter, Del completed his Air Force service and returned permanently to New Orleans—a veteran, a husband, a father, and a man with a plan. Finally, the good was getting better.

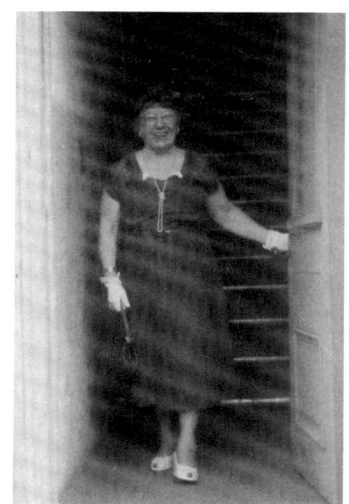

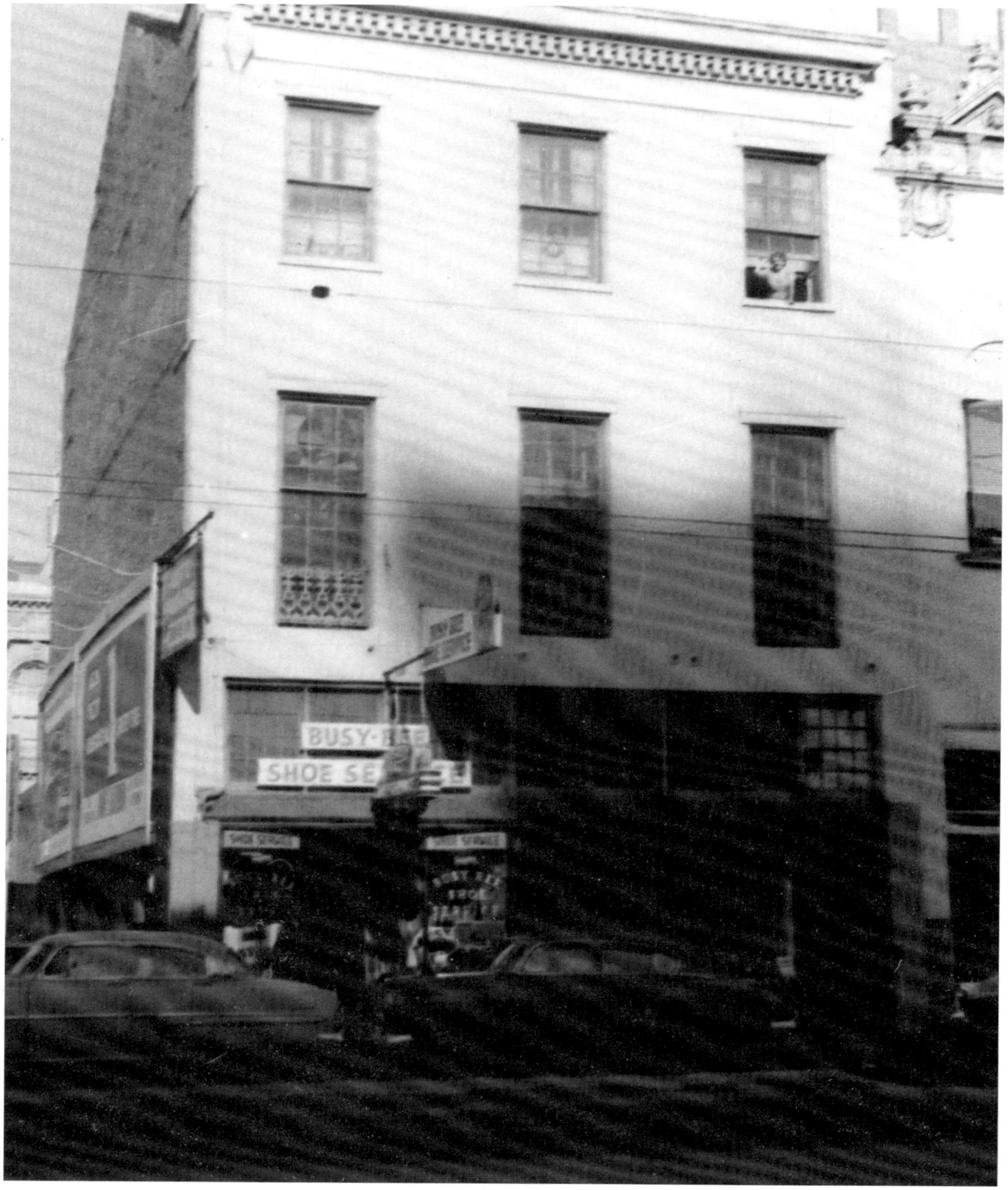

Na-Ma welcomes a visitor to her third-floor apartment at 129 South Rampart in New Orleans, where Del Hall was born in 1935. *Hall Family Collection.*

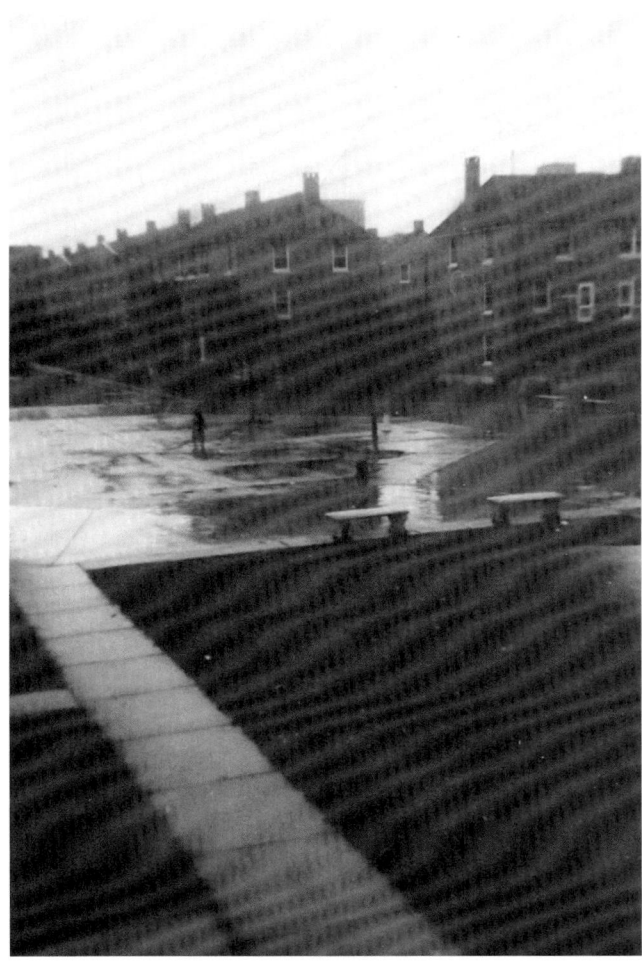

In 1940, Del's family moved into the segregated Iberville Housing Projects, seen here on a bleak winter day in the late 1940s. *Hall Family Collection.*

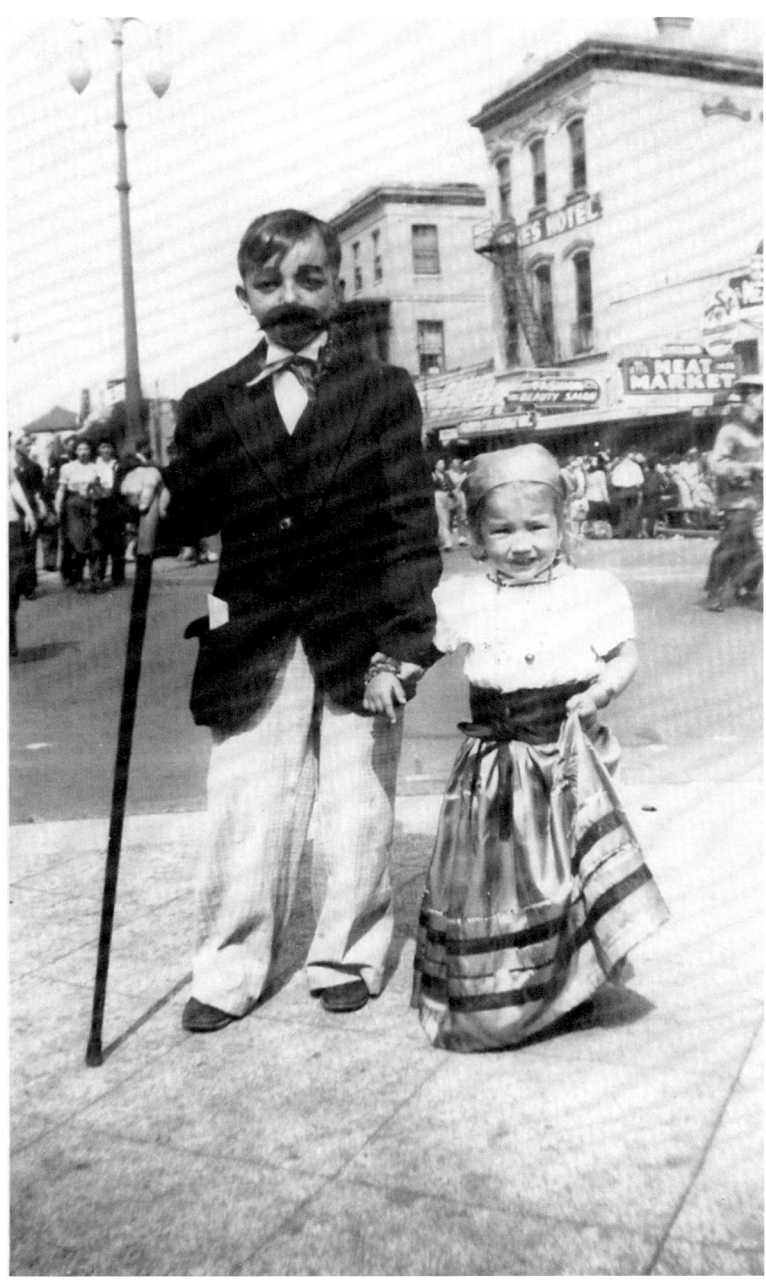

Del at Mardi Gras in downtown New Orleans with sister Sharon in the late 1940s. *Hall Family Collection.*

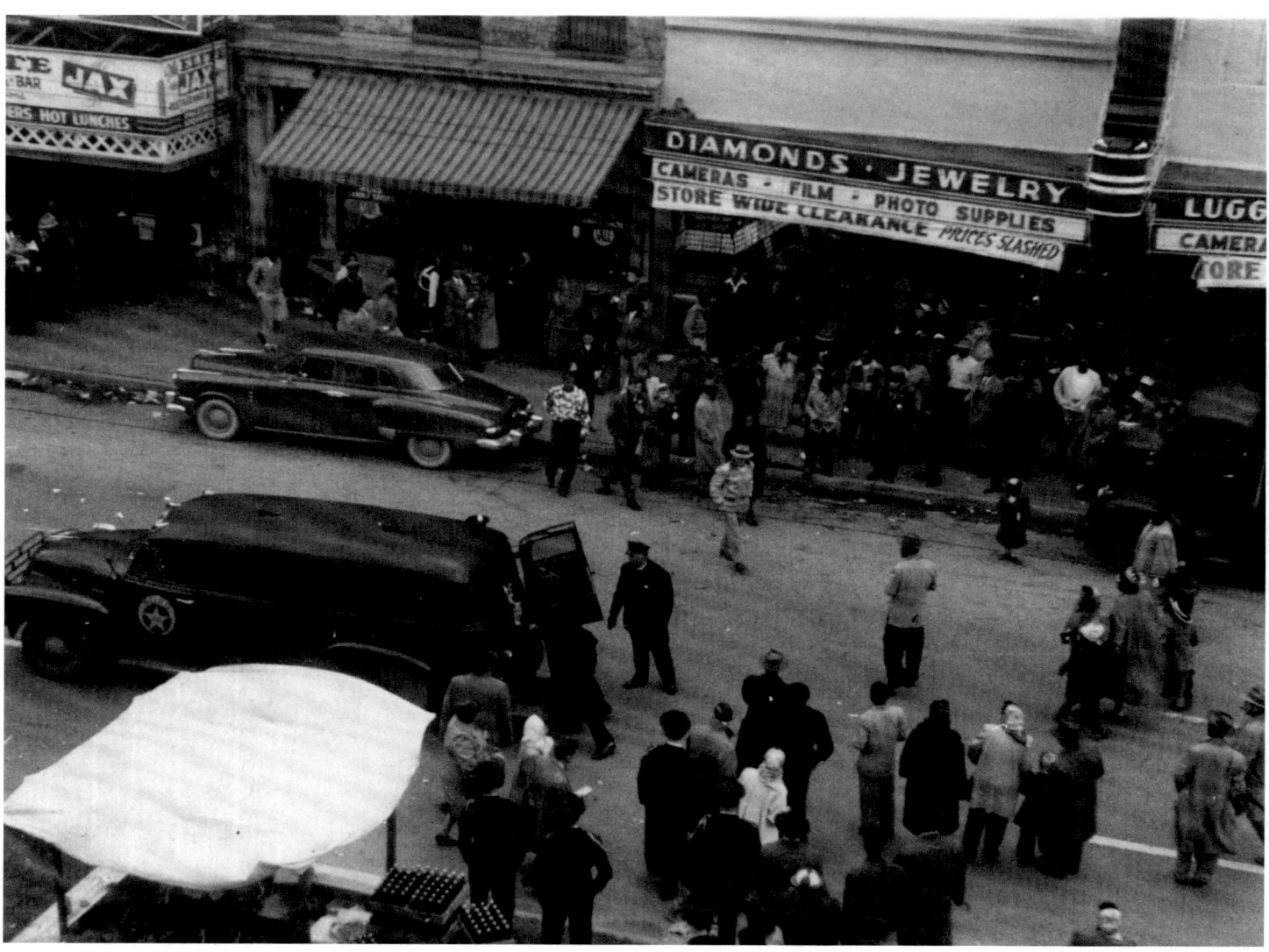

Into the paddy wagon: Mardi Gras zaniness in 1952 as seen through Del's viewfinder, positioned in Na-Ma's window on South Rampart. *Photos by Del Hall.*

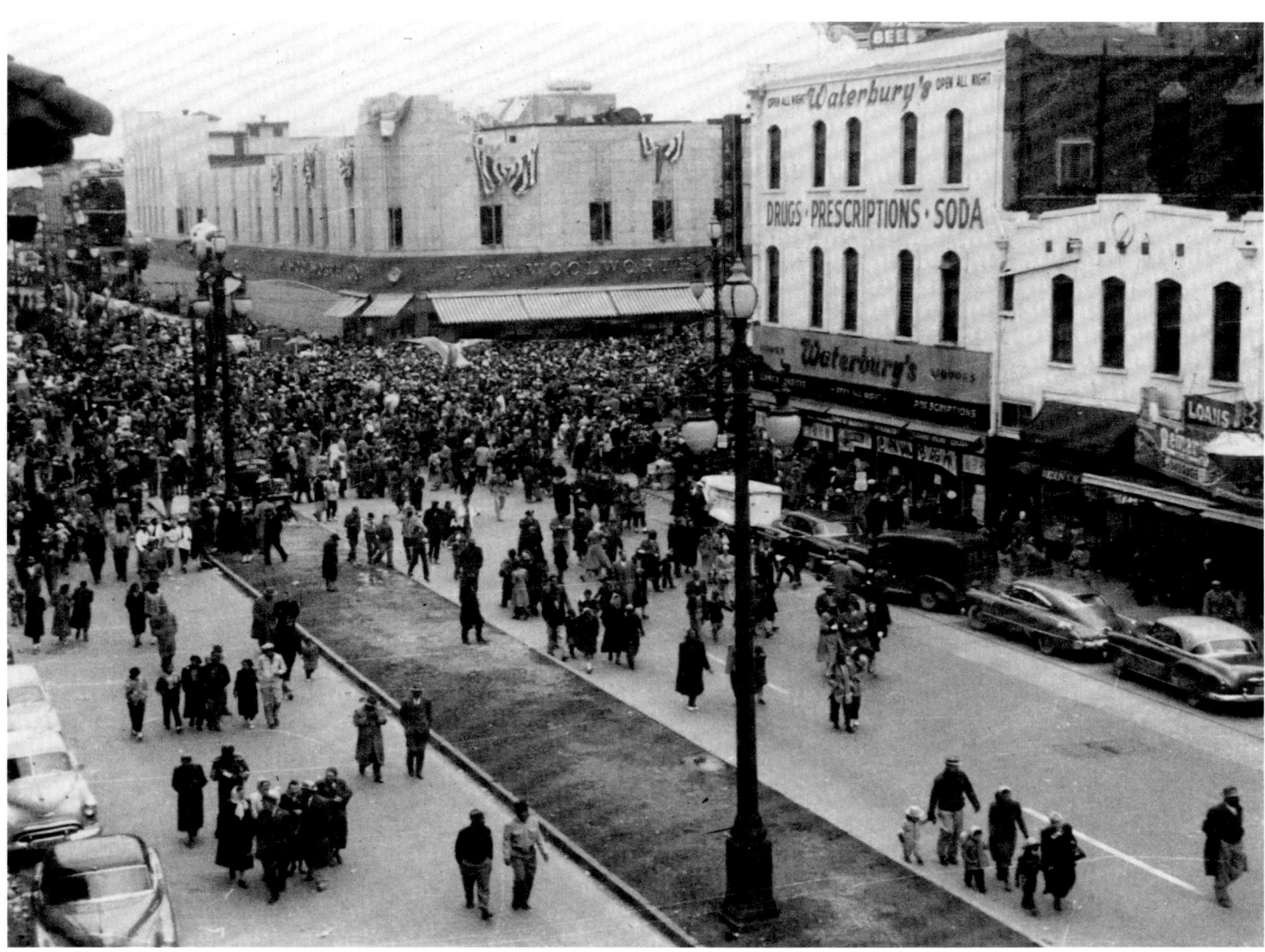

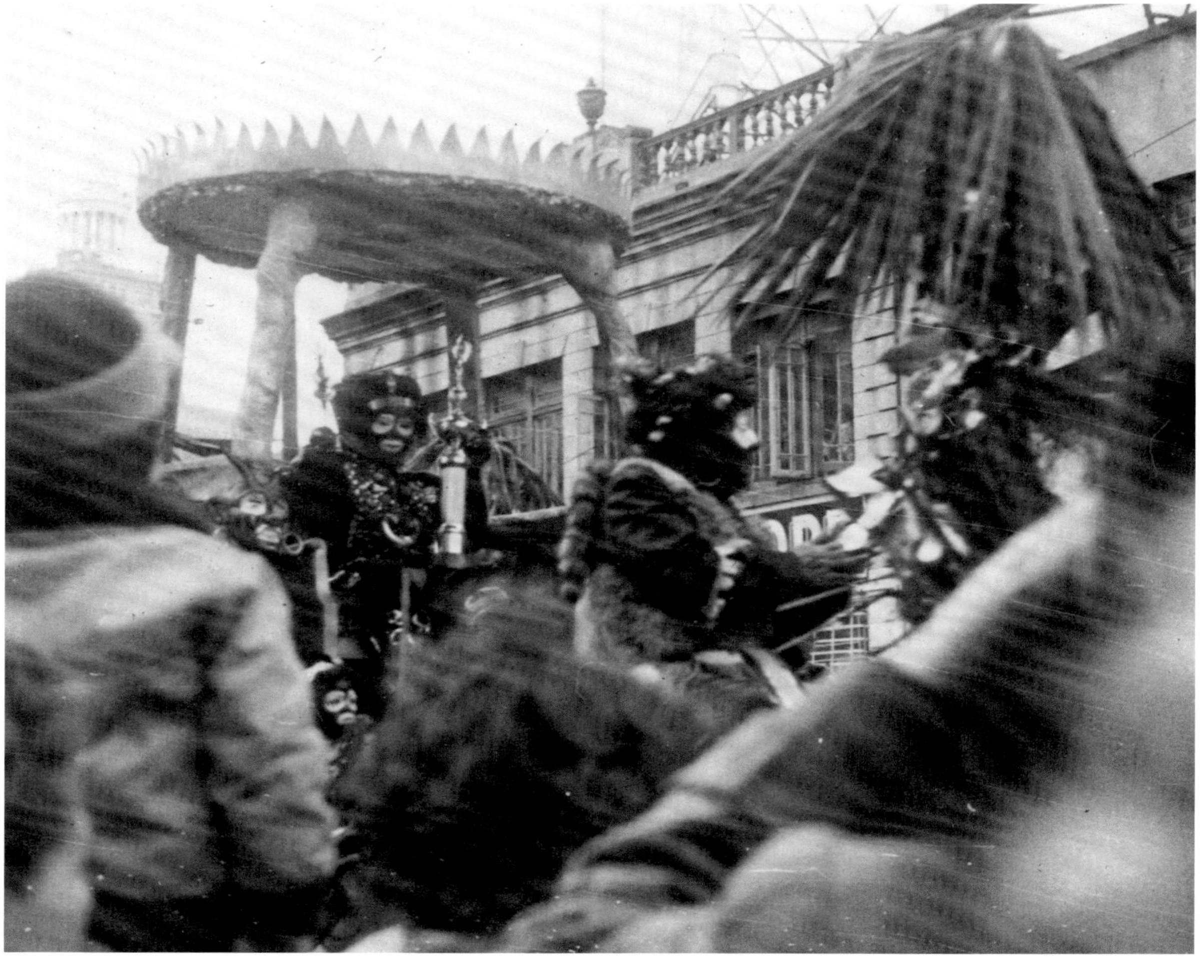

King of the Krewe
of Zulu. *Photo by
Del Hall.*

Del's sister and
cousins in front
of the segregated
entrance of Loew's
Theatre. *Photo by
Del Hall.*

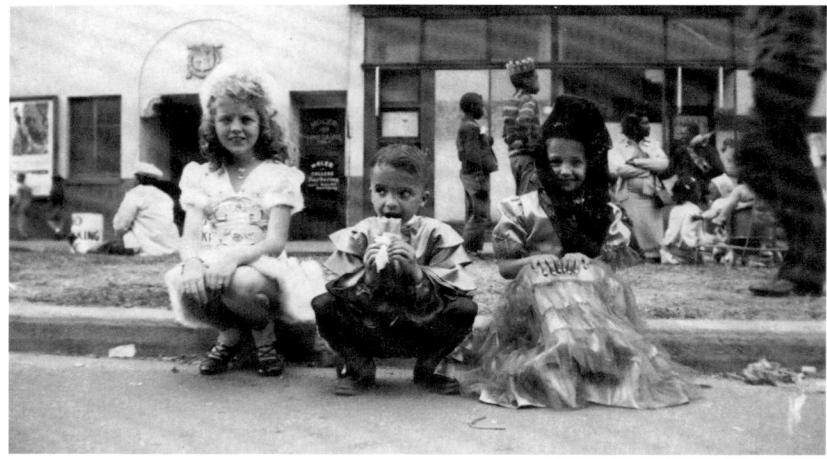

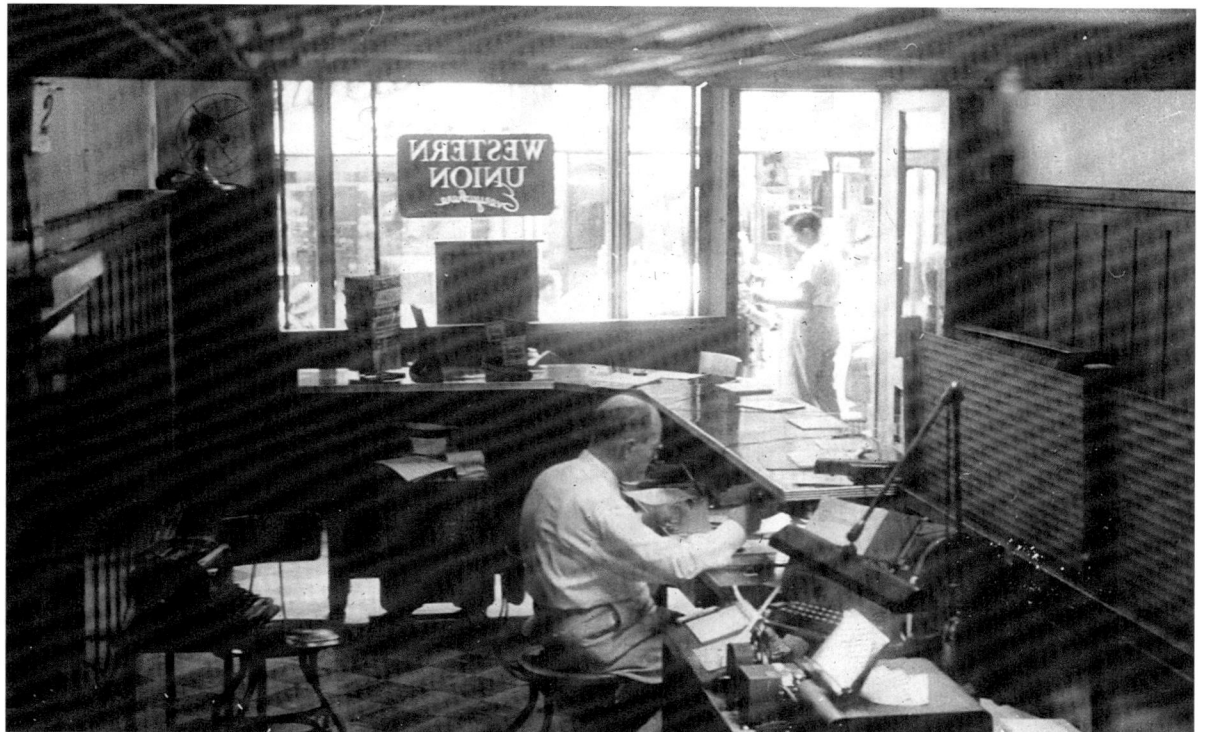

Western Union office in the St. Charles Hotel, where Del worked as a messenger in 1952. *Photo by Del Hall.*

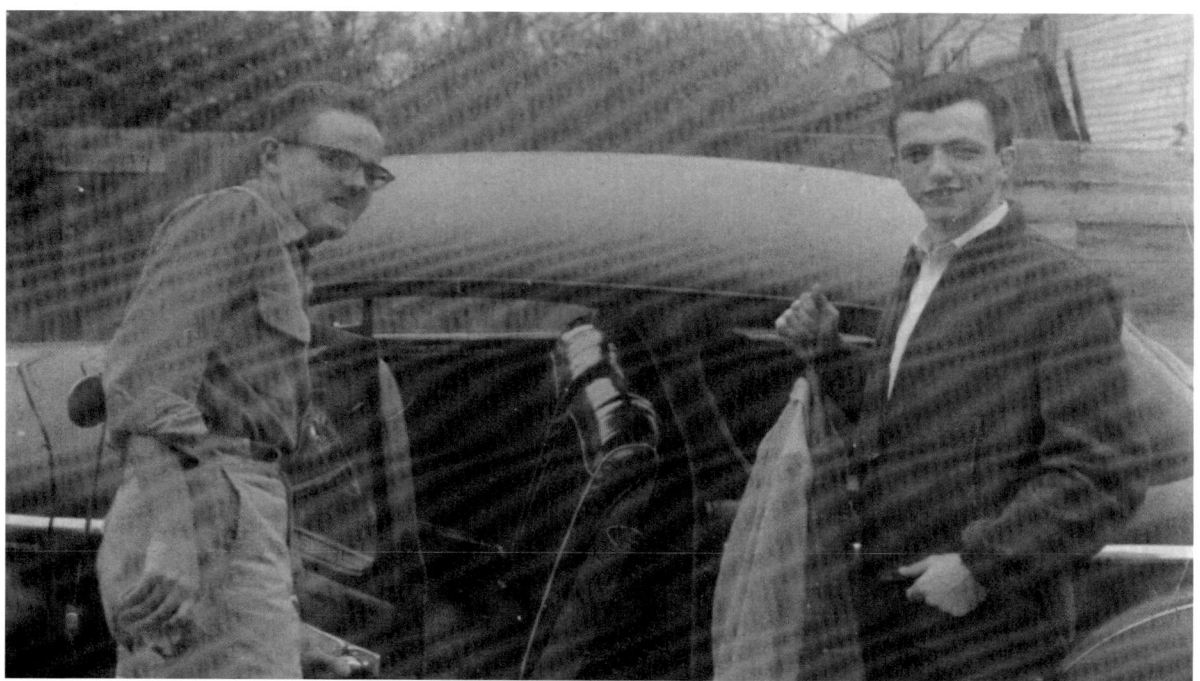

Off to college at Southeastern in Hammond, 1953; Dell at right. *Hall Family Collection.*

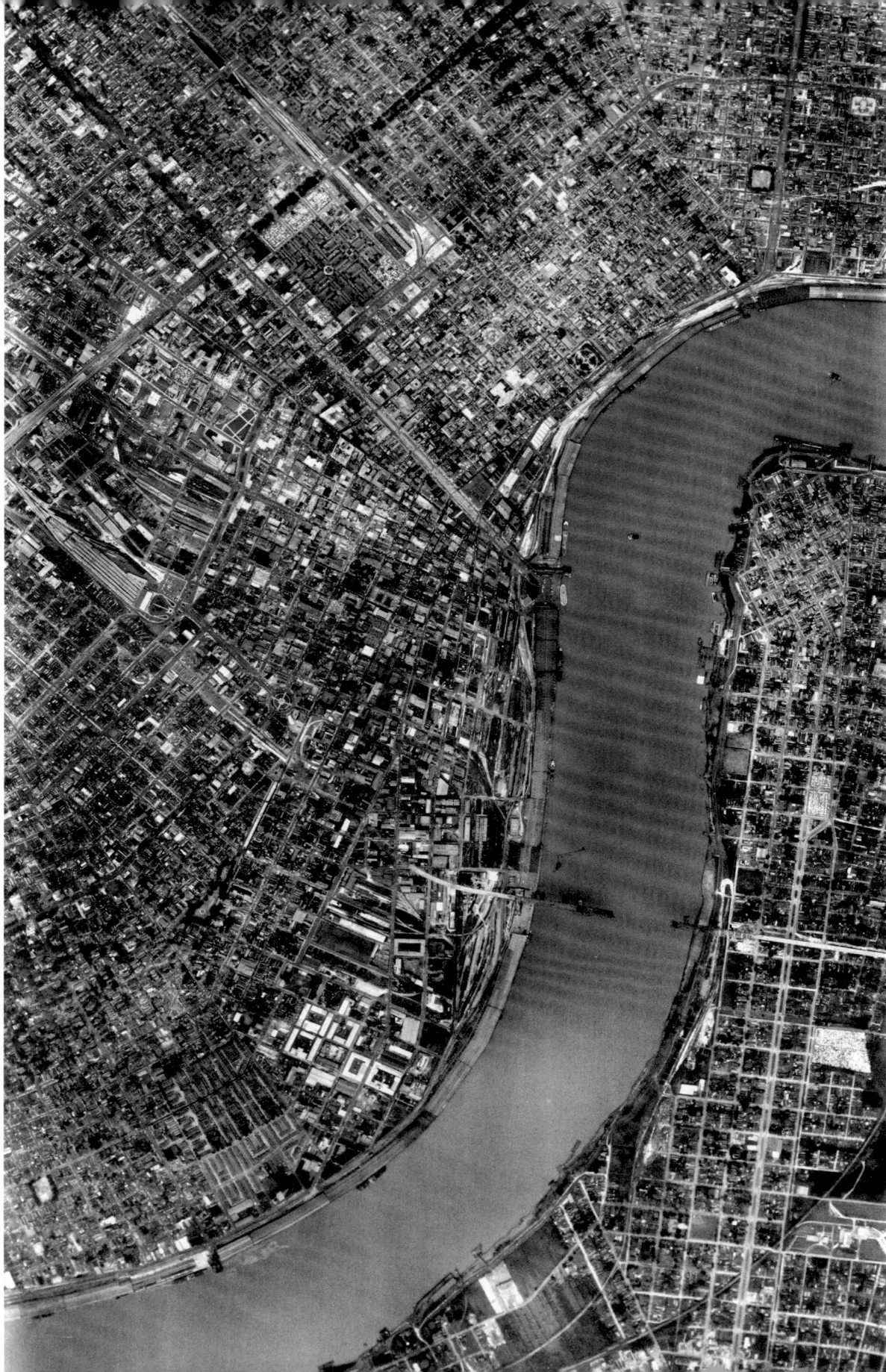

One frame of a series of aerial photographs of downtown New Orleans (note bridge under construction) captured in 1957, part of an Air Force mission organized by Del. *Photo by Del Hall.*

TAKE TWO

Popes, Protests, and War, 1959–1966

HAVING A PLAN points you in the right direction, but knowing the right person lands you a paying job. That connection came from Greta's uncle, who, as president of a local bank, knew his counterparts at the city's television stations. Chief among them was WDSU, the NBC affiliate and local leader, which broadcast from its prime Royal Street location in the heart of the French Quarter. Next was the Jesuits' Loyola University–owned WWL—for a long time the only church-owned commercial television station in the country—which, affiliated with CBS, competed fiercely from its 1024 North Rampart studio on the Quarter's edge. ABC-affiliated WVUE, meanwhile, operated on Cleveland Street, two blocks behind where Na-Ma used to live, and broadcast from the top of the Jung Hotel. It was WVUE's Joseph Paretti who agreed to see the banker's kin about a position. Del wisely brought his Bolex to the interview and cited his stringer jobs in South Carolina and his Earl Long coup as his experience. For a field that barely existed at the time, that was enough to set him apart, and Paretti hired him at $300 per month.

Del was thrilled to break into television, but had to pay his dues first, as floor director for the sort of low-budget, lowbrow variety programming (read: barn dances and bowling challenges) typical of 1950s local television. It was cheap, the viewers liked it, and the advertisers sponsored it. News, on the other hand, was costly, not particularly popular, and even less lucrative. But because stations were obligated to perform a civic function as part of their airwave agreement with the federal government, each formed a news division.

After paying his barn-dancing dues, Del edged into camera and editing work, building up his skills and gaining entry into the International Brotherhood of Electrical Workers, the closest thing at the time to a cameramen's union. In one of his first assignments with WVUE, Del covered Jimmie Davis singing his signature "You Are My Sunshine" while campaigning for governor against New Orleans mayor "Chep" Morrison, and filmed the May 1960 inauguration in which Davis replaced outgoing governor Earl Long. By summer, Del had made enough of a name for himself that Bill Reed, news director of the much bigger WWL-TV, asked him to join its crack cameramen duo of Larry Lala and Mike O'Connor. He accepted immediately.

With reporters Bob Jones, Henry Telles, and Rufus Rivers, led ably by general manager J. Michael Early and his erudite assistant Phil Johnson, WWL Channel Four had assembled what would later become recognized as a legendary team in early television news. The station benefited additionally from two tenants in its North Rampart studio, Dan Rather's CBS Southern Bureau and Roddy Mims's regional United Press International office, both of which partnered regularly with WWL's staff and paid them for their services. "[WDSU] Channel Six should have known it was going down in flames with a group like that!" says Jones today, looking back on the good-natured professional rivalry.[1] One of Del's first WWL assignments was the funeral of Earl Long, the rambunctious former governor who died suddenly of a heart attack four months after Del filmed him at Davis's inauguration—a time sufficiently long for the irrepressible "Uncle Earl" to re-emerge as congressman-elect. As cameraman, Del was not allowed to cover the funeral mass, so he improvised by filming foreboding thunderheads gathering above the church as Long's favorite song, "In the Garden," reverberated outside. Creative tactics like that, invented on the spot, garnered Del a rising-star reputation.

Del entered television news at a moment that, in retrospect, could be viewed as New Orleans's municipal zenith. The city's population peaked in the 1960 census—over 627,000 residents, largest in the South outside Texas—and, with new oil and gas money catalyzing the economy, infrastructure improvements and new subdivisions were blossoming hither and yon. Suburban parishes were developing under their own power, abetting rather than drawing resources from the urban core. New Orleans at the end of the 1950s seemed to be finally buffing off its nineteenth-century patina, and around their televisions New Orleanians gathered to witness local progress. For a kid from the Projects, landing a TV news job in this big city, at this halcyon time, was no picayune deal. His parents beamed, and former neighbors and Jesuit classmates took note.

Municipal progress, of course, did not reach all segments of the population. For blacks, the 1950s were all too much like the 1890s, and whatever rays of hope came out of *Brown vs. Board of Education* and the mounting national campaign for civil rights dimmed before they reached New Orleans. That began to change just as Del started with WWL, and for the next three years, civil rights dominated his assignments. Local stories broke almost daily, usually involving pickets of commercial arteries like Canal or Dryades, protest marches on City Hall, or White Citizens' Council meetings in the Municipal Auditorium, where, teamed with a young CBS Southern Bureau reporter named Dan Rather, Del covered

segregationist leaders rallying WCC members at a lectern draped in a Confederate battle flag.

Among the WCC's chief nemeses were the Congress of Racial Equality and its founder, James L. Farmer, who had adopted a direct-action strategy that actively defied Jim Crow wherever it showed its face, rather than passively protesting it in city-permitted marches. CORE's preferred technique was the "sit-in" at segregated public facilities, a tactic brought to national attention in February 1960 at a Woolworth's in Greensboro, North Carolina. Seven months later, CORE arrived at New Orleans and recruited students from Southern University and other regional colleges to sit in at whites-only lunch counters at Woolworth's, McCrory's, and Kress on Canal Street. Other sit-ins followed, growing in size and culminating with a December 16, 1961, event involving so many activists that it was more of an "occupy" than a sit-in. Del and his outspoken UPI buddy Roddy Mims recorded the escalating tensions between nervous waitresses, peeved regulars, and sixty anxious young black men and women, all in blue hats emblazoned with red CORE letters and the words "Support Freedom Rides." What put the authorities on edge, however, were Del's and Roddy's whirring cameras. Unlike street demonstrations, in which both sides had a point to make and saw the camera as an opportunity to make it, footage of sit-ins almost always ennobled the protestors and cast the white establishment in a highly unflattering light. The police realized this, and so did the managers, who also worried that the attention could not be good for business. Managers of both Woolworth's and McCrory's consulted with authorities and, moments later, had the police arrest both Del and Roddy for "disturbing the peace by creating a scene." As if to prove that the cameras were the real problem, the managers offered to drop the charges and have the police release them if they turned over their film.[2] They refused and were promptly driven to the police station, where the WWL news director later arranged for their release until they appeared in court. Del recalled someone murmuring to him as he was escorted to the paddy wagon, "If you weren't here, [the protestors] wouldn't be here." Two months later, both were found not guilty of disturbing the peace, although Mims was convicted of being "loud and boisterous."

Most eateries remained segregated for a few more years, and most hotels for a year or two beyond. Streetcars, on the other hand, desegregated earlier, in the late 1950s, as did other government facilities. When it came to the radioactive question of school integration, however, the white power structure both inside and outside government dug in its heels, Supreme Court be damned. Its strategy exploited a particular directive in *Brown,* ruling that southern schools should integrate "with all deliberate speed," and used its uncalibrated subjectivity to justify foot dragging and obstructionism. The white electorate penalized any politician who wavered, and reactionary leaders managed to defer and evade the reviled ruling.

For six years that strategy worked—until a local federal district court judge named J. Skelly Wright specified what the *Brown* decision did not: an integration deadline, set for Monday, November 14, 1960. In preparation, the NAACP began meeting with parents to select which children and schools would be first. Word got out that a little black girl would integrate William Frantz Elementary in the Upper Ninth Ward, and three others would enter McDonogh 19 in the Lower Ninth Ward. The whole nation was watching, because this was a first not just for New Orleans, but throughout the region.

On the appointed day, incensed white mothers arrived at the targeted schools prepared to remove their befuddled youngsters if black children were allowed entry. Backers gathered to support them, creating an ugly carnival-like atmosphere as the black families arrived. Del caught on film the spectacle of towering federal marshals escorting tiny girls; police in riot gear on jittery horses; vitriol and hatred (*"Nigger! Nigger! Nigger"*) flowing from adult to child; chants (*"2-4-6-8, We Don't Want to Integrate!"*); signs (*"Segregation or Closed Schools!"* affixed to a Confederate flag); and wickedly cynical props, such as nooses, effigies, and a little black doll in a child's coffin hoisted aloft by a smirking mob. His footage aired on WWL and on *CBS Evening News* nationally, and on this story in particular, his cameraman's axiom proved

true: *No matter what you say, they only remember what they see.*

History remembers one iconic scene from that morning because, a few years later, artist Norman Rockwell, drawing inspiration from the ongoing nationwide civil rights movement, painted six-year-old Ruby Bridges marching amongst the marshals into Frantz Elementary. The one salient memory that stands out in Del's mind, however, reflects the sheer absurdity of the spectacle. He recalls a tall, gaunt middle-aged woman across the street from the school, standing in a bird bath, waving her arms like a flustered hen, shrieking racial epithets maniacally at the black families. Further investigation indicates that the woman was no ordinary mother, but rather arch-segregationist Una Gaillot (Mrs. B. J. Gaillot Jr.), founder of Save Our Nation Inc. and ringleader of what John Steinbeck—in town researching what would become *Travels with Charley*—would later call "the Cheerleaders[,] blowzy women [filled with] insensate beastliness."[3] Through newspaper ads, letter writing, and leafleting, Gaillot called on legislators "to defeat the horrible, ungodly, satanical law of integration perpetrated on our nation" and later boldly admonished Catholic clergy "that God demands the segregation of the races and curses all integrators according to Scripture." Gaillot pushed her luck a bit too far in 1962 when she slammed the archdiocese for integrating Catholic schools. Archbishop Joseph Rummel took the extraordinary step of excommunicating her from the Church (along with notorious Plaquemines Parish political boss Leander H. Perez, whose views on race made Mrs. Gaillot look like Gandhi by comparison). The next day, Del's colleague at the Associated Press photographed Gaillot kneeling before the archbishop at a public event, seeking his blessing with apparent contrition—but explicitly not apologizing, even doubling down, at which point chagrined pilgrims dragged her away. That AP shot made it into national publications. Del, meanwhile, snapped a photograph of Leander Perez delivering a fiery segregationist speech to cheering rubes, his forearm bulging and fist clenched. Perez died a few years later, his name now synonymous with corruption and radical racism, but the bird-bath bigot fought on for decades, placing polemical ads "To Obey God's Blood Covenant—Law of Segregation" in the *Times-Picayune* as late as 1980. As of this writing, the nonagenarian lives in Metairie, reputedly unrepentant and still estranged from the Church.[4]

Three years after the sit-ins and schooling crisis, suffrage became the thrust of the civil rights stories Del covered. CORE and James Farmer, the same forces behind the 1960 Canal Street sit-ins and the 1961 Freedom Ride, had been conducting voter registration drives in Baton Rouge, and arrived at the nearby town of Plaquemine on word that officials had gerrymandered black precincts out of city elections. Farmer, as a close ally of Rev. Martin Luther King Jr., was particularly reviled by segregationists, and news of his arrival fomented local resistance. On August 19, 1963, Farmer led a slow-cadenced protest march through downtown Plaquemine under the most tenuous of police protection, based, according to Chief Dennis Songy, on an understanding that "the Negroes had promised not to sing." Defiantly, they sung—"We Shall Overcome," a thousand voices strong—and that's when the police fired multiple barrages of tear gas bombs. The intervention sent the marchers fleeing back to their Plymouth Rock Baptist Church and landed the organizers in jail cells. Neither side gave, each organizing boycotts and counter-boycotts and taking their message to the streets, while authorities secured a federal district court order against demonstrations. By week's end, over two hundred protestors had been arrested.

Del had been sent alone to investigate the unrest, and when he realized it was growing, he called in for the support of WWL-TV reporter Bob Jones. Townspeople on both sides eyed the pair curiously, almost opportunistically; when they saw Del's camera, both blacks and whites reacted with ingratiation, savvy to the power he wielded. To be sure, civil rights activists had well understood the power of the press in showing the world the spectacle of southern race relations—witness the Woolworth's sit-in—but what Del's experiences in Plaquemine and New Orleans reveal is that segregationists oftentimes felt the same way—that airing their point of view on camera would convince the world of their righteousness. The town sheriff, to whom Del introduced himself, succumbed to the camera's spell as well: next time they met, Del

noticed the lawman had adorned himself with a diamond-studded badge, wanting to look his dandiest, Louisiana style, for his moment in the limelight. "Neither side hated us," says Del. "The protestors didn't hate us[;] the white activists didn't hate us. They didn't seem to mind being part of this spectacle. They were probably pretty happy to see themselves on TV." The camera also helped protect the demonstrators, at least some of them some of the time, and probably Del as well, as he rendered himself nearly invisible—and maximally influential—when he crouched behind it.

The Plaquemine demonstrators took a hiatus in late August as their attention shifted to the March on Washington, which culminated with King's rousing "I Have a Dream" speech at the Lincoln Memorial. Farmer, meanwhile, languished in a Donaldsonville jail cell, all those in Plaquemine having been filled with demonstrators. He was finally released on August 30 and promptly resumed the struggle, deriding the police as "hillbilly cops" and rallying protestors at Plymouth Rock Church (which congregants had nicknamed Freedom Rock). So motivated, a group of teenagers marched down Court Street to City Hall, technically in violation of the federal restraining order, and were promptly chased down by mounted police and struck with cattle prods. Angered over the beating of their children, the demonstrators on Sunday, September 1, regrouped in the church to pray, sing, and strategize, as authorities milled about outside. Del noticed how a rookie cameraman from WAFB in Baton Rouge was shooting willy-nilly at any sign of discord. Del's instincts told him that the situation was mounting, not stabilizing, and that the setting sun meant he would have to preserve his battery for his camera's energy-draining light-and-shoot feature should something happen after dark.

Outside, helmeted police and state troopers on horseback grew impatient. With nightfall upon them, and legally emboldened by the restraining order, they decided to intervene. Bob Jones explained what happened next: "Suddenly, the cops surged into the crowd, the horses knocking down adults and kids[,] using cattle prods and clubs, hurting a lot of people. Then, without warning, the cops, wearing gas masks, filled the church with tear gas, broke down the front doors, and stormed inside, using high pressure hoses to all but level the sanctuary and knock out the windows. They drove the people inside out and then beat the hell out of them."[5] White and black men engaged in fisticuffs all around downtown, and protestors hurled enough rocks, bricks, and bottles to send twenty authorities to Plaquemine's sanitarium with injuries. Del himself was knocked down by a trooper on horseback, and both he and Bob "had to stop off at the Plaquemine clinic afterwards to have our eyes washed out." Farmer, target of the police action, escaped and went into hiding.

Racing back to New Orleans in the wee hours of September 2, Del and Bob realized to their chagrin they needed gas. While stopped at a late-night fueling station among the sugarcane fields along Highway 90, they happened to run into a familiar face in the New Orleans civil rights struggle. It was NAACP branch president Ernest N. "Dutch" Morial, returning wearily from voter-registration efforts—and, incongruously, at 4 a.m., sipping a Coke. None of them would have any inkling at the time, but fourteen years later, Morial would be voted the first black mayor of New Orleans.

Returning to the WWL studio at 5:30 a.m., Del had the film processed at the all-night Pan American Labs, edited it, and, at 8:00 a.m., "fed it" via coaxial cable to *CBS Evening News* studios in New York. His unique nocturnal footage of the Plymouth Rock Church assault was particularly significant because it aired on September 2, with Walter Cronkite anchoring and Dan Rather reporting, as part of the nation's first half-hour nightly news broadcast, previous shows having run only fifteen minutes. Coming on the heels of the March on Washington, the footage served as a reminder of the many wrongs that remained. Bob later wrote to Del, "You got everything on film. What really surprised me was how calm and deliberate we both were, you shooting very selectively and me taking notes until the tear gas got to both of us."[6] Their Plaquemine coverage, plus Del's work in the 1960 school integration crisis in New Orleans, had played key roles in the two moments to date when black Louisianans' quest for equality became the nation's leading civil rights story.

After the incident, both sides in Plaquemine requested intervention from U.S. Attorney General Robert F. Kennedy, insinuating that each saw itself as virtuous and victimized. Whites overwhelmingly directed their outrage at Farmer, who they viewed as the agitator of the discontent and instigator of the violence, and seethed as he described their community to national audiences as a "town under siege" and the violence of September 1 as a "night of wild terror." Mounted troopers hunted Farmer door to door in what supporters, who harbored him in a funeral home and handed him a loaded .45 to defend himself, viewed quite plainly as "a lynch mob" bent on killing him. Bloodshed was avoided when the supporters sneaked Farmer out in a hearse in an elaborate ploy complete with a decoy car, guided by maps of roadblocks and back roads through wildlife hunting grounds. Farmer finally made it back to the relative safety of New Orleans.[7]

Del had been immediately re-dispatched to cover integration protests at Murphy High School in Mobile, after which he had a chance to tend to matters at the office. Among them: seeking reimbursement for his green Haspel Brothers suit, which had been torn when the trooper's horse knocked him to the ground. Del still has the WWL expense report: "Replace suit ruined at Plaquemine riot 9/1/63 $30.00." A professional man in subtropical New Orleans, after all, is not properly dressed unless he's in a dapper seersucker from Haspel's. As he turned in the paperwork, a stranger came calling for him in the studio's visiting room. He turned out to be an FBI agent on assignment to piece together exactly what had happened in Plaquemine. Del told him everything he witnessed and showed him the footage. "I believe he chose to ignore anything negative, and made no notes of anything he did not want to hear," Del tells. "It left me with a bad impression."

By then the turmoil in Plaquemine had wound down, but the community had been forever changed. Farmer himself, speaking twenty years later, testified that "Right after the incident, blacks went on a voter registration and voter education campaign [and] threw the sheriff out of office. . . . There are now blacks on the police force of Plaquemine [and] holding key public office in both the parish and in the state. It has changed now, as it has changed in much of the South."[8] Change met particularly fierce resistance in the Louisiana mill town of Bogalusa, in Washington Parish. Located in the piney woods north of Lake Pontchartrain, this region had by some estimates the highest per-capita Ku Klux Klan membership in the South, in part because its industrialized, non-agricultural economy positioned whites and blacks in a competitive stance over mill jobs, and racial intimidation ensured that whites would gain more than their share of the better opportunities. Klansmen occupied positions throughout local government, and nighttime rallies of hundreds of hooded members saluting burning crosses occurred regularly.

Inspired by the success of civil rights protestors throughout the South, Bogalusa blacks took to the streets in early 1965 to defy the Klan presence and the white domination of mill jobs. Police suppressed them at every march, arresting as many as they could. "But everything changed," explains Del's partner Bob, "when the Deacons for Defense came to town." The turmoil in Bogalusa occurred at what proved to be a transitional phase in the nation's civil rights movement (1955–1965), when many black activists began to take up arms rather than patiently request equality. A new black militancy, in the form of the Deacons for Defense and Justice, thus arrived in Bogalusa, putting a twist on the prevailing narrative of nonviolent civil disobedience that surrounded the larger national movement. They and their cronies clashed head-on with the equally militant Ku Klux Klan and its allies. A bloody racial brawl ensued downtown, and was followed by numerous scuffles and flashpoints throughout the spring and summer of 1965, making Bogalusa a longer, more violent, and potentially more explosive situation than Plaquemine in 1963.

Also unlike Plaquemine, neither side in Bogalusa was particularly pleased to see journalists bearing cameras, a testament to the violence they were prepared to bring forth. Bob and Del did their best not to draw attention, such as renting a car rather than using a marked WWL vehicle, but nonetheless they pursued the story wherever and whenever it was, from all angles. "One Sunday night," Bob tells,

we covered a rally at a church in the African-American section of town[;] there was a decided lack of

streetlights so it was REALLY dark. I remember thinking to myself, "Here we are in this black neighborhood in this black church packed to the rafters . . . probably surrounded by every member of the Klan from at least four parishes. And we didn't even let the newsroom know what we were doing." Of course, those were the days when we both were just naive enough to believe that we were invincible and that nothing would happen. Thank God, on that night at least, it didn't.[9]

A day or so later, the duo in their unmarked car followed marchers to a segregated drive-in. As they parked between two cars in the lot, a beat-up pickup pulled behind them, locking them in. A burly ruffian then emerged from the drive-in and, indicating that a firearm was tucked in his clothes, "told us in no uncertain terms to get the hell off his property, and intimated we would be seriously sorry if we didn't." When Del and Bob acquiesced, he signaled to his accomplice in the pickup to pull back and let them out. They gingerly eased back onto the street, and noticed a dark sedan parked at the far end of the lot, in which two stone-faced figures were busily taking notes. They were FBI agents, and buoyed by their presence, the reporters felt safe enough to call the police department to request an escort out of town. "The police graciously complied with our request," recalled Bob sardonically. "Turns out, the three cops in the patrol car that day were later indicted by a federal grand jury and turned out to be members of the Ku Klux Klan."[10]

That was not their only run-in with the feared Bogalusa Klan. During another dispatch to the troubled city, Bob and Del discreetly covered an evening manifestation in the wooded outskirts. Del recalls it as a Klan rally; Bob remembers it as the animal stockade at the parish fairgrounds where police had detained protestors who had been arrested. As they filmed the scene, a man materialized out of the twilight and reproachfully asked them what they were doing. Their response was cut off by the man's swipe at their camera, followed by an incensed demand for their film. The two journalists hustled away, jumped into their rental car, and made off down a network of bumpy one-lane dirt roads. Bob was at the wheel, which freed up Del to try to film the man as he summoned fellow Klansmen and jumped in their vehicle. A chase ensued for three tense minutes, but as night had now fallen, Bob was able to throw off the pursuers by turning off his headlights and disappearing into the piney woods. They made it back to New Orleans, film and all. "You haven't been chased until you're chased by the Klan down a dark country road at night," Del says ruefully. "To me, Bogalusa was Philadelphia, Mississippi, in the making," added Bob, in reference to the murder of three civil rights workers during Freedom Summer in 1964. "That almost happened, but didn't."[11] (Del knew the Philadelphia story well: he filmed the recovery of the bodies at the reservoir via low-flying aircraft, and his colleague Bill Reed snapped the famous photograph of the smirking lawmen at their December 1964 arraignment, one of them cavalierly drawing tobacco from a bag of Red Man.)

Bogalusa's racial turmoil, like Plaquemine's, improved markedly by the 1970s but never quite disappeared. In 2008, Klan activity once again resurfaced in the woods outside town, making headlines nationwide and costing one troubled woman her life.

Not all civil rights stories yielded filmable moments. In fact, some important ones pointedly avoided them. One day, Del and Bill Reed drove to Baton Rouge to cover the state legislature about to vote on a major integration bill. The session had just opened when a representative immediately raised a motion to adjourn, which went straight to an up-or-down vote without debate. The motion passed, the session adjourned, and the integration bill had been successfully derailed, leaving Del with nothing to film for what in fact was a significant story. So he directed Bill to stand by the capitol and explain what had happened. With that, Del and Bill invented the "stand-up," in which a correspondent reporting from the site of a news story becomes the visual *for* the news story. Viewers in New Orleans had never seen it before, and shortly thereafter, colleagues and competitors adopted the tactic and used it regularly. "We were inventing this [business] as we went along," Del chuckles—"inspired," he adds, "by the movies."

Some civil rights stories were so close that Del and company all but missed them. Although WWL's studio lay within the confines of the city's oldest neighborhood, it bore a striking modernist façade (unchanged today) that contrasted starkly with the classic scenography of the French Quarter. Inside, however, was a design feature that was anything but modern, and anything but rare: there were two men's rooms in the main hallway, one labeled "White," the other "Colored." Segregation had ironically given the sole African American who worked at WWL, named Henry Turner, his own private restroom. (There was only one women's room because all the women who worked at WWL—more than the other stations, but only because they were paid less—were white.) The Jim Crow toilets, just downstairs from Dan Rather's CBS Southern Bureau office, remained so labeled at least through 1966, a time by which similar facilities elsewhere had been quietly removed.

Other news stories involving the African American population were coldly neglected—not necessarily out of explicit racial animus or misanthropy, but rather from a deeply institutionalized racism that rendered whites oblivious or indifferent to the disparities and injustices all around them. Del and his colleagues, for example, covered plenty of traumatic deaths: vehicular accidents, a hobo severed by a freight train, a couple asphyxiated by gas heating on a cold winter night. But, strangely, Del could not recall ever covering a murder. The reason was not because killings did not happen, though they were far scarcer than today. The reason was because the station had an unstated policy of disregarding crime in the back-of-town, where most murders occurred. Taking pains to transport listeners to the mindset of New Orleans in the early 1960s, Del explained in 2013, "We had a police scanner all the time, and whenever there was something on or behind South Rampart Street, we just ignored it. It wasn't like someone getting shot on Canal Street. No one thought it was wrong [to ignore it]; we just thought it wasn't really news . . . it wasn't out of the ordinary. You just couldn't cover every black shooting. 'Normal' is not the right word; it was *common*. You became immune to it. Like Viet Nam."

Producers ensured that hard news stories were more than

matched by lighter sports and pop culture fare. Del covered the entire 1963 LSU football season, and was among the first editors to post scores in a creatively dynamic manner, long before dazzling graphics became *de rigueur* in sports reporting. He regularly covered the Kentucky Derby in Louisville and the Masters Golf Tournament in Augusta, where, one time, he scored something of a cameraman coup. "We had a big platform at the 18th hole," Del remembered, "and Arnold Palmer was just about to make his putt, when he stopped and wanted all the cameras to pause—they were making too much noise. Well, I didn't have to stop because I was using my blimped [internally soundproofed] Auricon camera, which didn't make noise. . . . I was so happy I got that shot. . . . Palmer sunk his final putt and won the Masters that year, on my film."

Another dream assignment came Del's way toward the end of his stint at WVUE. He and sports director Al Wester, recently hired from WDSU after rumors of a payola scandal, were dispatched to balmy Florida to cover the 1960 Major League Baseball spring training season. Together with Wester's wife, two kids, and a dog, they drove across the pre-interstate Gulf Coast in a lumbering Cadillac ("I paid my dues," Del grins wistfully) and got to work. Del would shoot over 3,000 feet of sound-on-film interviews of a who's-who of midcentury baseball greats, among them Yogi Berra, Stan Musial, Hank Aaron, Whitey Ford, Warren Spahn, Red Barber, and the ever-cantankerous Casey Stengel. The material ran daily in the New Orleans market as well as throughout Texas, Tennessee, and Georgia, illustrating how affiliates would share stories of popular interest. One particular incident, however, soured his view of ballplayers. He remembers seeing an adoring little boy begging an aloof Whitey Ford for an autograph, to which the Yankees star finally gruffly complied. "Ha," snickered Ford to a teammate after he haphazardly scrawled his signature. "Dumb kid didn't even realize I signed that with my left hand." The incident vexed the kid-from-the-Projects in Del: *what a jerk.* On the drive back to New Orleans, Del found much nicer folks at Weeki Wachee Springs, where Wester, a real wheeler-dealer, finagled a story on the park's famously kitschy underwater dancing mer-

Covering a litany of greats for WVUE at spring training for major league baseball, 1960. *Del Hall Collection.*

maids. They deserved much better coverage than Whitey Ford did, and they got it.

Pop culture was a favorite respite for local news producers, particularly when famous celebrities came to town. Del got press access and plenty of photographs of the making of *The Cincinnati Kid,* including shots of Steve McQueen and local second-line bands milling about the set in the Iberville Projects. Another time, he picked up the Andrews Sisters at the Monteleone Hotel to drive them to the studio for a live guest show. (Whatever expectations he had of their coquett-

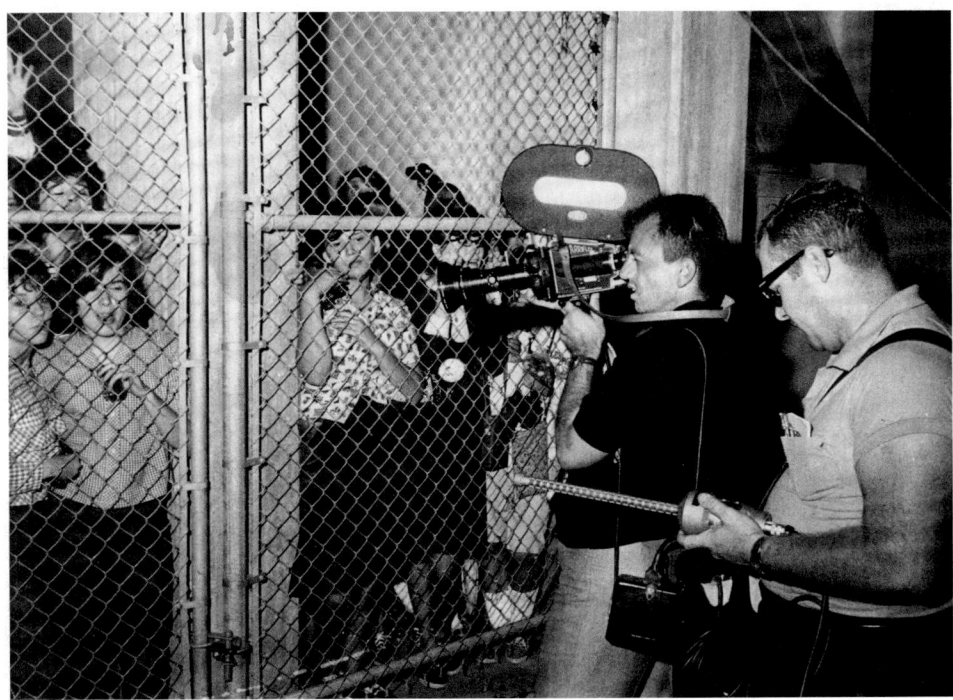

Del films fans awaiting the Beatles in City Park Stadium. *Photo by WWL-TV/Del Hall Collection.*

ish World War II days were dashed when all three singers, now middle-aged, spent the entire ride opening letters and chatting about family.)

His biggest pop culture assignment? Without a doubt, the Beatles. Seven months into their American invasion, the musicians landed at Lakefront Airport, lodged at the Congress Inn on Chef Menteur Highway, and arrived at City Park Stadium on September 16, 1964, for what would be their one and only performance in New Orleans. Emerging from their limo, the foursome ran past reporters and photographers shouting, "No pictures! No pictures!" which, of course, is exactly what reporters and photographers like to hear. Del filmed away. "During the concert," he recalls, "I could barely hear the Beatles because of all the screaming girls who began jumping out of the stands and running toward the stage. Cops were chasing them in every direction. It was surreal . . . little girls being chased by big cops—and tackled! . . .

Afterwards, the empty grass field, still brightly lit, was littered with shoes, sweaters and other bits. I climbed onto the empty stage and did something I knew I could brag about someday. I sat at Ringo's drums!"

Del was less likely to brag about the time he and a reporter were scheduled to interview Bette Davis. The Hollywood legend was in town for a performance of *The World of Carl Sandburg* at Tulane University and grudgingly agreed to meet with the twosome in her room at the elegant Sheraton Hotel on St. Charles—just upstairs, Del noted, from the Western Union office where he once toiled as a teenager. Now, he marveled contentedly, he was hobnobbing with Hollywood stars! Ever dependable, Del arrived early to Davis's luxury suite (mistake #1 for any man), checked himself over for seersucker perfection, and, with his trusty Auricon sound camera and tripod on his shoulder, rapped crisply on the door. It slowly swung open to reveal none other than—Bette Davis! In the flesh, just like in the movies! Those mysterious dark eyes, the cigarette drawn slowly from her lips, a hint of roguish sexuality! "Ummm, well hello, Miss Davis," he stammered, "good day to you; I'm, uh, I'll be filming the interview with you just as *sooooon* as my partner arriv—"

BAM! No sooner did the words leave his mouth did the aging star slam the door in his face. Apparently Bette Davis was above cameramen. Oh well. When the reporter finally arrived, she admitted them and did the interview, but Del doesn't remember anything after that. Who would?

Famed filmmaker Billy Wilder (*The Seven Year Itch, Some Like It Hot*) also came before Del's camera, but his problem differed from Davis's egotism. Wilder repeatedly sought assurance that Del would not confuse him with William Wyler

(*Ben-Hur, The Best Years of Our Lives*), a near doppelgänger who led a remarkably similar career, apparently to the irritation of Wilder. "I still have to think which is which," Del laughs.

WWL produced New Orleans features as well as covered news. One of Del's signature productions was something he co-invented with Leo Willette, his Air Force–era associate from North Carolina who now worked at WWL. Leo was an amazing person—smart, creative, skilled, hard-working, and daring, if a bit kooky. There was just one problem: everybody hated Leo. Everybody. Even Leo hated Leo. He rubbed people the wrong way—perhaps because he was aggressive and dismissive, because he was ahead of his time, or because some of his ideas seemed to have been phoned in from outer space. One time he had Del film women with curlers in their hair on Canal Street and aired the piece during the news—complete with legs-and-derriere shots—under the title, "Standing on the Corner, Watching All the Curls Go By." Another time he documented the various techniques of catching Mardi Gras beads—including tips for the blind. Even nuttier was his idea to add to the weather report a cigar-chomping midget named Carlos Marshmallow (a pun on local mob boss Carlos Marcello), decked out in a pinstripe suit and fedora, who made meteorology more interesting by wringing out a soaked sponge whenever the words "relative humidity" arose. Later, Leo was crazy enough to purchase the notorious Conti Street brothel of madam Norma Wallace.

For every few wacky ideas, however, Leo devised a winner. His premier brainchild was *Shades of New Orleans,* a series of beautifully filmed and poetically narrated three-minute vignettes of city life, a local forerunner of Charles Kuralt's *On the Road.* Del filmed for *Shades* stories such as the above-ground "Cities of the Dead," the Flying Horses at Audubon Park, Jackson Square "starving artists" like Johnny Donnels, the traditional jazz musicians at Preservation Hall, various social aid and pleasure club funerals and second-line parades, a charming portrait of French Quarter life entitled "Sunday on Burgundy" (Del's favorite), and a particularly valuable episode on the now-gone squatters of the batture along the wooded banks of the Mississippi. The black-and-white shorts aired at the end of Willette's Sunday evening news show, at which point he would intone, "And now it's time for another *Shades of New Orleans!*" The features improved after CBS Broadcast donated color projectors to its affiliates in 1961, for which Del acquired hundred-foot rolls of Kodachrome color film, the type that could only be processed by Kodak via mail. *Shades* thus became the first regularly scheduled color television programming in the city, and possibly the South. With about fifty stories running from 1960 through 1962, the vignettes enjoyed widespread popularity among New Orleanians, who had never seen their quirky city so lovingly depicted. *Shades* was also Leo's baby, and he promoted it relentlessly, almost obsessively. He coined "Smile, You May Be on *Shades of New Orleans*" and plastered stickers of the catchphrase on signs, walls, hallways, doors, toilets, everywhere, all over town. Building owners complained about Leo to WWL's program director, Rupert Copponex, who, needless to say, hated Leo. One day he called Leo into his office, cited the gripes, and took the opportunity to air his own grievances. Finally he delivered the bad news. "'Leo,'" Del tells today, giving voice to Copponex and chuckling at the memory, "'It looks like it's *curtains* for *Shades.*'" The show nonetheless remained popular under the direction of Jim Metcalf and eventually ran its course. Unfortunately, most, probably all, reels of *Shades of New Orleans* were either lost over time or destroyed in the Hurricane Katrina flood.

One day in 1962, WWL general manager Mike Early told Del to meet him at a particular bar out on Magazine Street. Why so far? Usually the television men rendezvoused in the Quarter. "Just keep it quiet," Early replied. Upon arriving at the darkened saloon, he found Early, Phil Johnson, and WWL ownership representative Father Aloysius Goodspeed huddled in the corner. Soon he learned why: they had a special assignment for him. He would go to Rome to cover Vatican II—not just for a news story, but something unheard of at that time: an hour-long color documentary with inside access to the Vatican. It was Early's idea, and he was able to arrange sponsorship from Progresso Foods, which had both

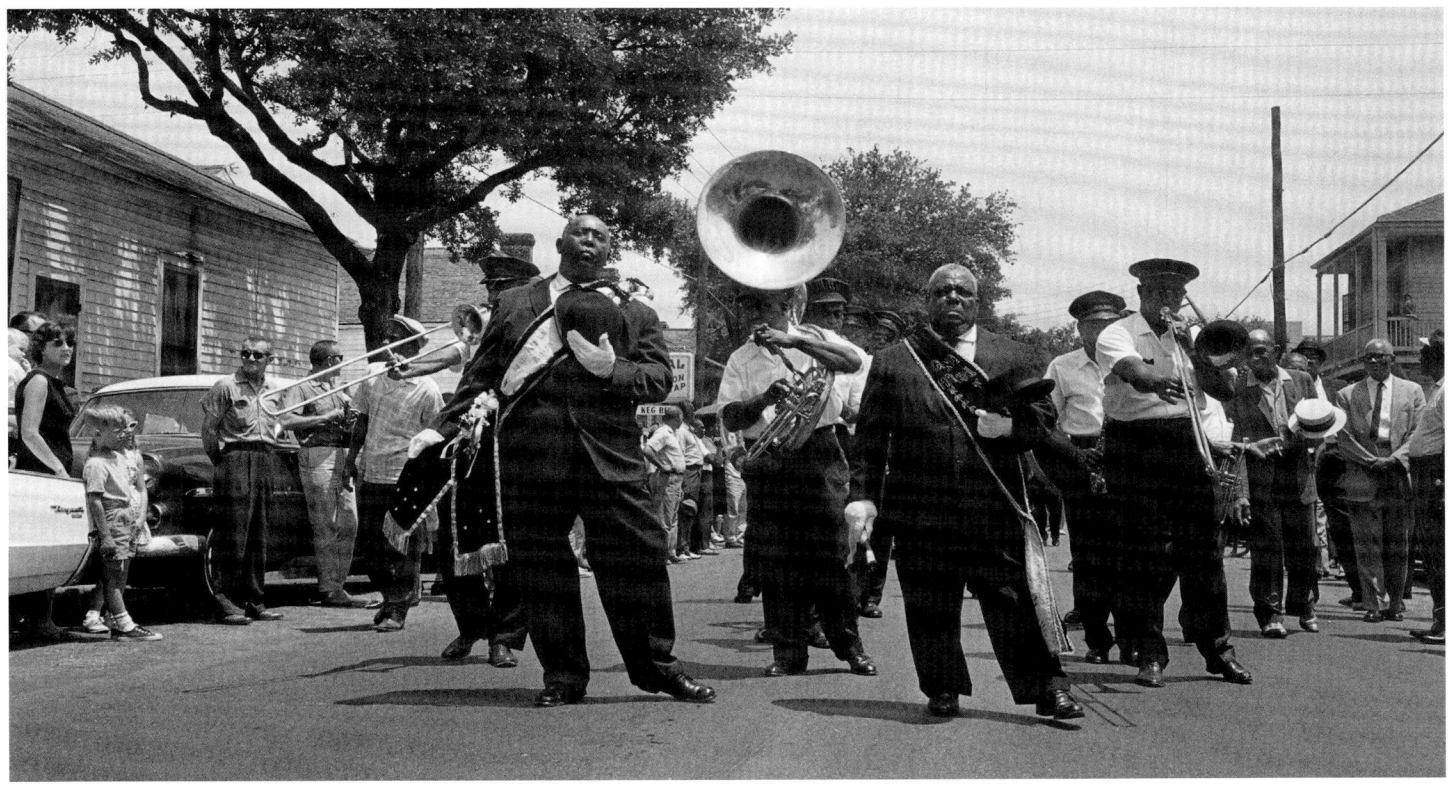

New Orleans jazz funeral, led by grand marshals Matthew "Fats" Houston (left) and probably Ace Watson, Eureka Brass Band, early 1960s. *Photo by Del Hall.*

New Orleans and Italian connections. Early recognized that the Ecumenical Council's pronouncements might deeply affect this majority-Catholic city, and that WWL's Jesuit owners were particularly obligated to cover them. But most of all, Early wanted to blow WDSU out of the water. Giving the documentary additional appeal was the fact that aging Archbishop Joseph Rummel and Coadjutor Archbishop John P. Cody would be participating in the Council, and could help Del gain precious access to the proceedings. Early entrusted Del alone with the project, and swore him to secrecy.

Del read everything he could on Rome and the Vatican, gathered his bulky CBS color camera and all the film he could carry, bid farewell to Greta and the children in Metairie, and departed Moisant Airport, bound first for Paris. His foray to the City of Lights allowed him to capture B-roll footage of famous sites, including the Eiffel Tower and the Arc de Triomphe, where he happened upon a ceremony featuring President Charles de Gaulle. The classic American in Paris, Del cheerfully asked a taxi driver to take him to see the Bastille, whereupon he learned, to his chagrin, that he was 173 years too late.

Upon arriving in Italy in early October, Del hired an electrician and a driver, and, communicating through cognates and sign language (his Italian peaked at *un espresso e due cappuccinos*), was ready to take on Rome. Unfortunately, no one told the Romans. He soon learned that the Eternal City went dormant from noon to about 3 p.m., which complicated everything he planned to do, including sending daily progress reports to WWL.

The assignment fulfilled Del's childhood daydreams—of

Life photographers in the field, covering world news in exotic locations. Inspired by *Life*'s "Behind the Scenes" feature, he photographed his spread of equipment at an iconic spot by the Coliseum and, with a bit of Hollywood directorial flair, had a local artisan chisel two rusticated plaques bearing the engraving WWL-TV ROMA 1962, to display in the documentary's end pieces. He later gifted one to his boss Early; the other, which actually aired, sits today on Del's shelf in Chicago.

Bishop Cody and Del forged a fruitful partnership in Rome, Cody benefiting from the coverage and Del from the access. "I pretty much kidnapped the Archbishop," Del chortles, recounting how he guided Cody to historic sites and let him explain them to viewers back home. They followed the chariot tracks of the Appian Way, visited the church where Cody had been ordained, walked the banks of the Tiber River, and toured the Coliseum, which was free, wide open—and infested with cats. Together they met with Rev. Pedro Arrupe, the influential Jesuit and survivor of Hiroshima who would later become the Superior General of the Society of Jesus, the so-called Black Pope. Del also filmed Bishop Cody saying Mass in the Catacombs, and when the rudimentary electrical lighting flickered out, Cody continued the liturgy in cavelike darkness, his Latin echoing off the walls timelessly. (Not all was solemn: the two also made off to Cody's favorite drinking hole, where, Del remembers, the archbishop ordered a Tom Collins.)

As the Ecumenical Council opened on October 11, eyes throughout the Catholic world fell on the 2,600 participating religious leaders and the charismatic Pope John XXIII. The best media perches within St. Peter's Basilica were reserved for engineers and cameramen of the Italian Television Network and a Roman movie company. But "Hall's ingenuity," as Mike Early later wrote, "got him into the Basilica [as] the only television news[man] to photograph in glorious color. . . . [He] managed to bluff his way past the Swiss guard with his camera under his coat and from that vantage point high in the Basilica, caught all the majesty and beauty of the opening day ceremony."[12] Roll after roll he shot of that and subsequent events, returning nightly at 11 p.m. to his hotel, where he would report back to WWL. Distinctive for his specialized equipment and chipper American demeanor, Del came to be a familiar sight around Vatican press circles, so much so that Archbishop Cody was able to arrange for him to meet the pope. Relishing the opportunity, Del thought back to the nuns at St. Joseph and the priests at Jesuit. Here he was a decade later, about to meet the spiritual leader of two billion Catholics, at the moment he would change the Church forever.

A meeting with the pontiff starts with a foray into the Vatican's inner chambers. Del was driven, along with the two New Orleans archbishops, into a courtyard serving the papal quarters. From there they proceeded down a narrow hallway, through room after room, until they entered a large chamber with a series of cubicles, each filled with other guests awaiting their papal appointment. Del recalls that one distinguished-looking American clergyman in regalia, Cardinal Cushing of Boston, eyed the New Orleans contingent suspiciously, as if to say, "How did those clowns get in?" Finally they were called into the papal library, and there was Pope John XXIII, smiling warmly, arms open in welcome. He held out his ring for Del to kiss, and Bishop Cody introduced him as a television cameraman from his home diocese. The pope nodded approvingly and responded, through Cody's translation, "This is good, because we need all methods to distribute the Word." The statement signaled Pope John XXIII's embrace of modernity and presaged the liberalizations and reforms forthcoming from the Second Vatican Council by the time it closed in 1965. Vatican II changed the lives of Catholics in New Orleans as much as anywhere, and Del got its opening session on film, in color, roll after hundred-foot roll, 8,000 feet in all.

He shipped the cache home and got permission to fly to Berlin for a very different story, the recently completed Berlin Wall dividing the Soviet-dominated East from the Allied-protected West. "The effect of the war was still visible even though it had ended almost twenty years ago," Del recounts. All day on October 22, he shot footage of the front line of the Cold War, including scowling armed guards, floral memorials for those killed trying to cross, and bleak deserted streets lined with bombed-out buildings on the other side.

Returning to his hotel late that night, he tuned in the Voice of America to catch up on news back home. What he heard was an anxious voice announcing that President John F. Kennedy would address the nation at 7 p.m. Eastern Standard Time on a matter of pressing importance.

Del felt as though he knew the young president; he had photographed him up close on the steps of New Orleans City Hall just five months earlier and had chatted with the then-senator during the 1960 presidential campaign. Now, on his transistor radio, he heard President Kennedy announce that Soviet missiles had been discovered on Cuban soil, opening up a new and potentially hot front in the Cold War. Early the next morning, he contacted WWL in expectation of being deployed to Havana, and promptly flew home. He was a bit nervous, given his experience a year and a half earlier, when he was scheduled to cover the Bay of Pigs invasion but backed out when he grew suspicious as to how a "secret" attack could be so plainly and openly scheduled. WWL's inside contact on the planned invasion was one Sergio Arcacha Smith, a virulent Castro foe with murky ties to the underworld and a flair for old New Orleans–style Latin American filibustering. Del's instincts proved correct; the invasion turned out to be a bloody fiasco, and a stain on Kennedy's foreign policy record. Now, eighteen months later, the president redeemed himself by defusing a superpower showdown that, in retrospect, ranked as the closest humanity has ever come to an all-out nuclear war. Del was happy to stay off Castro's island a second time; the movies had inspired him to be adventurous, but the Projects had taught him to be shrewd, and with a wife, family, and career now in high gear, he'd rather be shrewd and alive than adventurous and dead. As for Sergio Arcacha Smith, he was worth holding askance. The firebrand later found himself embroiled in a bizarre court case in which he was suspected for the murder of none other than President John F. Kennedy.

The resolution of the Cuban missile crisis allowed Del to proceed with editing the vast amount of raw footage from Rome. Once he assembled the best scenes, complete with his stone WWL-TV ROMA 1962 plaques and an amusing sponsor tableau of a toy Roman centurion perched on a Progresso tomato can, he passed the reel to Jim Kincaid to write the script. Kincaid's narrative, however, struck the sprightly tone of a tourist travelogue, and missed the majesty and solemnity of the event. Mike Early tasked Phil Johnson to rewrite the script with the requisite gravitas, which Johnson, who came out of the newspaper world, delivered in a manner that would later make him revered by a generation of New Orleanians for his eloquent baritone on-air editorials.

Vatican II achieved all of WWL's aims, and then some, having won Del the Catholic Broadcasters Association's Gold Bell Award and a rare letter of accolade from the General of the Society of Jesus in Rome. A year later, after Pope John XXIII died, Del returned to Rome to capture the coronation ceremonies of Pope Paul VI. "I had to secure a tripod position a day ahead," Del says, "by climbing up a ladder and securing a perch [overlooking] the outdoor platform next to the base of St. Peter's statue." There he got the best seat in the house covering the last pope to be crowned ceremonially. Another successful hour-long color documentary resulted, complete with behind-the-scenes access and close-up footage of President Kennedy's visit to Rome's Pontifical North American College. Entitled *Apostle to the World,* the work cemented Del's reputation as a master of his craft.[13] He didn't have much time to regroup before its September 15, 1963, airing, however, because he was busy covering the civil rights unrest in Plaquemine. And when he wasn't covering breaking news, he took on additional documentary work as part of Early's new Special Projects department, headed by Phil Johnson and equipped with the city's first state-of-the-art recording and dubbing studio, plus one of the first German-made 16 mm Arriflex cameras in the United States.[14]

Special Projects' goal was to build on its *Vatican II* success with similar documentaries on topics of interest to WWL's viewership. With Del at the camera, the department went on to pioneer the television news "feature" and "investigative" story format, with pieces on topics such as the Chinchuba lip-reading school for deaf children (*A Tree in the Forest*), traffic fatalities (*Wheel of Death*), President Lyndon B. Johnson's new Medicare program, the New Orleans coffee industry (*Million Dollar Bean*), religious vocations (*A Priest Forever*), plus two biographies on archbishops Cody and Hannan, a school-board and levee-board taxation investigation (*The Million Dollar Question*), and a special on the 1965 hurricane-induced flood entitled *72 Hours of Betsy,* which Del edited and Larry Lala and Mike O'Connor shot. Managers Bill Reed and Rufus Rivers, who did the assigning and dispatching, generally sent Lala and O'Connor to cover everyday local incidents, such as the one on August 9, 1963, when O'Connor filmed some character passing out Communist leaflets on Camp at Common after he locked horns with Cuban exiles and got himself arrested on Canal Street.[15]

Del's daily schedule became increasingly relentless. It started before dawn at his family's home in the Lynette Park subdivision of Metairie and had him shaving in the WWL car as he sped down Airline Highway to the downtown studio, listening to Don McNeill's Breakfast Club (*"brought to you from the Tip Top Tap, high above the Allerton Hotel, overlooking the Magnificent Mile in downtown Chicago"*). A police scanner kept him apprised of breaking incidents, and a two-way radio kept him on short leash with the studio. Traffic was light but thickened more and more each year, as the first wave of white families fled the integrating schools for the mostly white subdivisions of Jefferson Parish. It was there where he and Greta were raising their family. Del's focus, however, tipped increasingly toward his career, and in the fiercely competitive marketplace of the job he loved, he found himself investing fewer and fewer hours in family life and the couple's growing number of children—five by 1965. One particular moment is illustrative: a vessel on Lake Pontchartrain crashed into the Causeway Bridge on the same day that Greta was about to give birth to their second child. Del got the call, raced to his car—and drove to the crash scene. The couple began to grow apart, and Del recognized his role in the drift. Greta had her own demons, traceable to her troubled childhood, and they began to manifest themselves in the form of a drinking problem. Stress on the home front made work that much more enticing, which of course only widened the distance.

Then there was Del's dad. A lifelong smoker and drinker who lived what family members wistfully described as a "don't-worry-about-tomorrow" lifestyle, Pops had been diagnosed with cancer in 1963. The disease spread swiftly and claimed his life in November. After a solemn burial in Greenwood Cemetery, the Halls convened for a luncheon at a nice restaurant, as if to turn over a new leaf and refocus on family.[16] It was early afternoon, and a daytime drama droned on the television set above the dining din. Suddenly a newsflash came on the screen, and the crowd hushed. An announcer reported that shots had been fired at the president's motorcade in Dallas. Shortly thereafter, a visibly shaken Walter Cronkite came on the air and told the nation that President Kennedy was dead.

For once, Del did not race to the studio; he had the weekend off on account of Pops's passing. Like most Americans, he sat glued to the television, exchanging phone calls with the studio in the hopes of gleaning inside information from CBS. Authorities in Dallas had arrested a suspect, he learned, and upon seeing his face, Del pulled close to the screen. This Oswald character seemed familiar, and word from the station was that the suspect did indeed have New Orleans ties. Two days later, Del saw Oswald shot and killed on live television, an act that immediately catapulted the assassination into the realm of conspiracy theories. A nation reeling from a sudden tragic change of government now desperately needed to know who this Oswald character was.

Amid a flurry of phone calls, Del and his colleagues finally pinned down that vaguely familiar face. It was the man Mike O'Connor had filmed back in August distributing leaflets on Camp Street! Other stations shot the scene as well, but O'Connor's two minutes of footage were of the highest quality. Del explains, "After the JFK assassination, this film became very valuable. [*Life* photographer] Flip Schulke put the positive in our enlarger and projected a single 16 mm frame onto a 4 × 5 film holder to make a negative. He later printed it, and it became one of the more famous images of Oswald before the assassination."

What made O'Connor's footage uniquely valuable was the plainly visible words HANDS OFF CUBA on the leaflet, quite literally linking Oswald with that political ideology. That

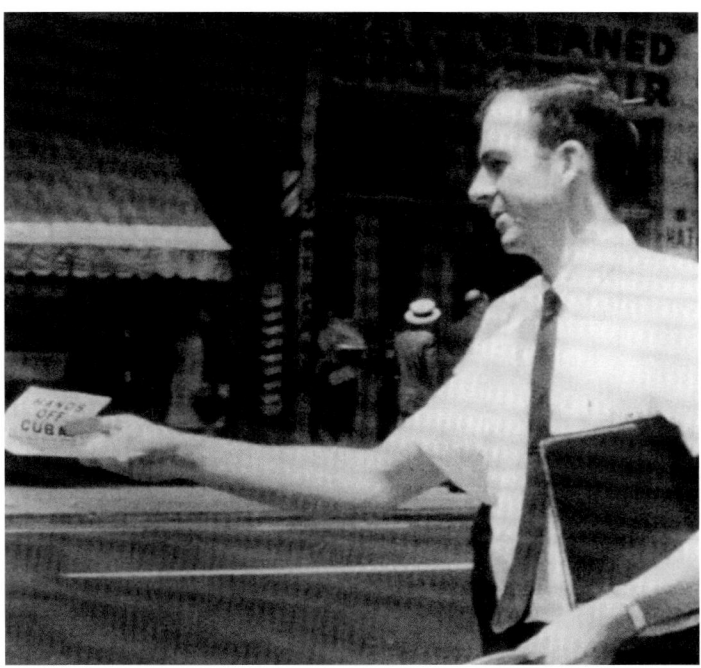

Mike O'Connor's footage of Lee Harvey Oswald on Camp Street in August 1963 included this frame, in which the words HANDS OFF CUBA are clearly visible on the leaflet.
Film frame by Mike O'Connor.

link was later upheld by conservatives as evidence that Kennedy's assassination was the work of leftists, and probably a lone one at that. Liberals, meanwhile, viewed Oswald's association with the committee that published the leaflet, the New Orleans Chapter of Fair Play for Cuba, as a reactionary counterintelligence operation aimed to discredit the pro-Castro group, as suggested by the fact that the "544 CAMP ST." address stamped on the leaflet actually belonged to an anti-Castro group with CIA ties. They also later pointed to declassified documents revealing that the Cuban exiles who had tussled with Oswald in the August incident were also CIA affiliated and, they inferred, had carefully set up a public fracas on Canal Street for the police and the media to put "on the record."[17] Hence the importance of O'Connor's footage.

Cross-town rival WDSU, meanwhile, got a scoop of its own. After covering Oswald's leafleting back in August, re-porter Bill Slatter and cameraman Michael Lala, brother of WWL's Larry Lala, invited Oswald over to their studio on Royal Street for an interview. A minor story at the time, the interview film, after airing, "was thrown into one of three film boxes: current month, last month, and two months old," Del explains. "On the first of each month, the boxes were rotated and the oldest box of film was thrown away, and that empty box started new for this month's film." It was Mike Lala together with his colleagues who, hours after the assassination, immediately made the connection between the wry face flashing on the television screen and the interview he had done three months prior. Lala was a fascinating character—brilliant, visionary, oblivious to his own eccentricity, and meticulous to the point of obsessive-compulsive. His contribution to history came in the form of rescuing the Oswald interview within a few days of its scheduled destruction. In it, a slight and vaguely smirking young man waxed glibly on Marxism, communism, socialism, geopolitics, and American slights to Cuba. The August 1963 footage of Lee Harvey Oswald helped lay the groundwork for the full range of hypotheses explaining the murder of the president. One—that of the Warren Commission—would hold Oswald and Oswald alone responsible, and many others would construe conspiracies involving a host of New Orleans characters, some of whom were well known to WWL staffers, among them Bay of Pigs freebooter Sergio Arcacha Smith and mobster Carlos Marcello.

Topping the list of conspiracy builders was Jim Garrison, the towering and rather peculiar Orleans Parish district attorney who had gained renown for a widely publicized crackdown on Bourbon Street vice. With a craving for heroism and a propensity for reckless dot-connecting, Garrison concocted a theory that positioned civic luminary Clay Shaw at the center of an elaborate plot to murder the president. Shaw happened to be a member of the French Quarter closeted gay community, and Del's UPI buddy Roddy Mims, who lived next door to Shaw, witnessed the stag parties that Shaw pained to conceal from public attention—and that Garrison, bully-like, used to his advantage. The 1969 trial, which garnered national attention and marked the only time the JFK assassination went before a court of law, ended abruptly with a not-guilty verdict—but not before financially and physically wrecking Shaw. Twenty years later, director Oliver Stone restored Garrison's damaged reputation, and further trashed Shaw's, in his highly revisionist 1991 movie *JFK,* starring Kevin Costner in the title role and Tommy Lee Jones as Shaw. Del worked with both Stone and Jones in the 1990s and was tempted to share with them his local perspective, but decided it probably wasn't worth his time. Mike Lala, ever the obsessive perfectionist (he would groom his Gentilly lawn using a string to ensure grass height consistency), later became a successful restaurateur in a meticulously renovated historic complex in the French Quarter, and remained a close friend of Del's for decades to come.

JFK's death portended an era of intensifying change in New Orleans and the nation. The trickle of white families flowing to the suburbs starting in 1961 grew to a torrent, and set New Orleans on a half century of precipitous population decline. Del's old neighbors in the Projects were among those who fled, as Iberville, now integrated in a *de jure* sense, swiftly resegregated toward becoming *de facto* all black and overwhelmingly poor. Downtown, while still relatively vibrant, witnessed changes all its own, as rows of nineteenth-century storehouses were razed for parking lots (including much of old South Rampart Street) and workers laid the groundwork for new federally funded interstates. Hurricane Betsy struck in September 1965, and while it was not recognized at the time, the storm would mark an era in which environmental deterioration accelerated at a pace faster than levee improvements and would ultimately lead to the Hurricane Katrina catastrophe forty years later. (Del and Bob Jones, while working on *72 Hours of Betsy,* were in City Hall when Mayor Vic Schiro uttered his now-infamous adage, "Don't believe any false rumors, unless you hear them from me.") Also in 1965, two new skyscrapers rose to heights never before attempted on New Orleans's soft soils. The strikingly modernist Plaza Tower in particular was enabled by a new piling-coupling system which so impressed Del that he storyboarded a documentary on the technique and tried to sell it to the engineering firm. He failed in that effort but held on to the idea of topical documentary filmmaking, an idea he would one day develop into a successful business.

Del captured on camera other transformations of the 1960s. He filmed the last streetcar on the last Canal Street line one dawn in May 1964, as the century-old rails were ripped up and replaced with modern buses. He captured the last bell at the historic New Orleans Cotton Exchange, as government price supports negated its function and cotton production shifted away from the Mississippi Valley. He photographed the agony of the Morrison family in their Coliseum Square parlor, as they awaited the fate of their father in Mexico, where the airplane of the ever-sunny mayor-turned-diplomat had disappeared. Six months after Morrison's untimely death, Archbishop Rummel, who had led the New Orleans archdiocese since 1935 and desegregated its schools, finally passed away, and Del got an amazing overhead shot of his funeral in St. Louis Cathedral.

This being New Orleans, Del also covered Mardi Gras annually, and a close inspection of his photographs (some of which appeared in *Newsweek*) heralds the coming social revolution in everything from attire and public behavior to gender relations and sexuality. Bourbon Street and the French Quarter, where the photos were taken, were also changing. One can see in Del's 1963 Carnival photographs, for example, the circa-1892 Sisters of the Holy Family girls' school on Orleans and Bourbon, a bastion of the neighborhood's old black Catholic Creole population. When Del photographed revelers in the same spot two years later, one can see the massive Bourbon Orleans Hotel rising where the school once stood, signaling the Quarter's shift from an old hometown neighborhood of grandmothers and children to a tourist destination with a small gentrified residency. Along with six other new corporate-owned hotels in the French Quarter, the Bourbon Orleans would serve tourists now flying and driving into New Orleans by the millions. Their presence drew more and more workers into the low-paying service economy, while containerization and labor strife killed thousands of better-paying jobs in the shipping sector. Tourism was overtaking the French Quarter Del had known since his youth; in fact, just across the street from his favorite hangout, Larry Lamarca's Gunga Den, developers had leveled a nineteenth-century brewery for yet another mega-hotel, the Royal Sonesta. All this came on the heels of Jim Garrison's crackdown on the classy nightclubs and burlesque venues that had made Bourbon famous in the 1920s–1950s; now, tawdry joints and grimy bars dominated the scene, and great old places like the Gunga Den—and leathery old locals like Lamarca—were becoming a thing of the past. Reminisced Bob Jones in a recent conversation with Del, "All those nights on Bourbon Street, sitting in the Gunga Den with Larry Lamarca . . . I always found it a bit difficult to talk politics with Larry at the bar while his wife Linda was stripping less than ten feet away."[18]

Dominating the news in the mid-1960s was Washington's increasing involvement in Vietnam, the Cold War's hottest conflict since the Korean War. The Johnson administration by March 1965 had escalated Kennedy's "police action" in South Vietnam to the level of a U.S. ground war, aimed at pushing back the Soviet-backed Viet Cong incursion from the Communist North. Young men from Louisiana and Mississippi abounded among the recently deployed troops, and WWL general manager Mike Early felt their actual experiences on the ground were getting lost amid the political debate about the conflict. He decided to dispatch Del and Phil Johnson to the war-torn nation to create an ambitious documentary along the lines of *Vatican II.* This would be a first for any station in Louisiana, and a competitive advantage over rival WDSU. But the WWL brass had something else in mind. Unlike civil rights, which the station covered with pointed detachment, Vietnam brought out the innate conservatism of the Catholic-owned station. Early made it clear in a press release "that the coverage is aimed at counteracting anti-draft, anti-war outcries and at showing wholehearted support for the nation's fighting armed forces."[19] In its planning of the Vietnam tour, however, WWL appears to have had mostly human interest in mind. This was not intended as an investigative news story, but rather a public service to raise the spirits of New Orleanians at war and on the home front. The station asked from its viewers the

names and bases of local soldiers, sailors, and Marines currently deployed, with the promise that it would mail them a fruitcake for Christmas. Responses poured in.

Del and Phil departed Moisant Airport and changed planes in San Francisco and Honolulu. "We boarded a military plane for the final leg into Saigon's Tan Son Nhat Airport," Del recounts. "Instead of a low and leisurely approach, the plane took a last-minute dive toward the runway. They always landed like this to avoid attracting gunfire." The chaotic capital was crowded with the transients of war: rural refugees, conscripts, American soldiers, journalists and stringers, adventurers and profiteers, plus millions of native city dwellers. Their first stop was to check in with the CBS Bureau at the renowned Caravelle Hotel, where they had to rouse a napping Morley Safer for assistance. Unfortunately there was no room at the inn, so the two New Orleanians were escorted to a decidedly second-rate boardinghouse on Tudo Street and given a small room to share. The upside was it adjoined the well-known Minh Tailor Shop, where Americans enjoyed having custom-fit field outfits made within twenty-four hours. Del still has his today.

Del was a bit apprehensive about his hardware. He had to shoot using a double-system sound technique, which used separate tracks for film and audio. Equipment all tested and packed, the duo set out into the troubled countryside. "We traveled by jeep, car, and plane to find our New Orleans men," Dell tells. "Our very first interview was with an injured Cajun boy lying in his hospital bed. He talked to us on-camera, [despite his] pain." The hospital was full of wounded Americans and South Vietnamese. "As we left and walked outside, I swear there was a total eclipse of the sun casting an eerie red glow on everything, including many Vietnamese families camped outside to be near their loved ones." What Del witnessed was the annular solar eclipse of November 23, 1965, which indeed passed directly over South Vietnam.

Phil and Del filmed rice paddies, villages, jungles, and rugged peaks, and interviewed as many soldiers and villagers as they could. On one occasion, they covered the Marines' Min Cam booby-trap training school, where advisers demonstrated an array of diabolical devices—with nicknames like the Roadside Companion, Pongee Stick in a Hole, the Trap-Door Spider, the Mouse Trap, and the fearsome Malaysian Whip—all cleverly camouflaged, for which Del had to use a variety of techniques to make visible to the camera. On another occasion, they learned that their position had been the scene of an ambush just hours earlier. Amid all this was a memorable Thanksgiving with the troops in a mess tent, and rarely was a feast enjoyed with such gratitude.

Not wanting to neglect the sailors on their list, Phil and Del arranged with the Navy to meet up with the targeted vessel, the *Kitty Hawk.* "We were on our way in a twin-engine Navy plane somewhere over the South China Sea," Del says. A storm brewed as they circled over the carrier, while sailors cleared the deck and finished refueling from a tandem vessel. Winds and rains whipped up just as they got word to land. The pilot pulled back, approached low, and finally plunged onto the gyrating deck, two moving objects grinding into each other on tempestuous seas. Del almost couldn't believe that they didn't crash and, from the blank expression on the pilot's face, that this apparently qualified as a normal landing. Having less than an hour on board, Phil and Del tracked down four Louisiana sailors and interviewed them, the storm raging outside. "I was confident they wouldn't allow us to take off in that weather, [but] I was wrong, and we were on our way back to Saigon." That evening they enjoyed a leisurely dinner at a French bistro on the roof of the Caravelle Hotel, complete with an ice cream dessert served in a coconut shell. But even there, Del remembers, "we could hear shelling and see smoke in the distance." Just a year before, a bomb had been detonated in the Caravelle itself.

Del, a former airman, wanted to get aloft to shoot panoramic vistas of the countryside. Cargo planes and jets would not suffice, and he had no luck getting aboard a helicopter. There was, however, room for him in a Piper Cub, the perfect low-flying top-wing aircraft to shoot a camera from. It was also the perfect craft to shoot *at*—and the Air Force knew it. This particular Piper Cub was a spotter plane, and its ostensible mission was aerial reconnaissance. Only later did Del come to understand that its unofficial job was to attract enemy fire and reveal its positions. Del

climbed, nervously but gamely, into the cramped back seat and donned his flak jacket, only to be told not to wear it but to sit on it. Of course. They took off, soaring over rice paddies and dense jungles, and flew to the bend of a river where lay a hamlet suspected of harboring Viet Cong guerrillas. The pilot circled low and slow, tempting them. Moments later, they heard metallic retorts from below, each followed by a faint whizzing whistle all but a few dozen feet away. "Did you hear that?" the pilot said, almost elatedly. "Bullets!" Just a few months earlier Del had been chased by the Ku Klux Klan in the Louisiana night; now the Viet Cong were shooting at him in the Asian sky. He felt for the flak jacket beneath him and tensed as the pilot banked upwardly. "We circled at a slightly higher altitude, as the pilot called for air support [and] pinpointed the target with a smoke rocket," he recalls. Then "the fighter planes did their job with napalm and bombs." Del caught the jets swooping in and explosions rising around the village. He later learned that the pilots dubbed that particular Piper Cub "Ol' Magnet Bottom" for its ability to draw enemy bullets, and nineteen holes in the wings and fuselage proved their point. "To this day I wonder about the casualties of that anonymous act, and came to understand [feelings such as] guilt and [post-]traumatic stress," Del reflects. "I still have a hard time talking about that day."

One night Del and Phil found themselves so far afield they decided to sleep in Da Nang, hundreds of miles north of Saigon. They roomed at a former brothel that had one big open room filled with bunks, each with an armed stranger on it. When they returned late the next evening to their Tudo Street room in Saigon, Phil unlocked the door, flipped on the bare incandescent light bulb—and found a beefy foreigner jumping out of his bed. "What the—who the hell are you?" asked Phil, his heart pounding. Without missing a beat, the man responded in a thick Russian accent, "Khrushchev! Who are *you*?" They shortly figured out that the manager had re-rented their room and, after a hearty laugh, made other arrangements for their new comrade. They did ponder, however, what a Russian was doing in downtown Saigon. As for these two Americans, it was time to go home. They stopped en route in British colonial Hong Kong, where Del photographed scenes all but extinct now in Victoria Harbor: picturesque junks, fish drying on wooden docks, and an ivory dealer with "tusks from a hundred elephants." This being before the era of environmental values and a worldwide ban on the ivory trade, Del and Phil bought a piece and had it engraved "WWL-VIETNAM-1965," to match the 1962 Rome plaque on Mike Early's shelf.

Viet Nam '65: A Distant Christmas, ninety minutes of Del's color double-system film and audio (which, thankfully, worked perfectly) set to Phil's graceful prose, aired locally as over a thousand holiday fruitcakes were sent overseas, as promised by WWL. The documentary won widespread popularity as well as official praise. General Wallace M. Greene Jr. of the U.S. Marines headquarters in Washington personally sent Del his accolades, as did Louisiana congressman Hale Boggs. Critical acclaim followed, in the form of a letter from Rod Serling, president of the National Academy of Television Arts and Sciences, informing Early that the documentary had been nominated for an Emmy. Phil, Del, and Father Goodspeed attended the Eighteenth Annual Emmy Awards banquet at the Hollywood Palladium on May 22, 1966, where they did not win but nonetheless enjoyed at their table the company of childhood hero Gene Autry and vaudeville-era comedian Ed Wynn, who died only weeks later.

Del's experience in Vietnam reminded him who the real heroes were, as did the letters he received from Louisiana parents, wives, and children. "Seeing and hearing my husband meant more to me and my two little girls than I could ever express," wrote one Metairie housewife.[20] Del emotionally reports that, after tracking down "the fruitcake list" a number of years later, he learned to his relief that all the servicemen involved had made it home safely.

Today, fifty years later, Del's hometown is now also home to 15,000 Vietnamese-Americans, nearly all of them refugees or their descendants from the war that was just starting to burgeon in 1965. Mostly Catholics from the former French colony on the Mekong Delta, the refugees arrived starting in 1975 to the Catholic former French colony on the Mississippi Delta. They came on the invitation of New Orleans archbishop Philip Hannan, whose elevation to that rank Del and Phil had covered in Rome in 1965. So effectively did the two work together in WWL's Special Projects department that their colleagues nicknamed them "Del-Phi Productions."

Despite his childhood solitude and proclivity for quiet observation, Del in adulthood developed a penchant for civic and professional society. New Orleans is a clubby sort of town; people join organizations reflecting their aspirations and social position—the Boston or Pickwick Club for men, Le Petit Salon or the Orleans Club for women, or Carnival krewes such as Comus, Momus, Proteus, or Rex. For journalists, the group to join was the New Orleans Press Club. Organized in 1957, the Press Club had become by the 1960s the see-and-be-seen networking-and-connections hub for media professionals citywide. Politicians yearned for invitations to its soirées, and its annual award banquet was the hottest ticket in town. Del won four Press Club awards between 1963 and 1966, for Best Spot Newsfilm, Best Human Interest Story, and two Best Documentaries. He also served as president of the Press Club in 1966 and became a charter member of the Gridiron Club, an exclusive society known for its annual satirical show featuring local luminaries.

One summer night during his tenure as president, Del presided over the Gridiron Show at the club's well-appointed 201 Chartres Street rendezvous. A lavish party followed, where circulated a who's who of the city's elite. Among the special guests was a twenty-three-year-old beauty named Ginger Fann, an adventurous Hoosier who fled to New Orleans "like a migratory bird going to a more congenial climate," as Tennessee Williams once wrote of his own escape into this last refuge of Bohemia. Ginger had a marvelous time that evening; "they had the best entertainment," she recounts, and "everyone asked me to dance. I felt like Cinderella." She stepped outside to take a break in the steamy French Quarter night, a place that can bring out the passions in even the most stoic of souls. "Lo and behold, coming down the street, were three men," she tells. One of them caught her attention, to say the very least. Speaking forty-seven years later, she states with airtight certitude, "I *imme-*

diately fell madly, *eternally* in love, before I said one word to him. Saw him coming, fell in love with him." The group proceeded back into the gala, Ginger tracking the striking stranger. She shortly learned he was the club president, and there he sat, coolly and dispassionately at the bar, while nearly every other fellow at the party flirted with her. "He *never* asked me to dance," she laughs, "whereas I swear every other man in the entire room asked me to dance." No wilting flower, Ginger took charge of the situation, a trait that would someday make her an ideal professional as well as personal partner. "So I went up to Del . . . and asked *him* to dance." Del recalls that Ginger did not ask if he was married, but rather how many children he had. "I answered truthfully, five. . . . I was shocked by the question, and even the answer." "[I] got my hooks in him," Ginger says today, "knew he was meant for me for life, and absolutely pursued him. . . . I confess to that."

Later that same summer, CBS's man in Chicago, Dan Bloom, stopped by the WWL studio. Bureau chiefs frequently made use of affiliates' facilities while in the field,

and Bloom got to know Del through his collaborations with Dan Rather upstairs. Dan and Del once flew twice in one day to Jackson for an exclusive interview with Ole Miss integrator James Meredith, which aired on Cronkite's *CBS Evening News.* Bloom heard additionally of Del's camerawork and editing talent, something the Midwest Bureau needed. One day he called Del and abruptly posed a question to him (bureau chiefs never minced words). "Say, fellow, you want to work for CBS in Chicago?" Caught off guard, Del did what many New Orleans natives do when the outside world comes calling: he listed all the reasons why such a move was impossible. Hanging up the phone, he immediately lamented to Bob Jones, "I just blew the biggest chance of my life." Not two minutes later, Bloom called him back. "OK," he said. "I got you a plane ticket." This time, it clicked—that knack of his to see what lies over the horizon, and to set forth toward it with a minimum of sentimentality. Reflecting on that moment, Del remembers, "I made up my mind to leave everything in New Orleans behind as I was climbing the steps to the plane."

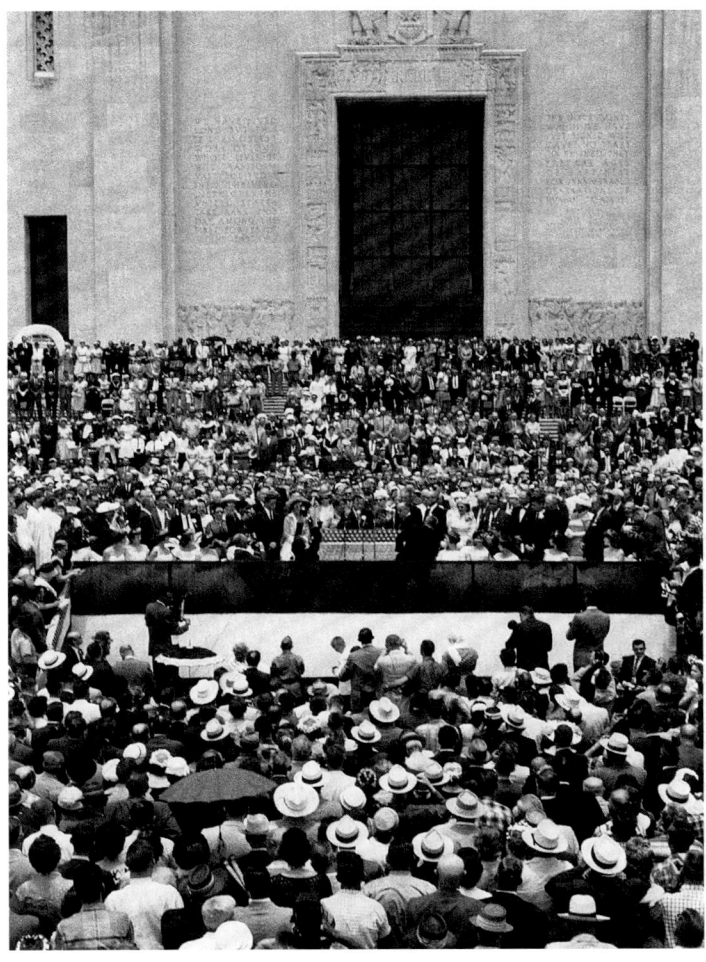

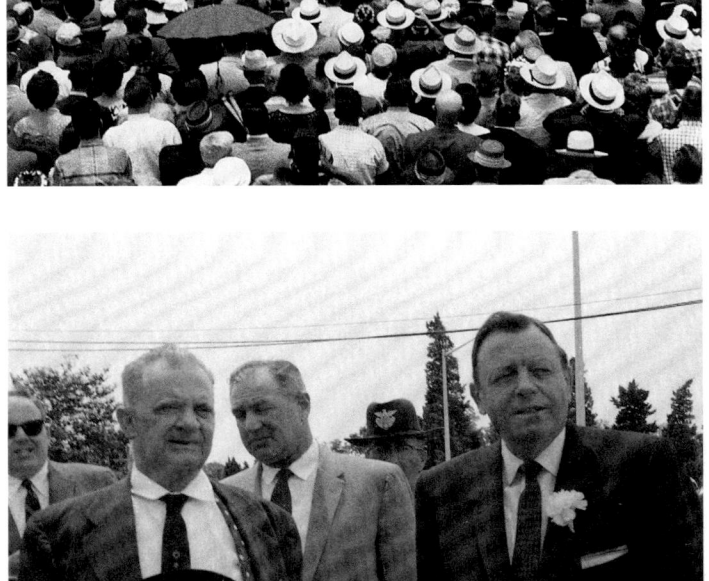

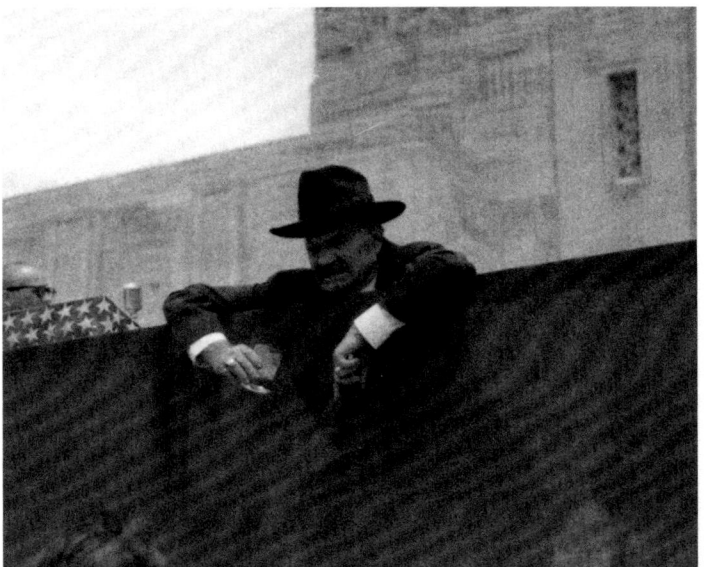

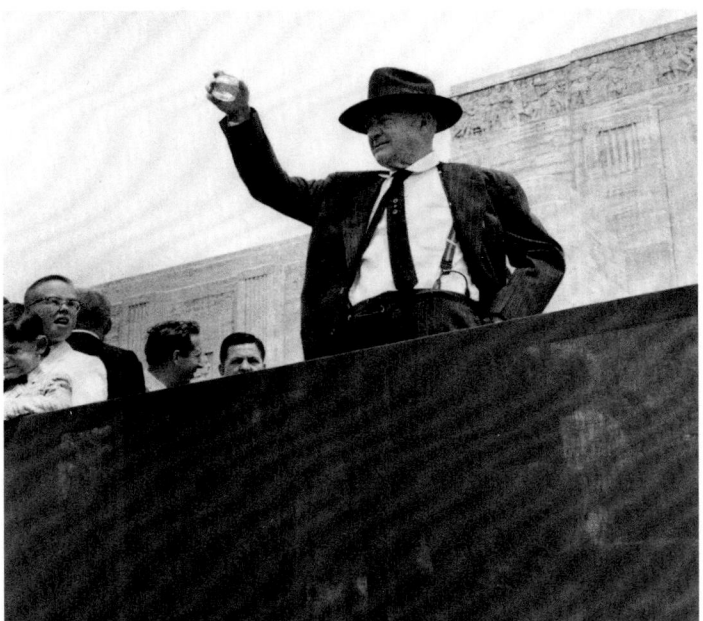

Only in Louisiana: Governor Earl K. Long steals the show at the inauguration of his replacement, Jimmie "the Singing Governor" Davis (with flower on lapel, at left). Three months later, Long managed to reinvent himself as congressman-elect. Shortly thereafter, he was dead. *Photos by Del Hall.*

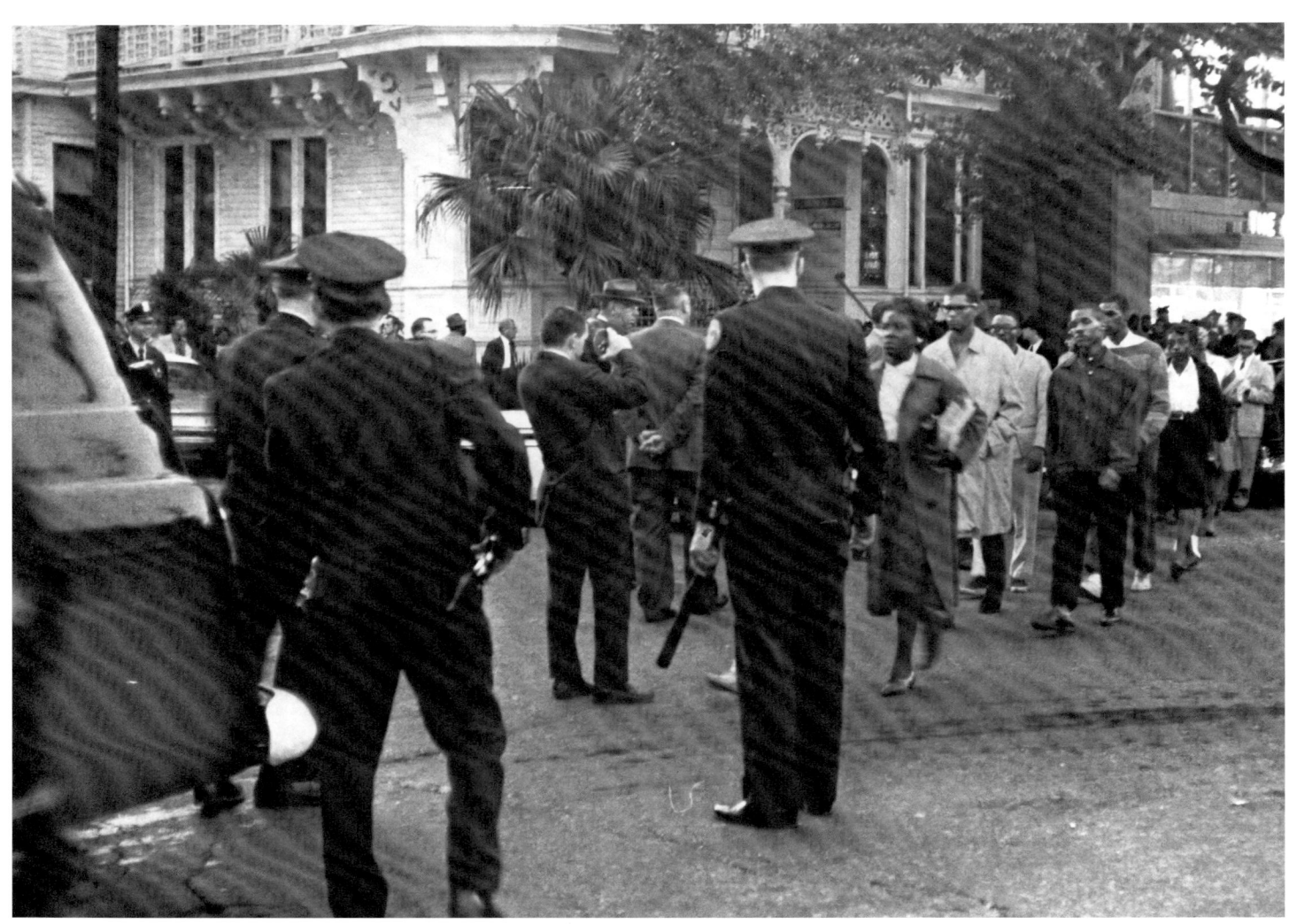

Civil rights protest
on Canal Street.
Photo by Del Hall.

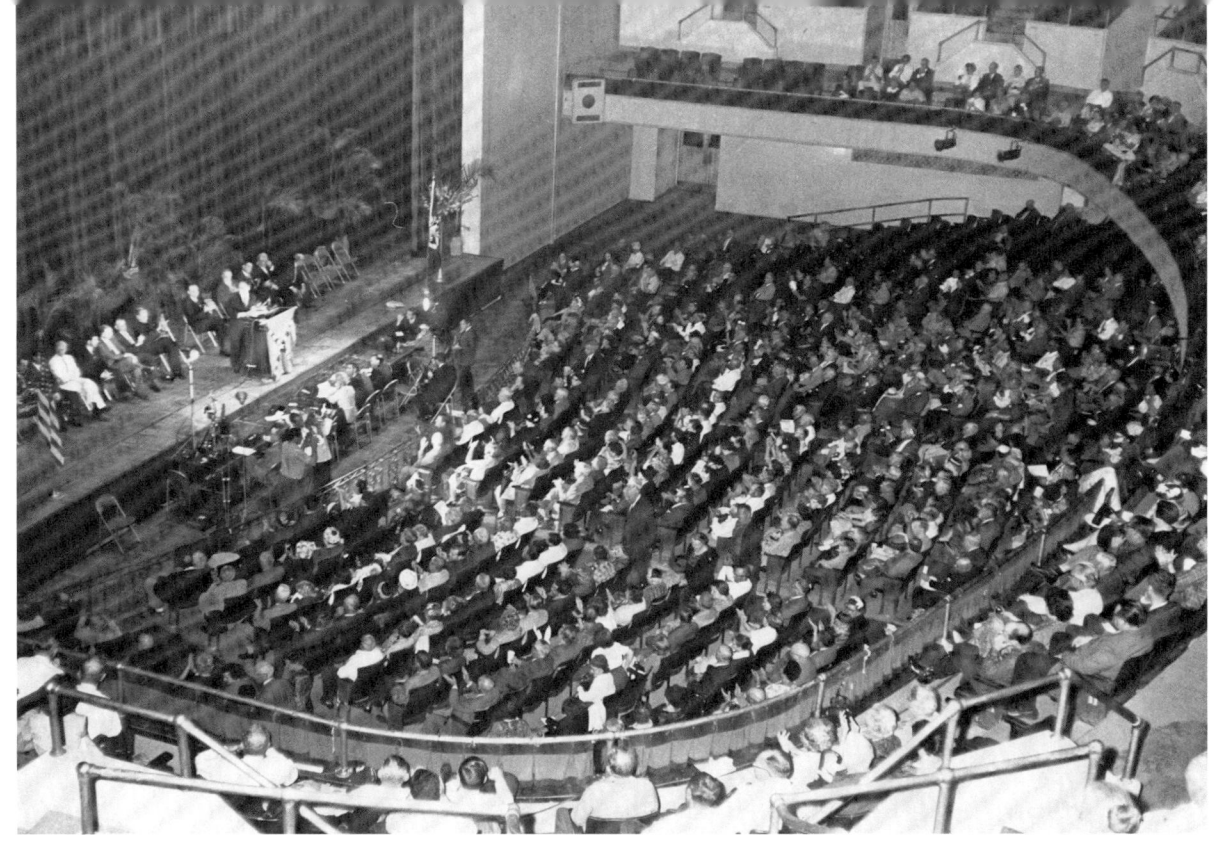

A White Citizens' Council strategizes its resistance to school integration. Note Confederate battle flag draped over lectern. *Photos by Del Hall.*

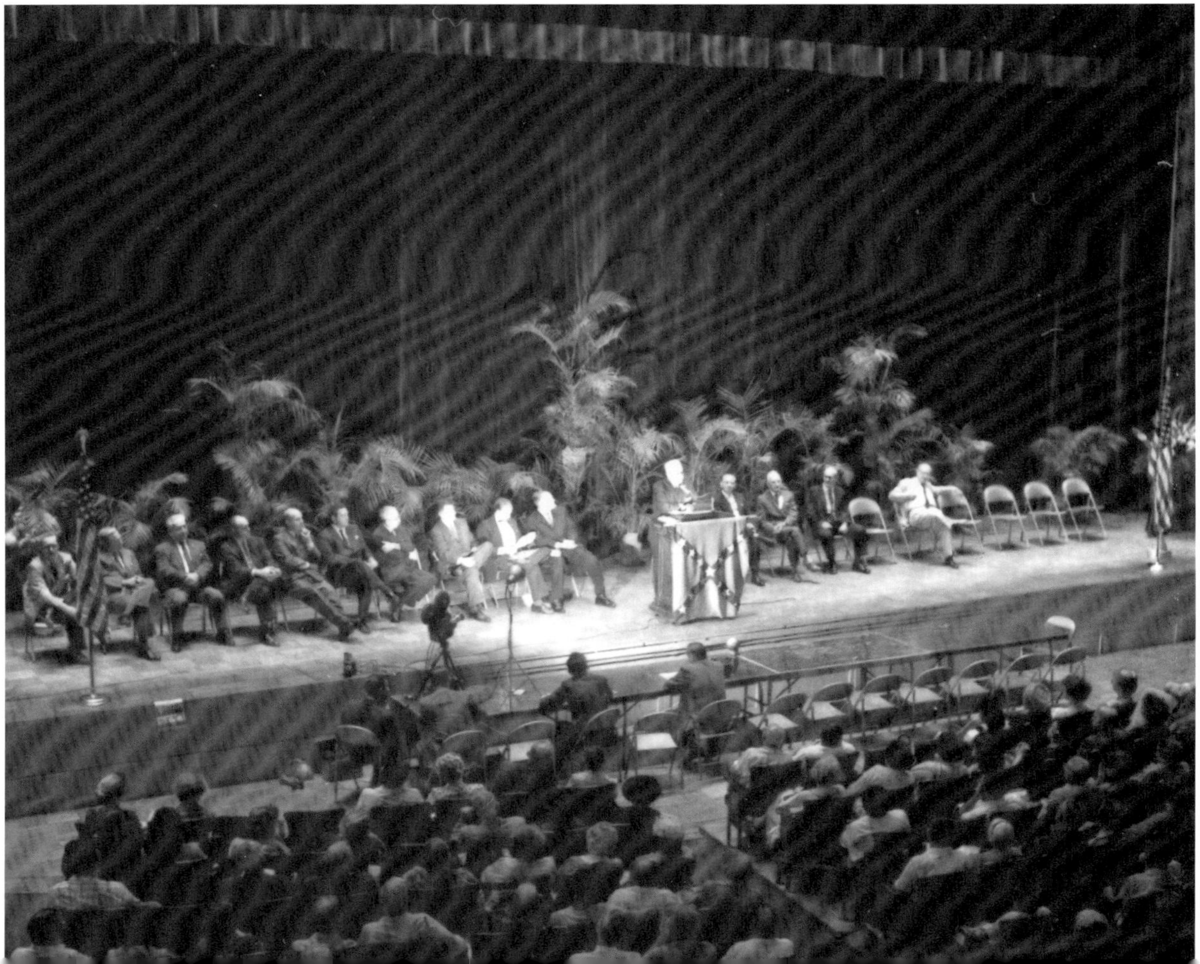

In December 1961, Del filmed a civil rights sit-in at Woolworth's on Canal Street and got himself arrested in the process. Top frame: a black woman (center right) seats herself at the lunch counter. Next frame: whites leave in a counter-protest. Third and fourth frames: the manager and police intervene, and, at bottom, arrest and arraign Del as well as Roddy Mims of UPI. *Film frames by Del Hall and Roddy Mims.*

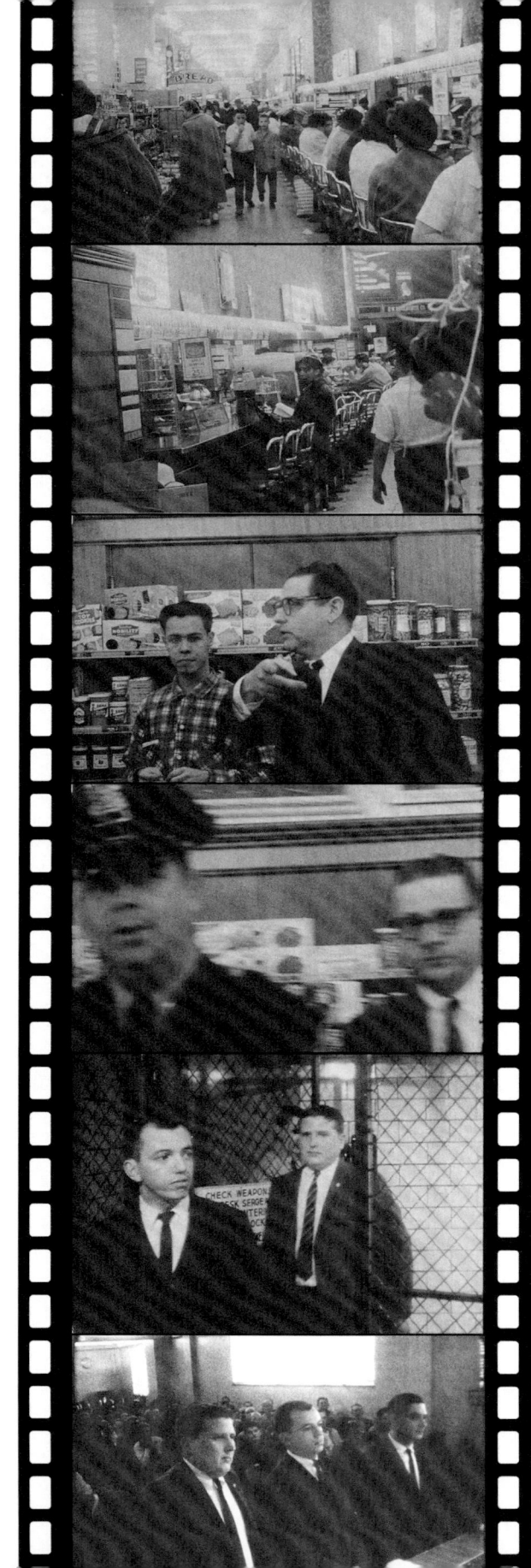

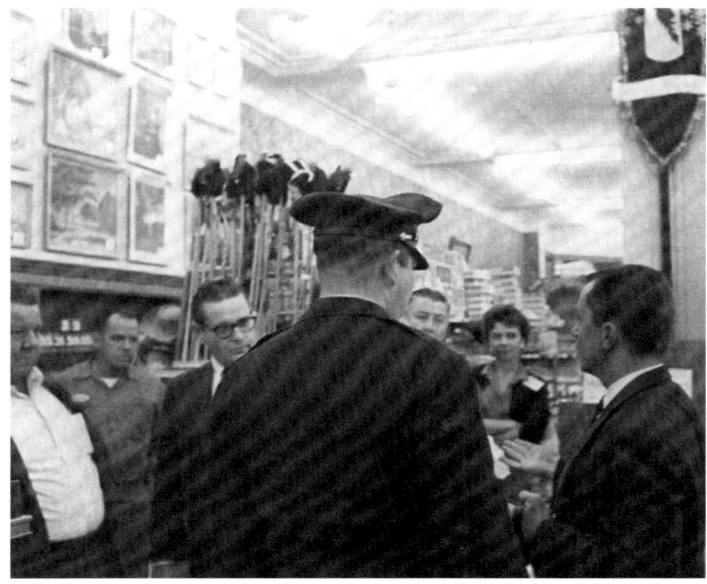

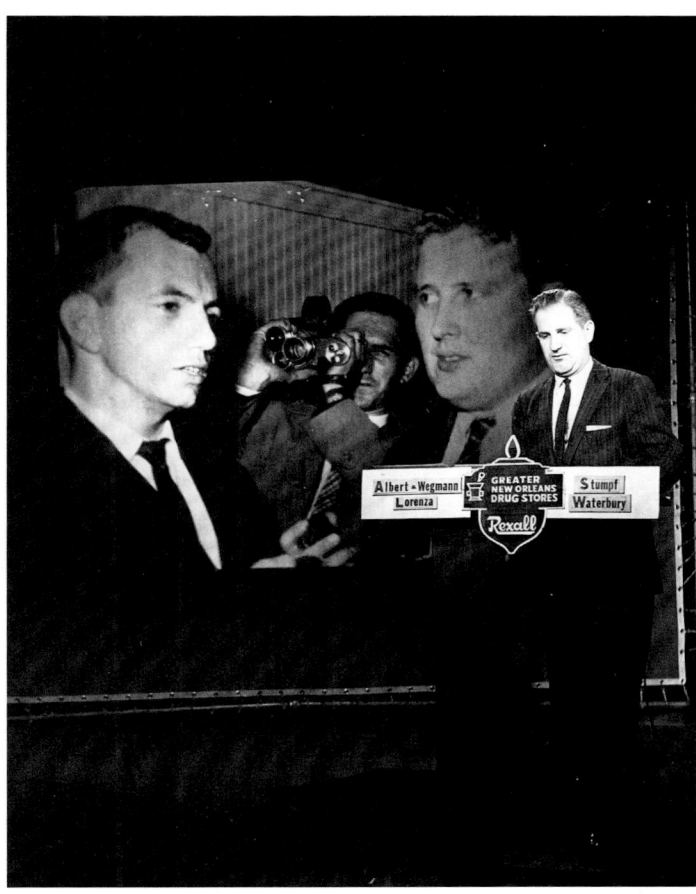

Leo Willette reports the incident on WWL. *Photo by WWL-TV/Del Hall Collection.*

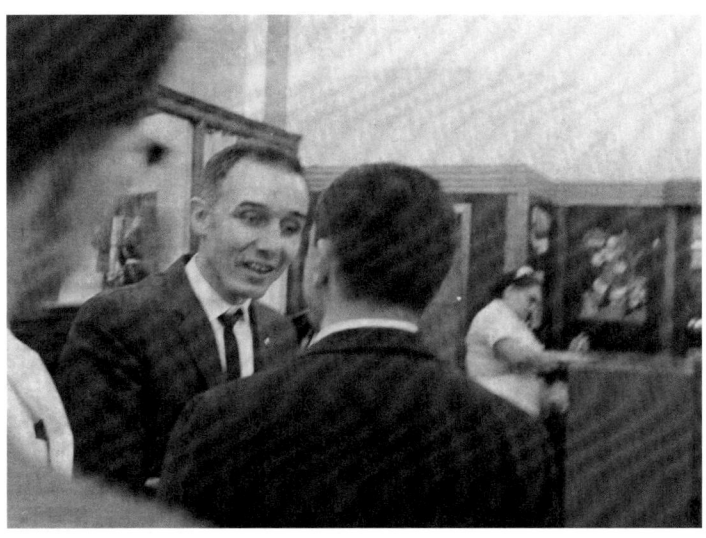

The managers offer to drop charges in exchange for the film, which Del and Roddy both decline. *Photos by WWL-TV/Del Hall Collection.*

Plaquemines Parish political boss Leander Perez gestures his fierce resistance to integration to a crowd of appreciative constituents. *Photo by Del Hall.*

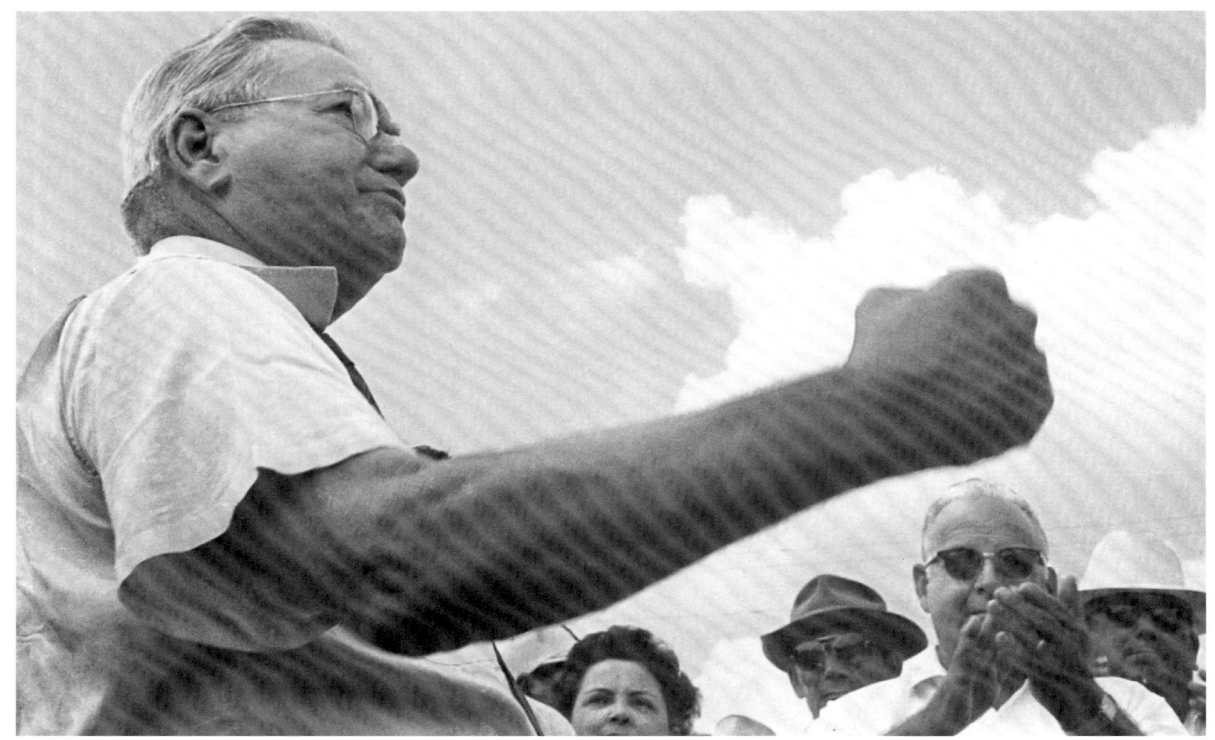

New Orleans police officers keep a watchful eye on a public school at the height of the 1960 school integration crisis. *Photo by Del Hall.*

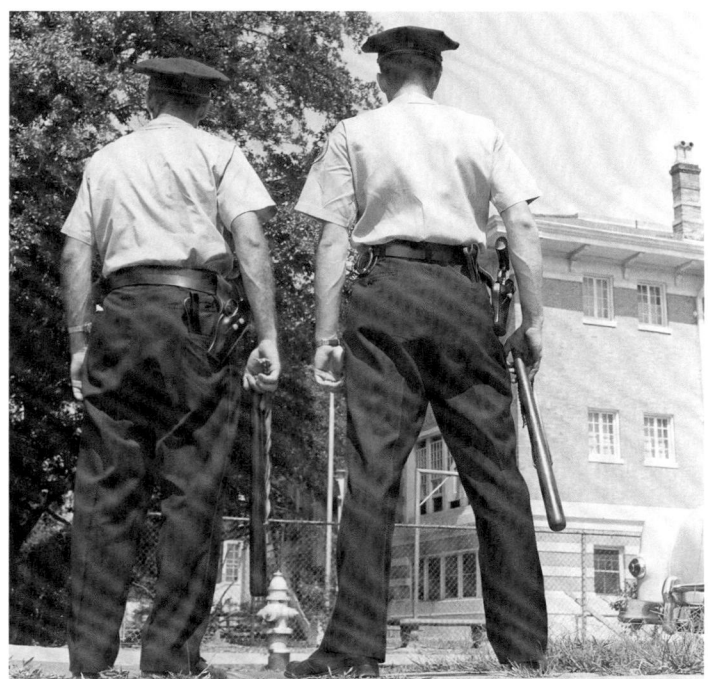

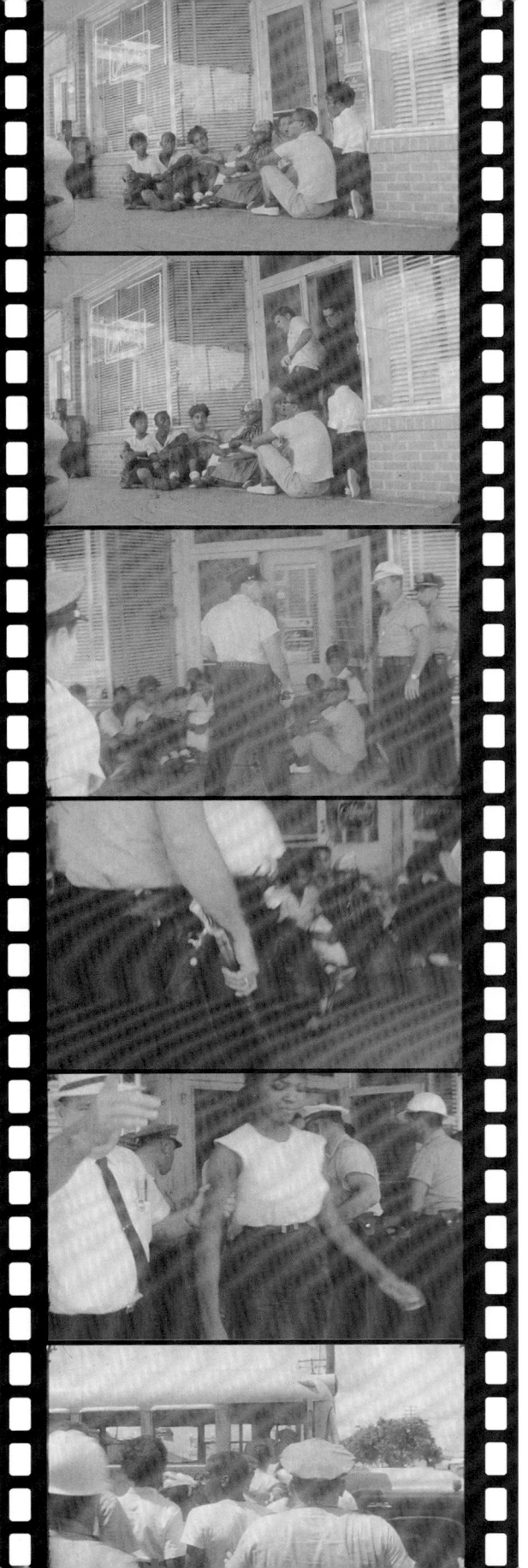
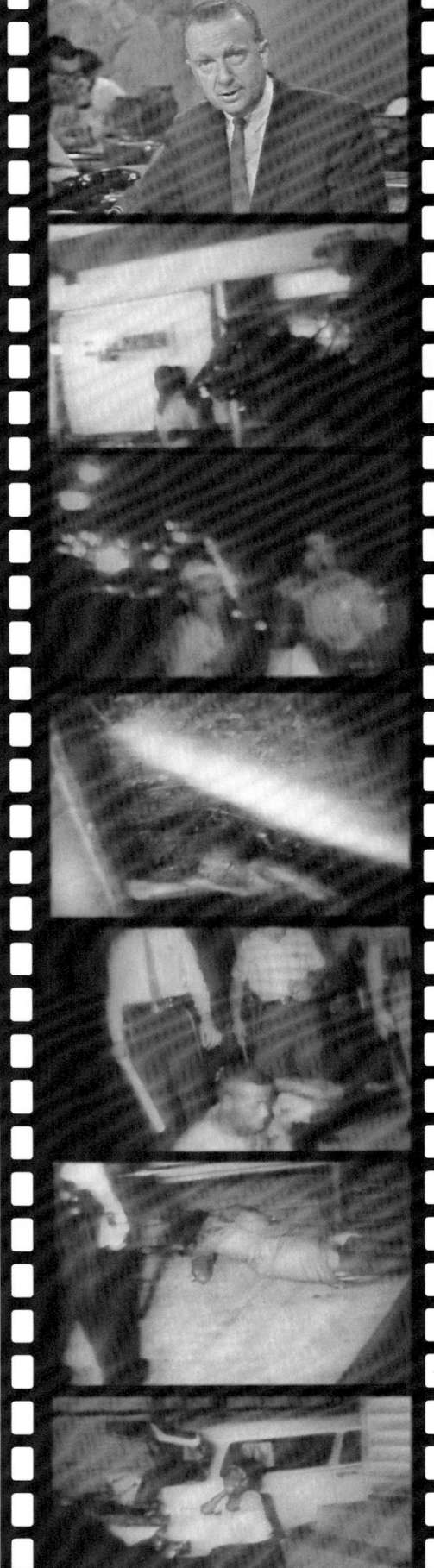

At first it started off peacefully: black youths (upper left) protest a segregated lunch counter in Plaquemine, August 1963, as white patrons step over them. Police soon arrive and haul the protestors to the Iberville Parish Jail (lower left). Tensions mount by the end of the month, and on the evening of September 1, riots engulf the town. Del's unique nighttime footage of the mayhem landed on the first 30-minute broadcast of Walter Cronkite's *CBS Evening News.* *Film frames by Del Hall.*

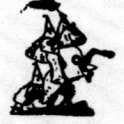

APPLICATION FOR CITIZENSHIP

IN THE

INVISIBLE EMPIRE

NATIONAL KNIGHTS OF THE KU KLUX KLAN

ASSOCIATION OF AMERICA

National Headquarters

Tucker, Ga. P.O. Box 107, Area Code 404

Phone 938-5921

I, the undersigned, a native born, true and loyal citizen of the United States of America, being a white person of temperate habits, sound in mind and a believer in the tenets of the Christian religion, the maintenance of White Supremacy and the principles of a "pure Americanism," do most respectfully apply for membership in the National Knights of the Ku Klux Klan Association of America.

I guarantee on my honor to conform strictly to all rules and requirements regulating my "naturalization" and the continuance of my membership, and at all times a strict and loyal obedience to your constitutional authority and the constitution and laws of the fraternity, not in conflict with the constitution and constitutional laws of the United States of America and the states thereof.

If I am accepted as a Klansman and prove untrue or violate my oath as a Klansman, I will willingly resign as a member, upon notice in writing received by me from any of my superior officers. I further certify that I am not, nor have I ever been a member of the communist party. I know that I owe allegiance first to my God, second to my country third to my family and last, but not least, to this organization.

This is to certify that I donated the sum of _____ dollars, the required "klectokon" to the propagating fund of the National Knights of the Ku Klux Klan Association of America.

Signed...........................Applicant

Residence Address.......................

City & State........................

Phone.......................

Date................, 19

*From The Desk of The Grand Dragon State of Illinois
Invisable Empire Knights of The Ku Klux Klan*

NAME_____

ADDRESS_____

SHIP TO_____ NO._____

ARTICLE_____

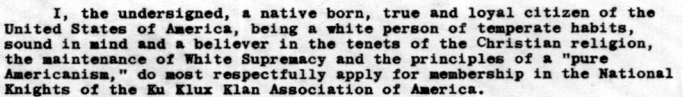

ROBE MEASURE

1 TO 2	
3 TO 4	
3 TO 5	
3 TO 6	
7 MEASURE AROUND CHEST	
SIZE COLLAR WORN	
SIZE HAT WORN	

Chest Measure (AROUND BODY)

Measure Sleeve length 1½ inch longer than Coat Sleeve

Measure close around chest at 7 and add 3 inches for full Measure

Size of HAT and COLLAR very IMPORTANT

TAKE MEASURE WITH COAT ON

Ku Klux Klan paperwork circulating through the South and North during the 1960s. *Del Hall Collection.*

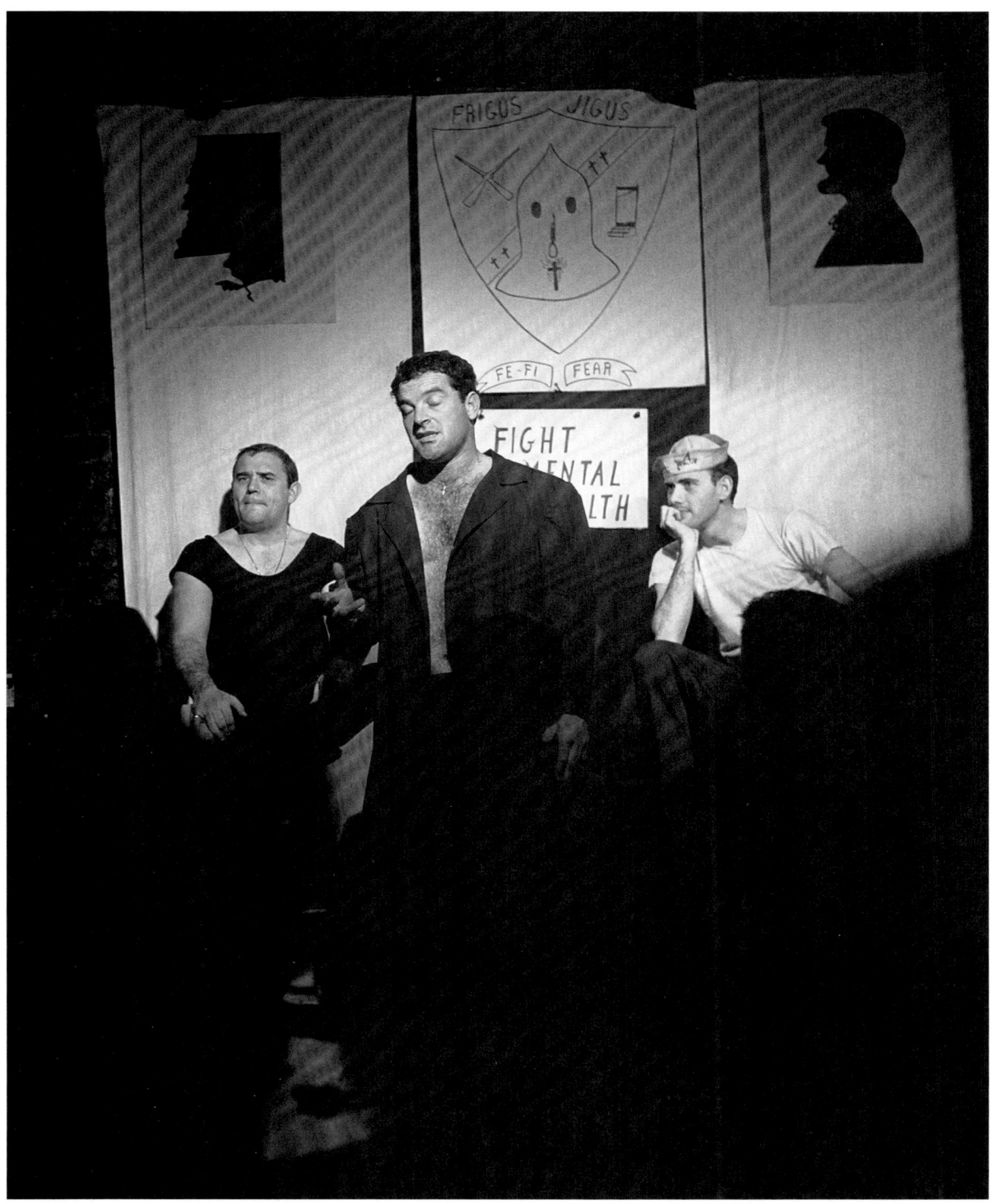

Bourbon Street comedy troupe Fudgeripple Follies pokes fun at the civil rights movement with characters such as Martin Luther Queen and skits entitled "At the Lunch Counter" and "Hill Billy Citizens Council." The Follies' motto: "No cow is too sacred to milk." *Del Hall Collection.*

Del shoots a scene for WWL's influential *Shades of New Orleans,* a predecessor of sorts to Charles Kuralt's *On the Road* vignettes. *Del Hall Collection.*

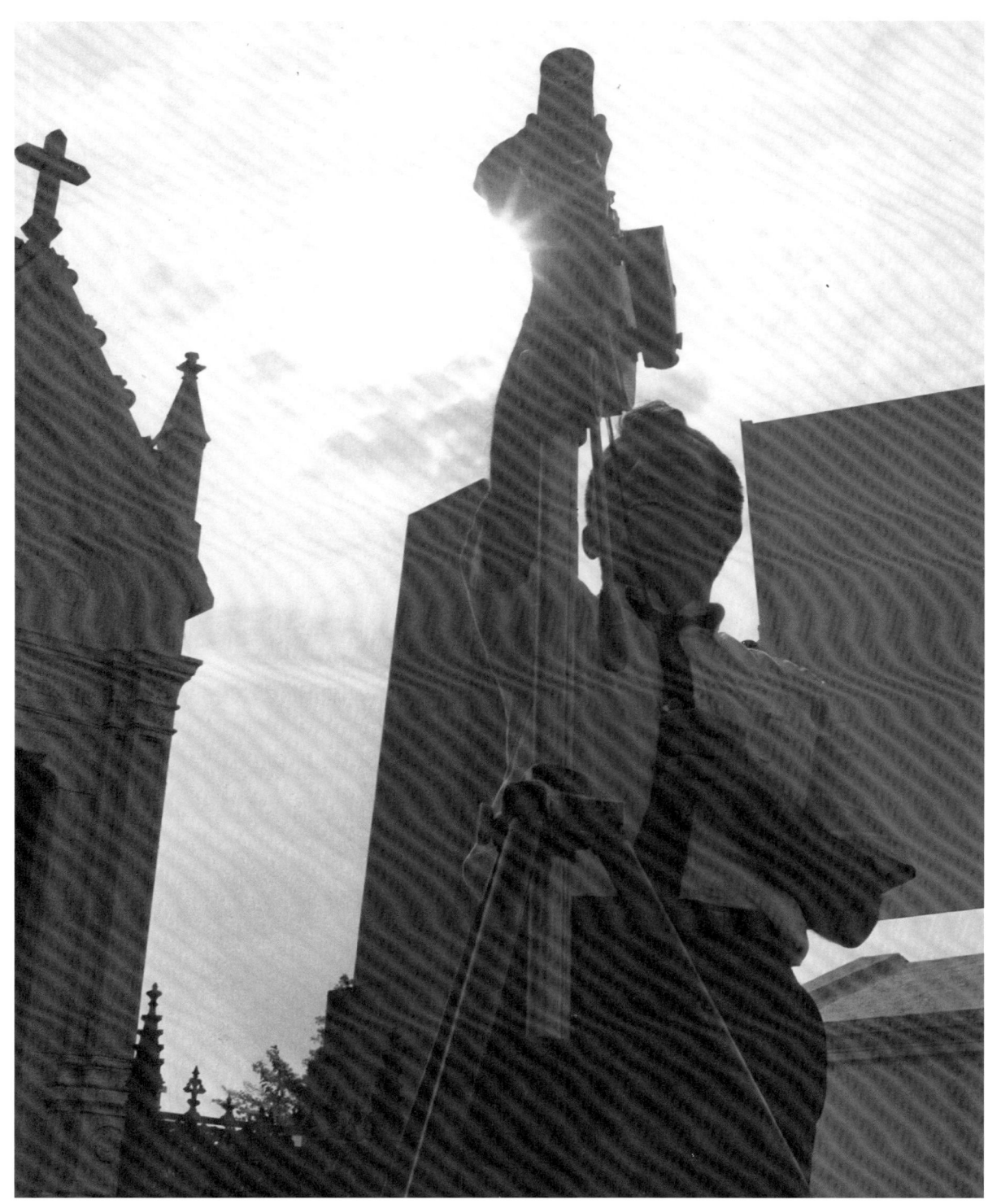

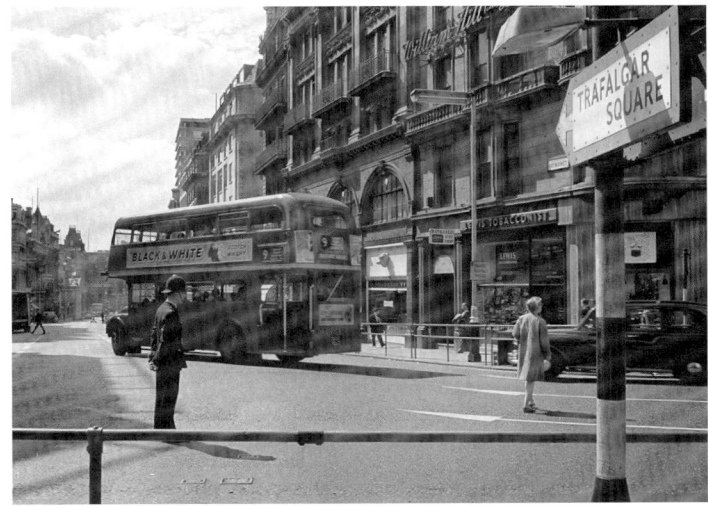

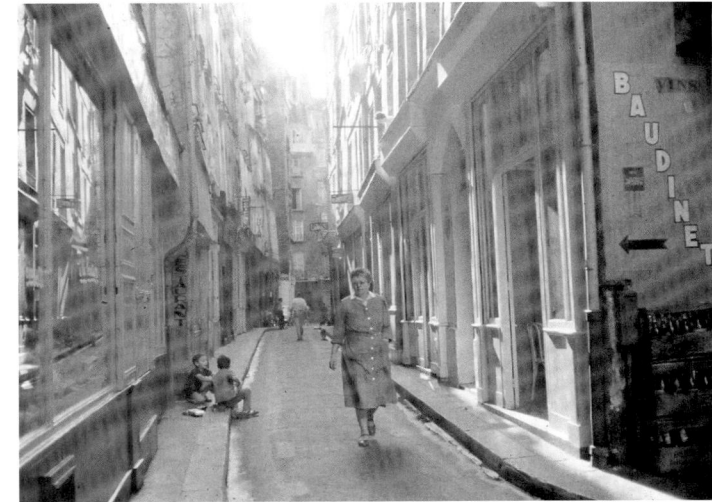

Through Del's lens, scenes from London, Paris, and New Orleans in 1962–1963. *Photos by Del Hall.*

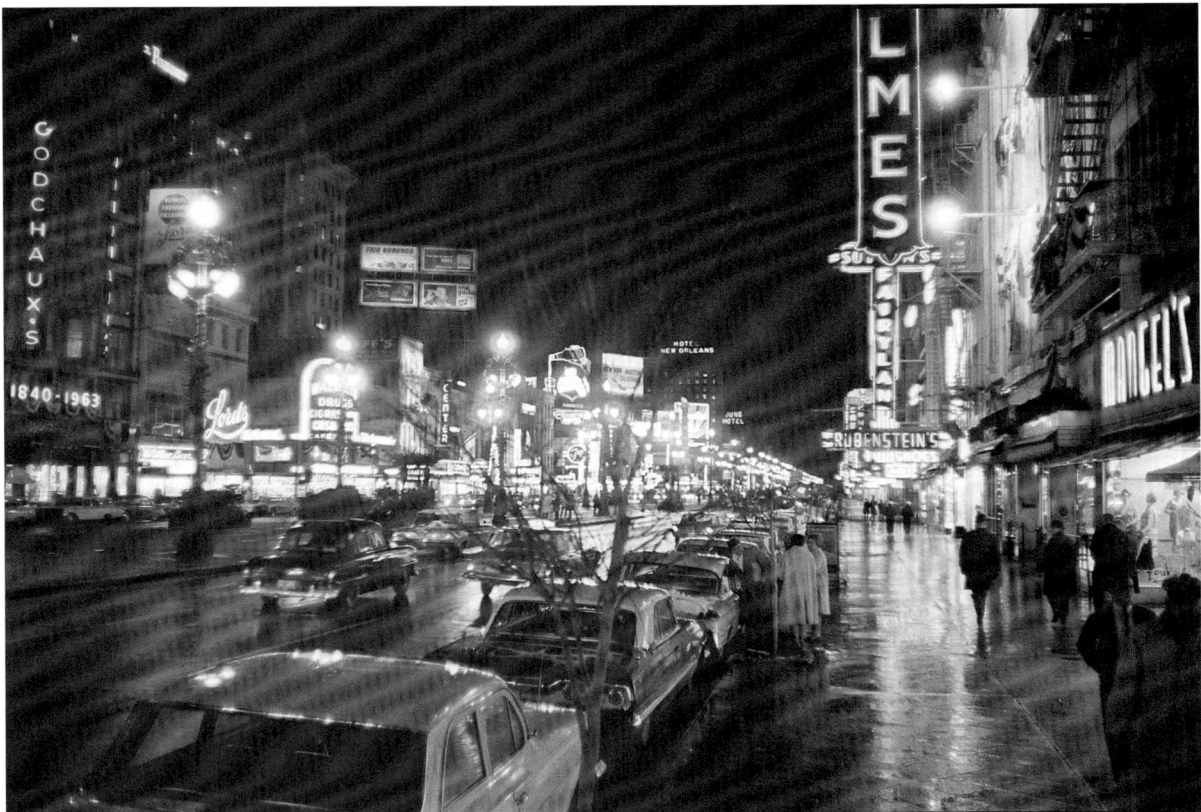

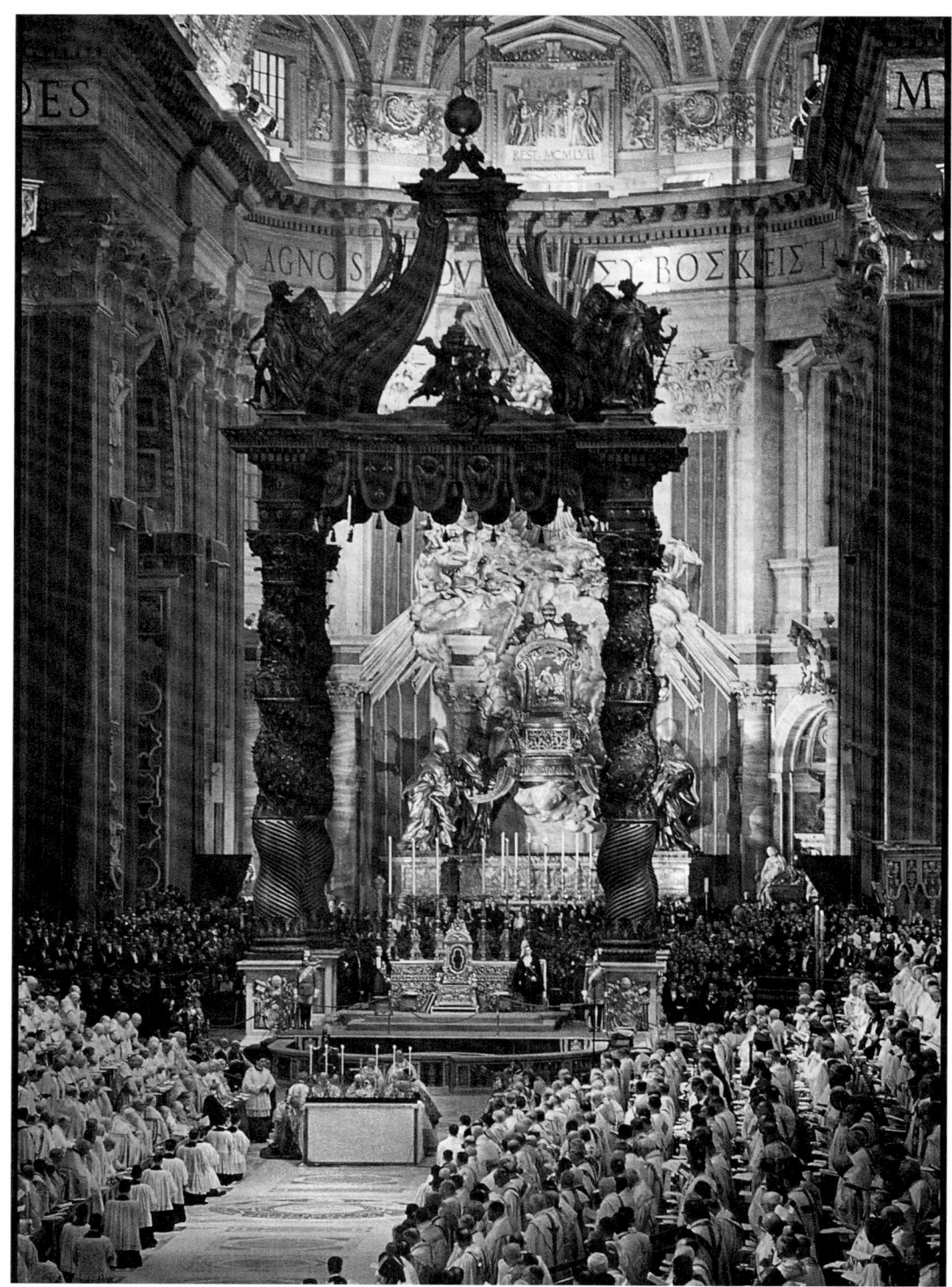

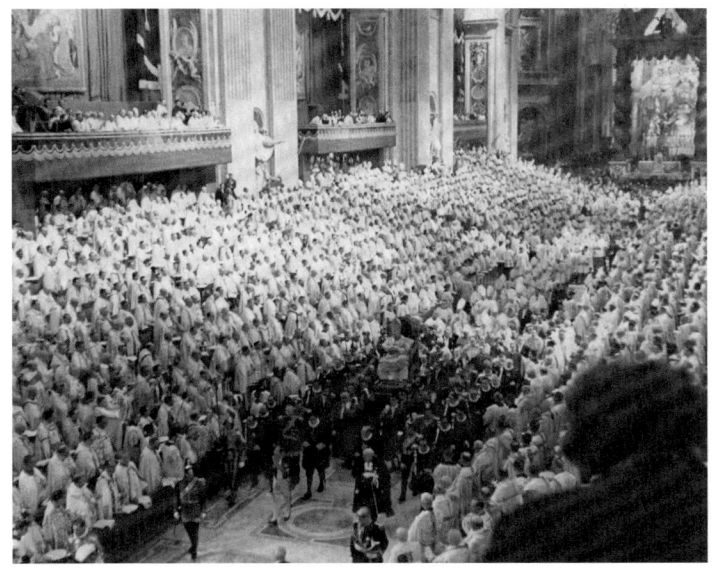

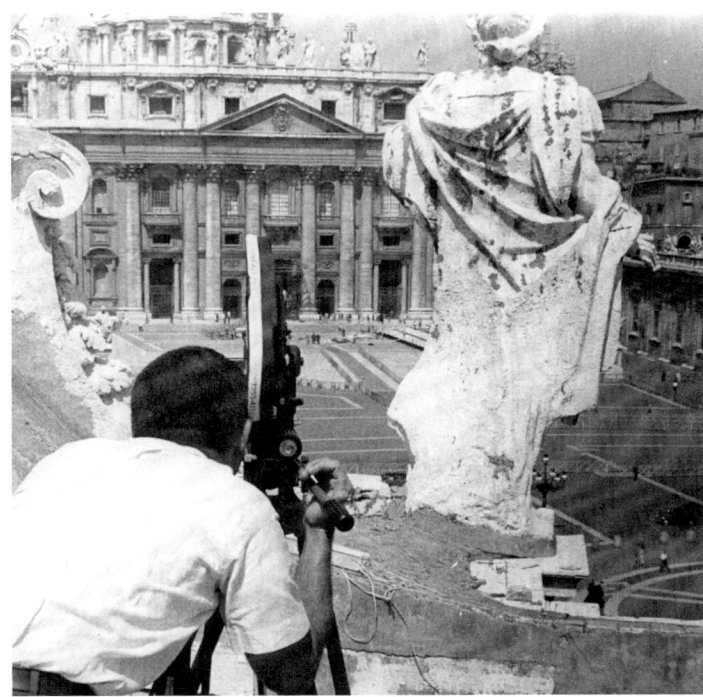

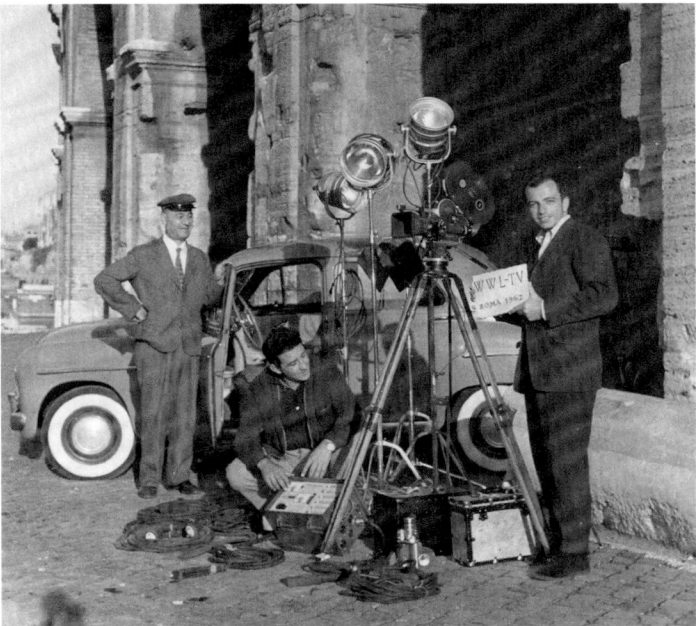

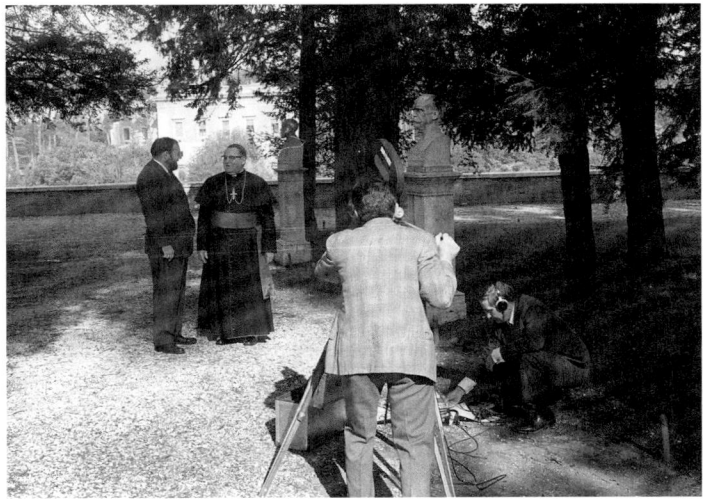

Scenes from Del's one-of-a-kind coverage of Vatican II and the subsequent coronation of Pope Paul VI. The Vatican II coverage resulted in the South's first hour-long, color local news documentary. *Photos by Del Hall, some using auto-shutter.*

President John F. Kennedy emerges from New Orleans
City Hall to greet a racially integrated crowd in 1962.
Photos by Del Hall.

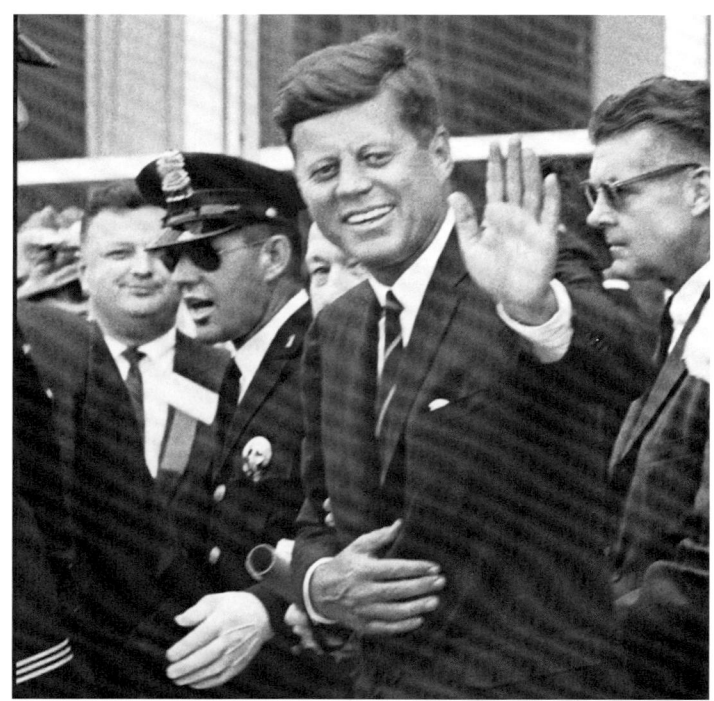

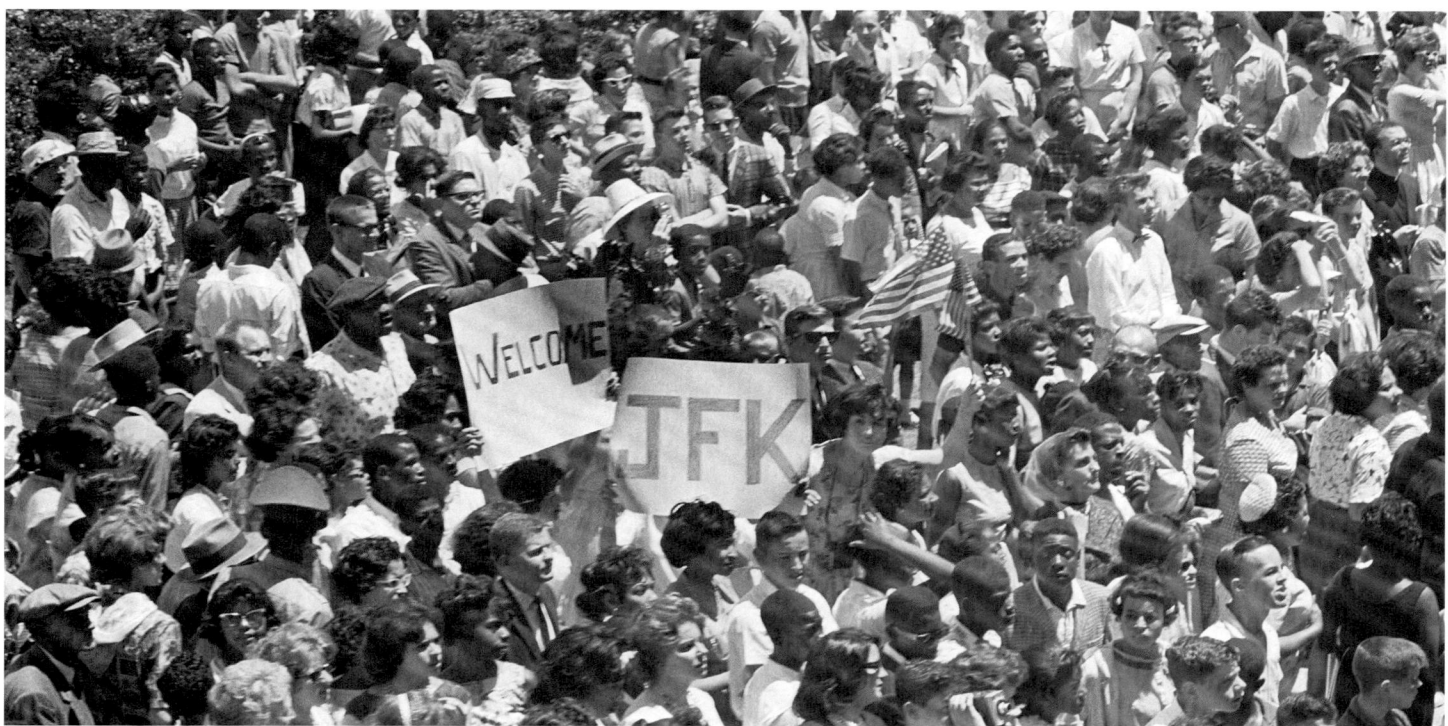

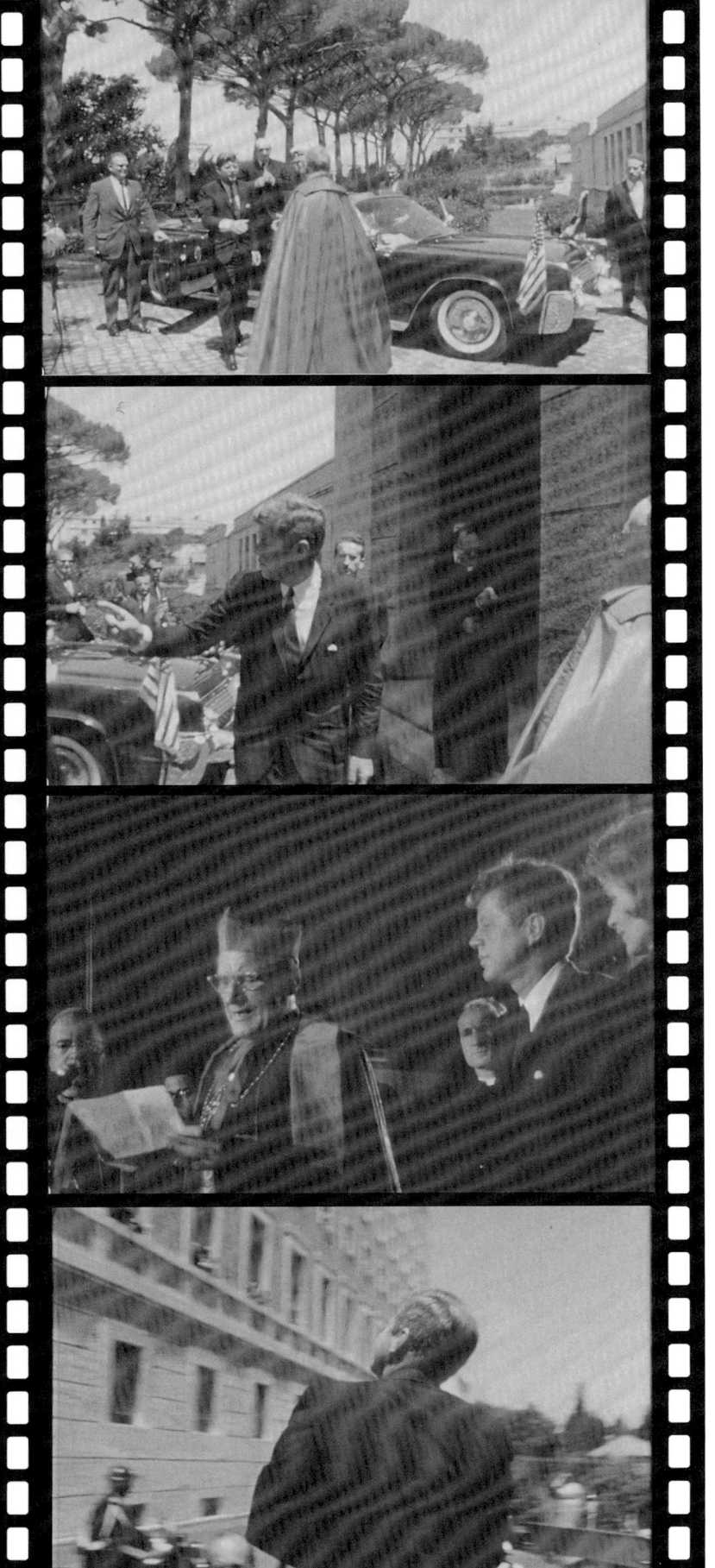

Del covers President Kennedy's visit to Rome's Pontifical North American College in 1963. *Film frames by Del Hall.*

Life along the Berlin Wall in October 1962. A few hours after Del filmed these scenes, President Kennedy took to the airwaves to announce that Soviet missiles had been discovered in Cuba. *Film frames by Del Hall.*

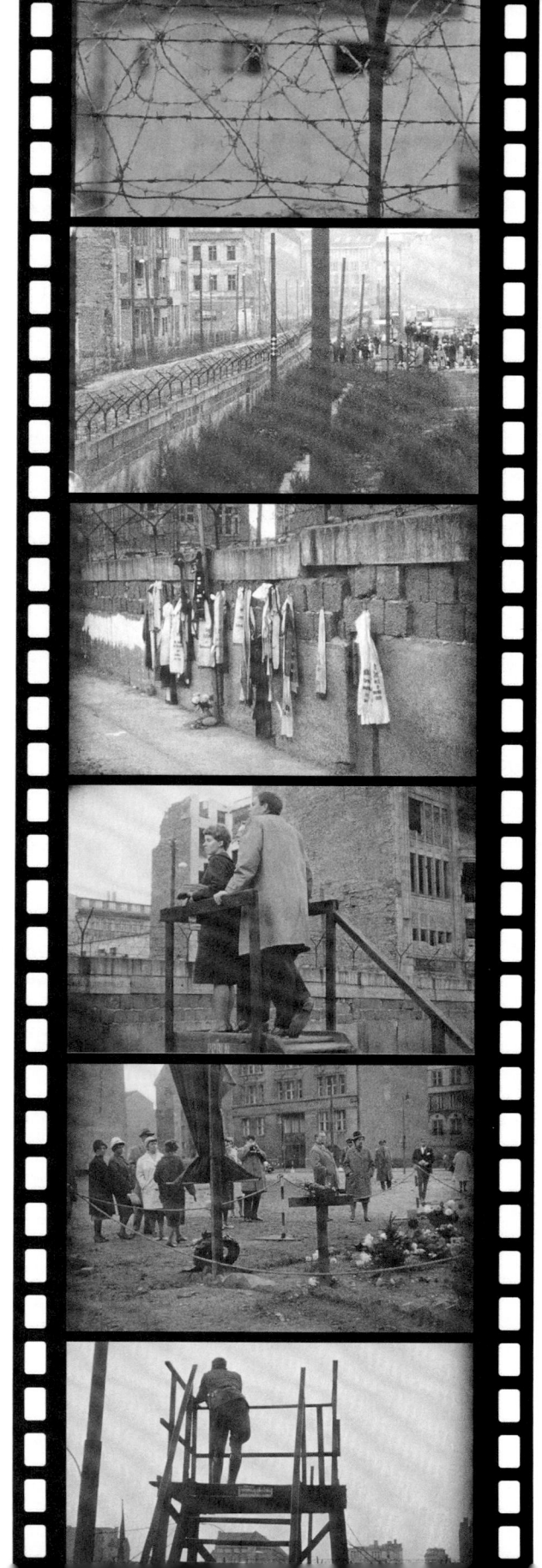

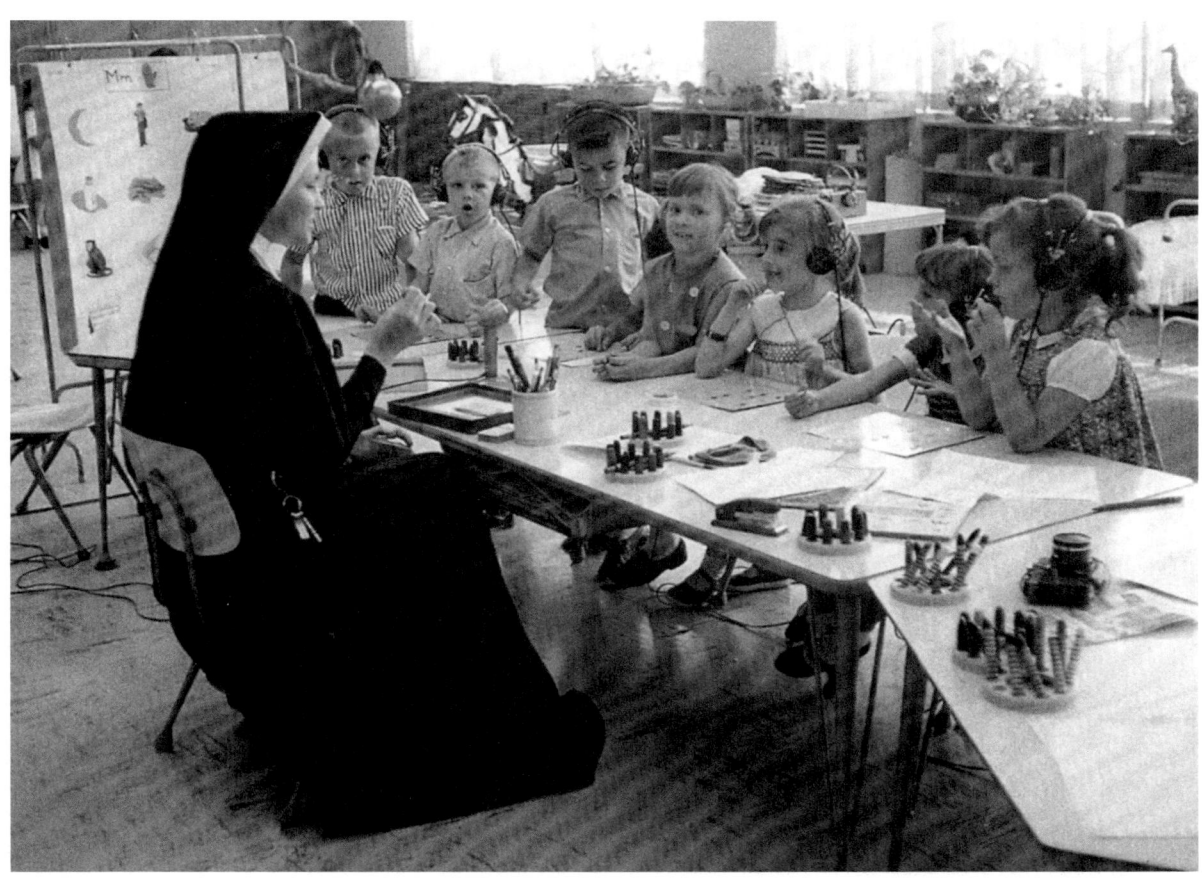

A feature story at the Chinchuba Institute for the Deaf in New Orleans. *Photo by Del Hall/WWL.*

Louisiana governor John McKeithen plays to Del's camera. *Photo by WWL/ Del Hall Collection.*

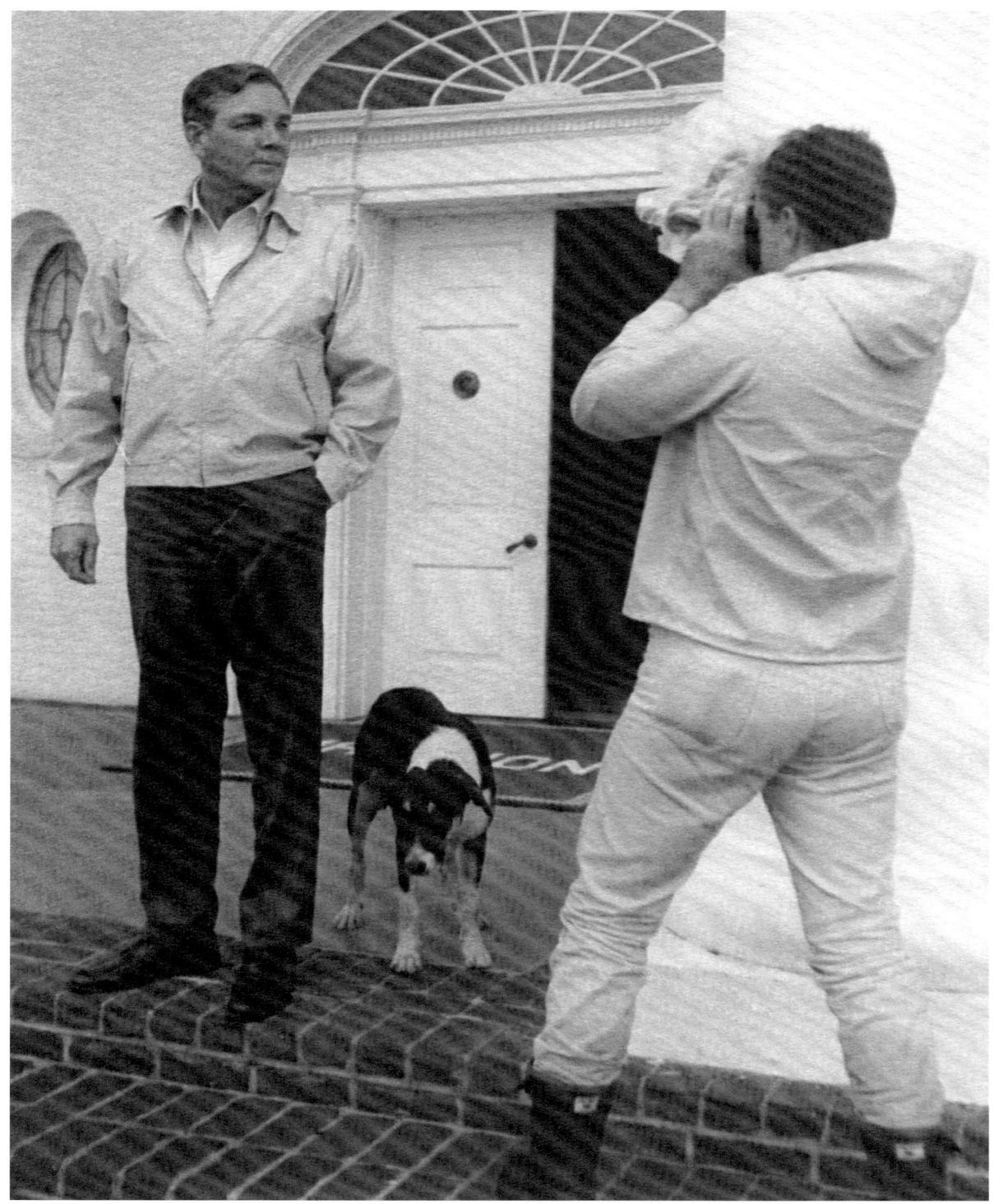

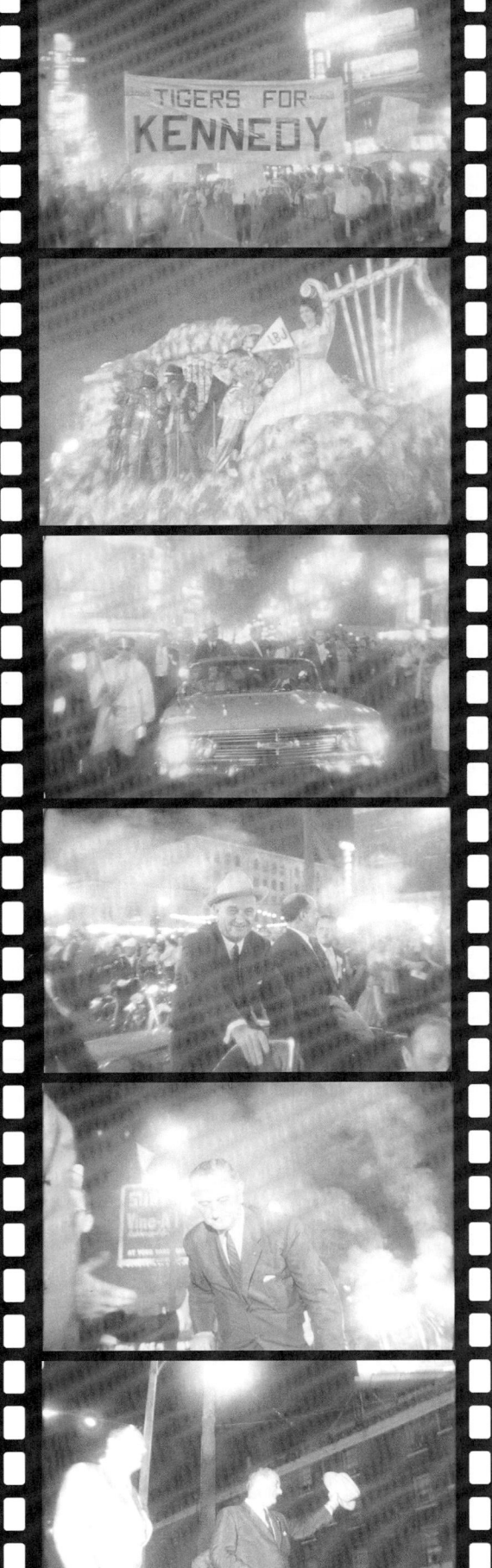

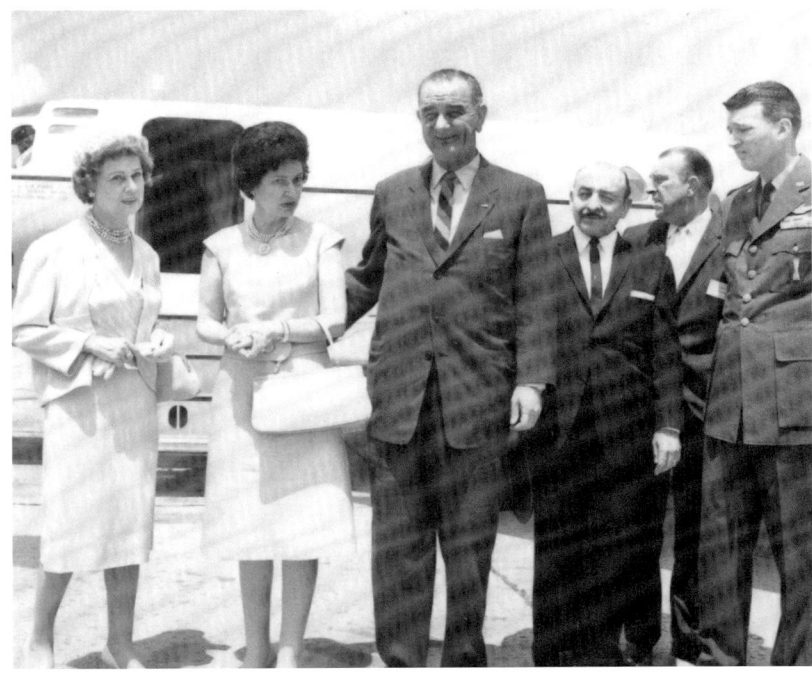

Politicking, Louisiana-style . . . At left are frames from Del's coverage of Vice-President Lyndon Johnson's whistle-stop campaign to win over the South for the 1960 presidential election, which culminated with a wild Mardi Gras–like reception on Canal Street. Five years later, President and Lady Bird Johnson meet with a much shorter New Orleans mayor Victor Schiro. *Film frames and photo by Del Hall/WWL.*

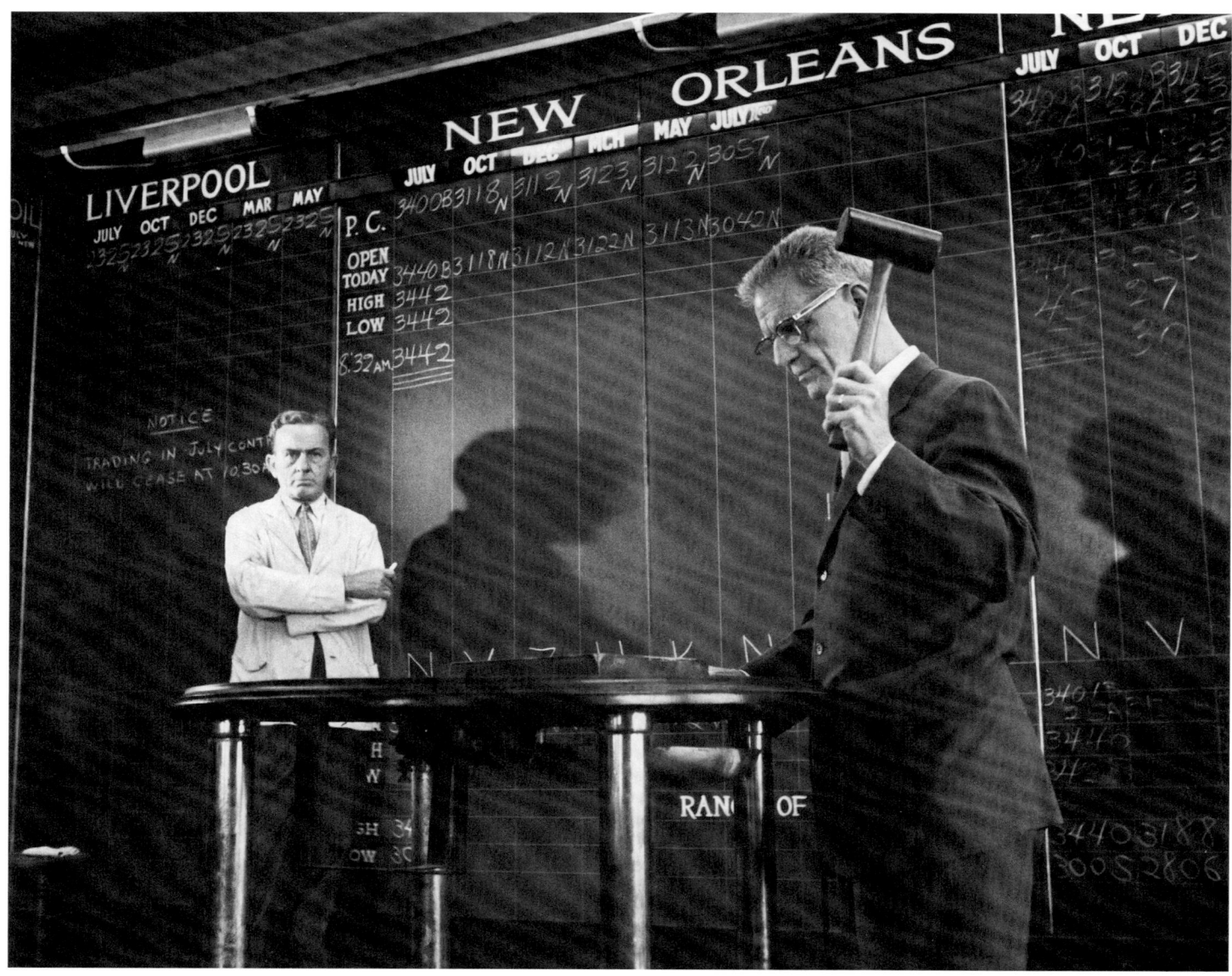

Last gavel at the New Orleans Cotton Exchange, 1964. *Photo by Del Hall.*

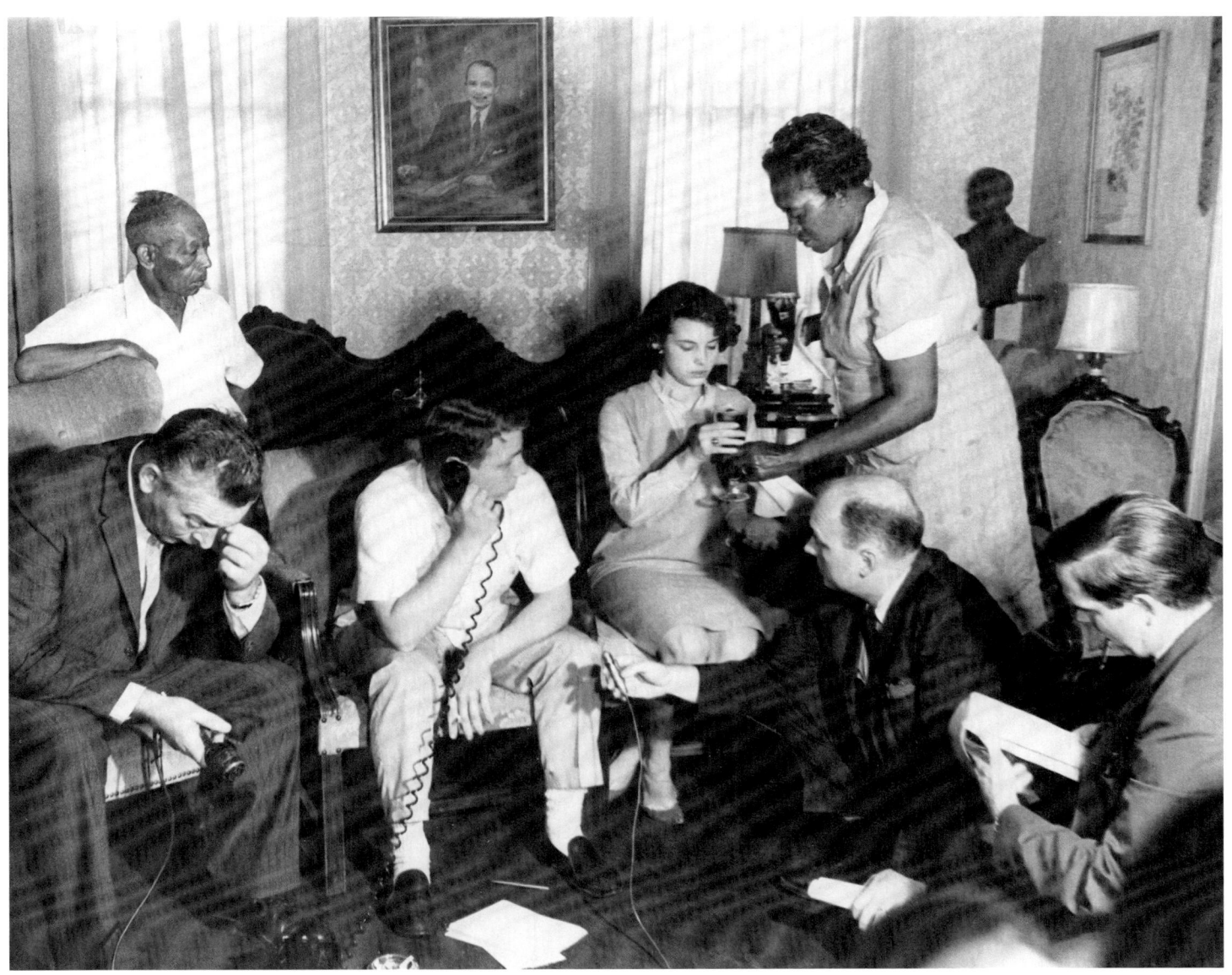

The Morrison family awaits updates on the fate of former mayor Chep Morrison, whose plane had disappeared in the mountains of Mexico. *Photo by Del Hall.*

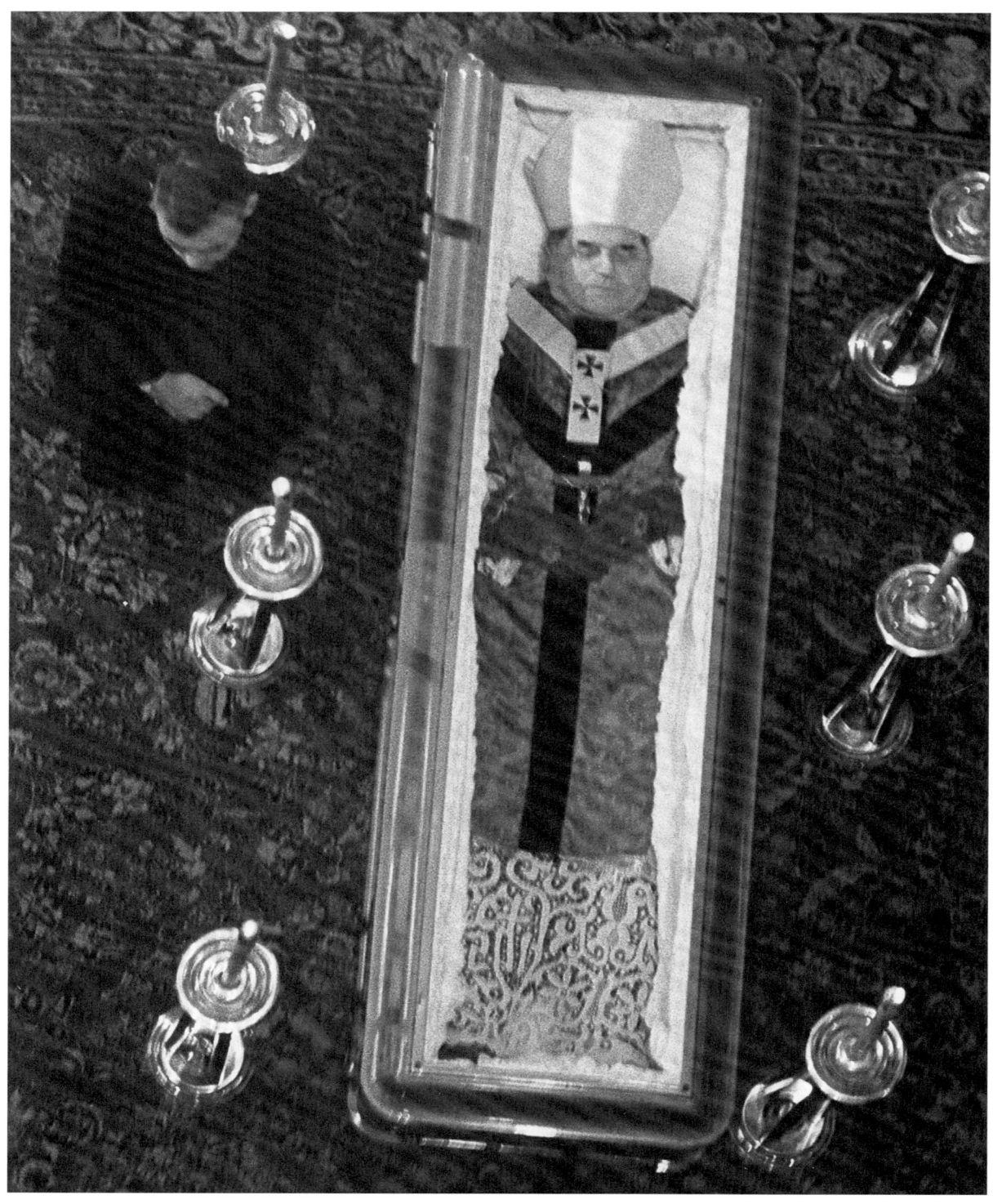

Archbishop Rummel's casket at St. Louis Cathedral. *Photo by Del Hall.*

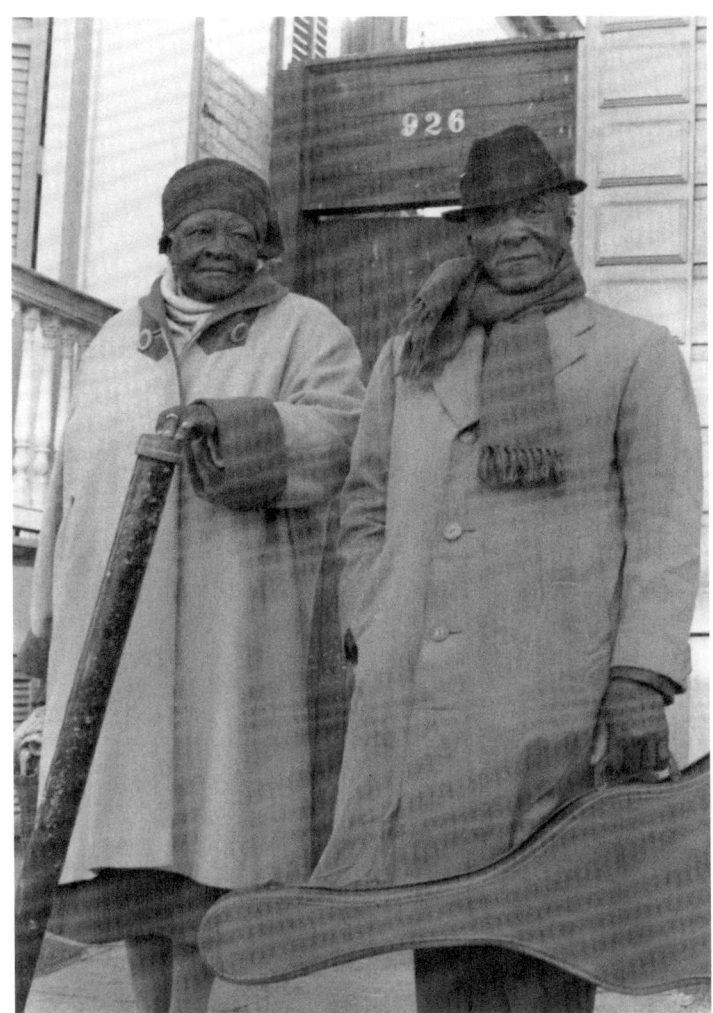

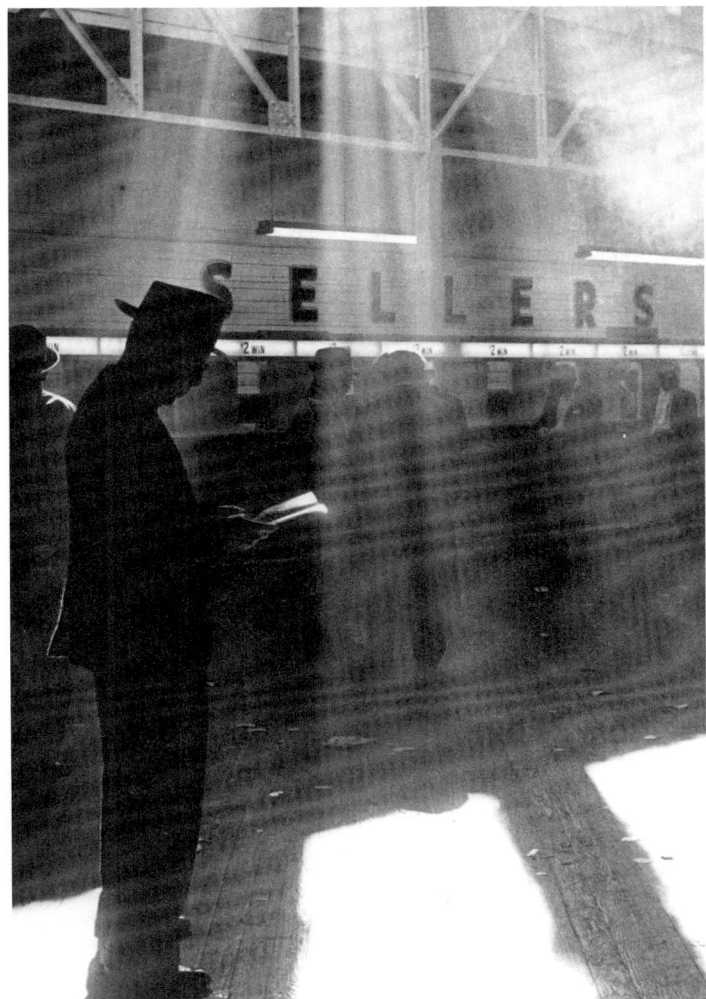

Left, an elderly musician and his wife head home on a cold day in the French Quarter. Right, picking a winner at the Fairgrounds. *Photos by Del Hall.*

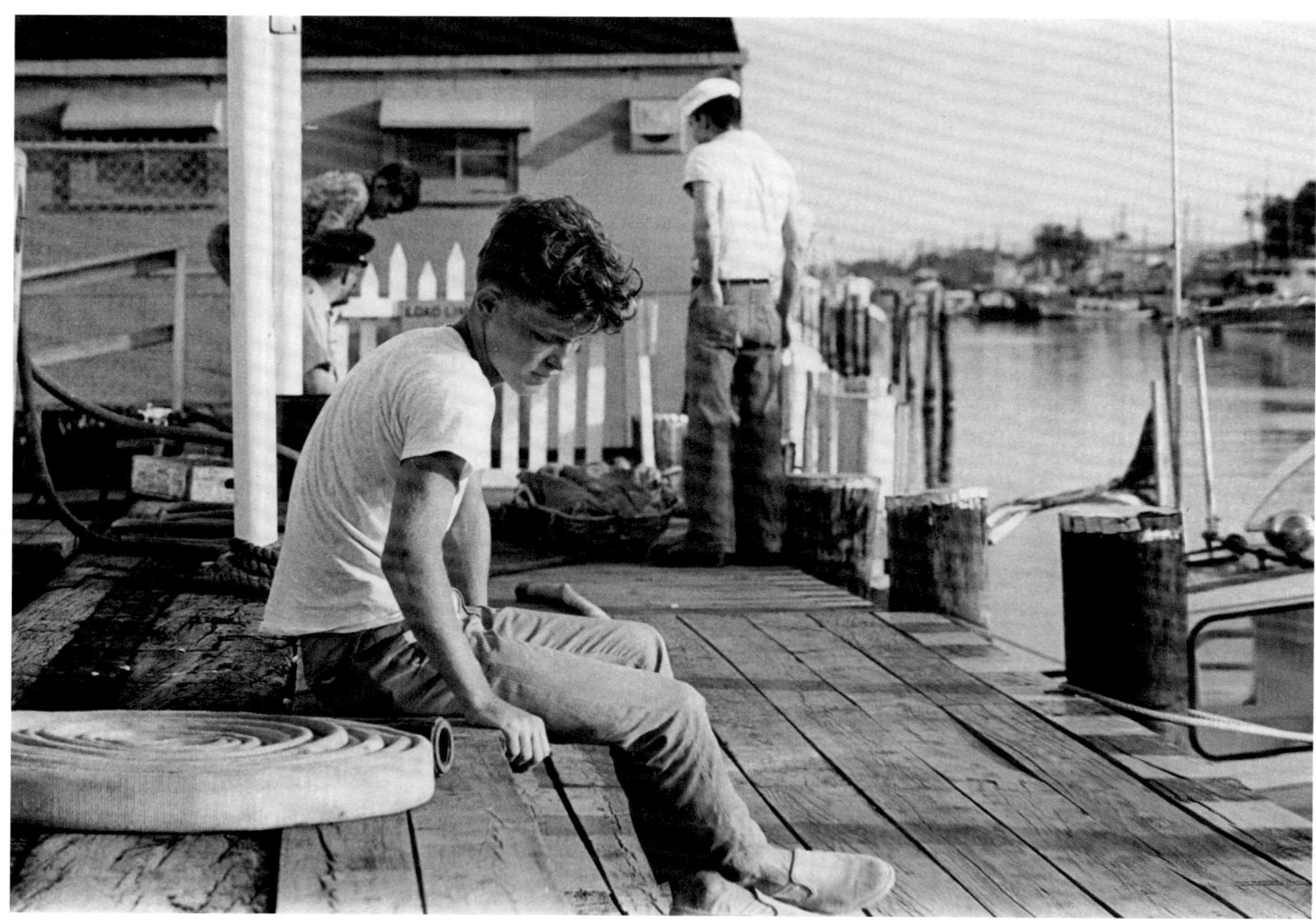

A fourteen-year-old contemplates the drowning death of his older brother in Lake Pontchartrain. *Photo by Del Hall.*

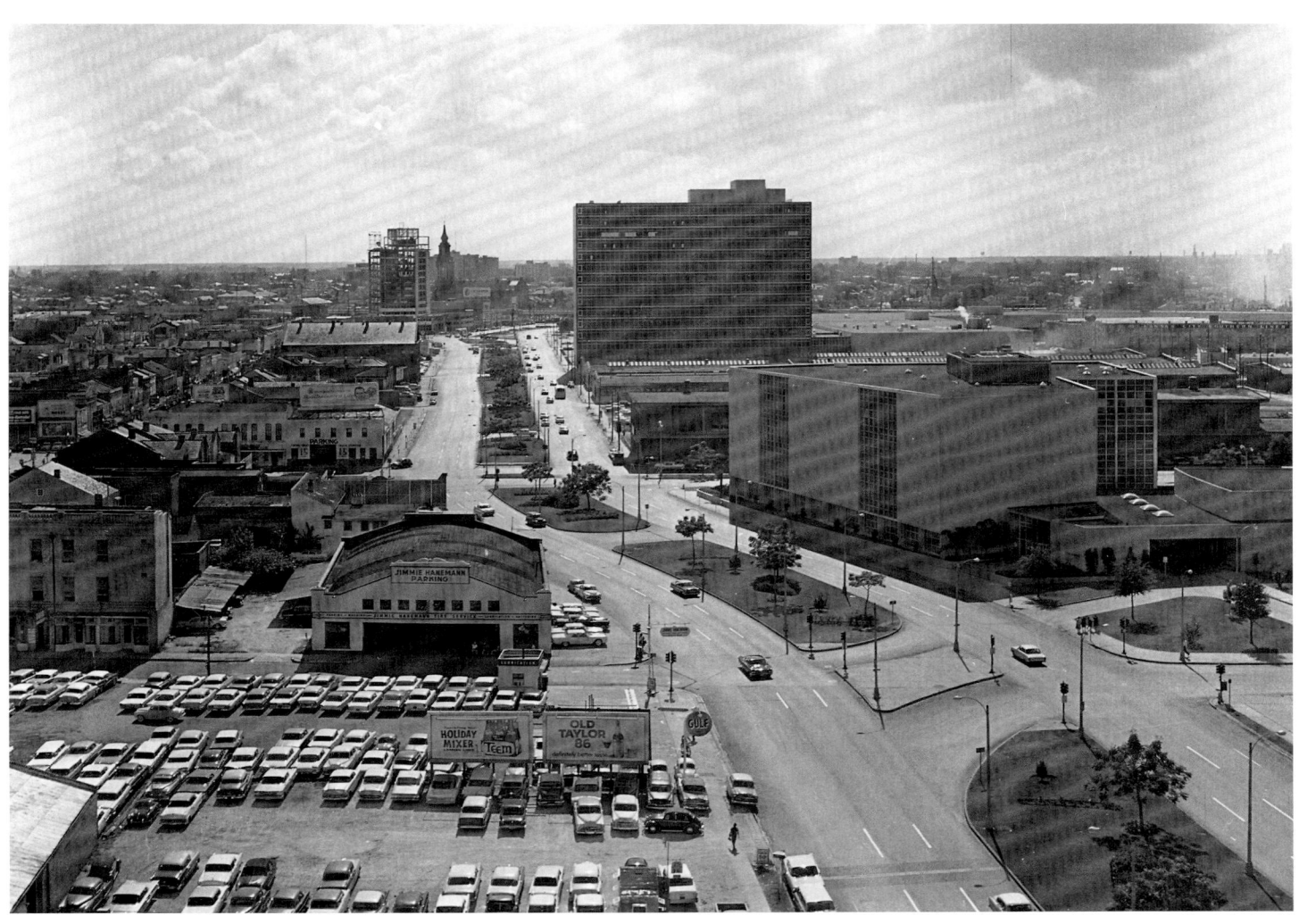

Plaza Tower, New Orleans's first modern skyscraper, under construction in distant center, left, and other urban renewal projects along the recently widened Loyola Avenue. *Photo by Del Hall/WWL.*

The last ride of the Canal streetcar line in New Orleans. *Photo by Del Hall/WWL.*

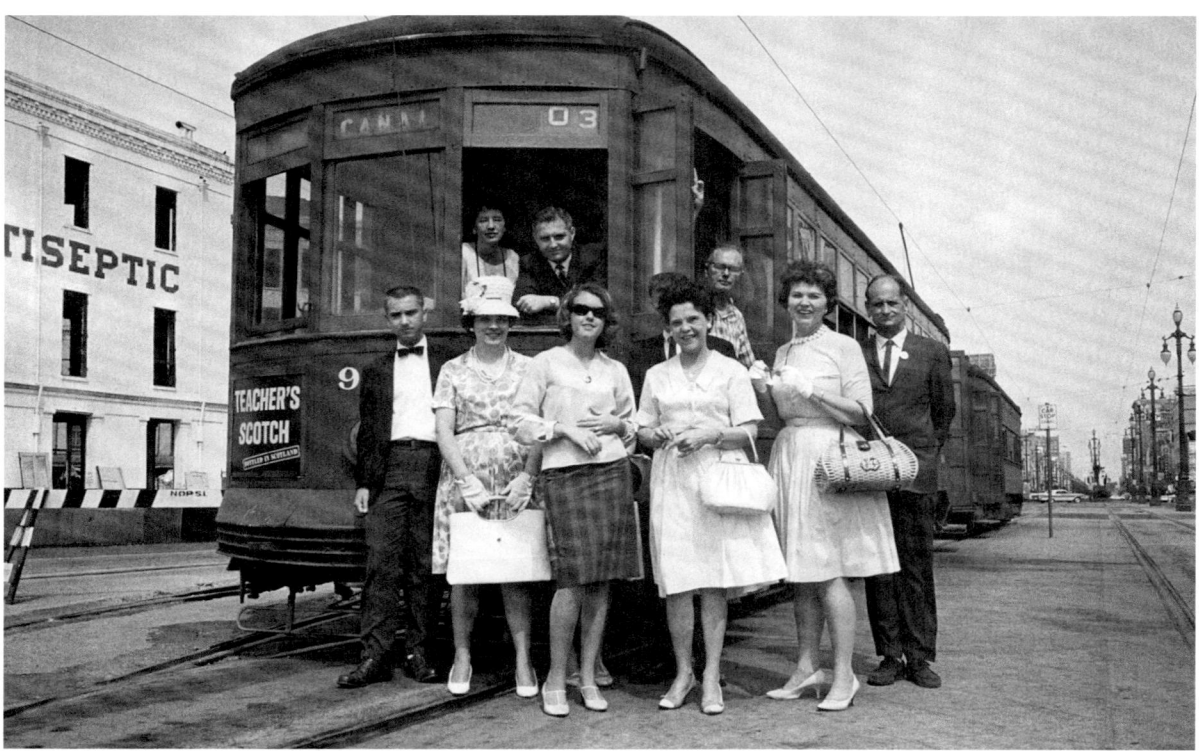

Covering politics at City Hall. *Photo by WWL/Del Hall Collection.*

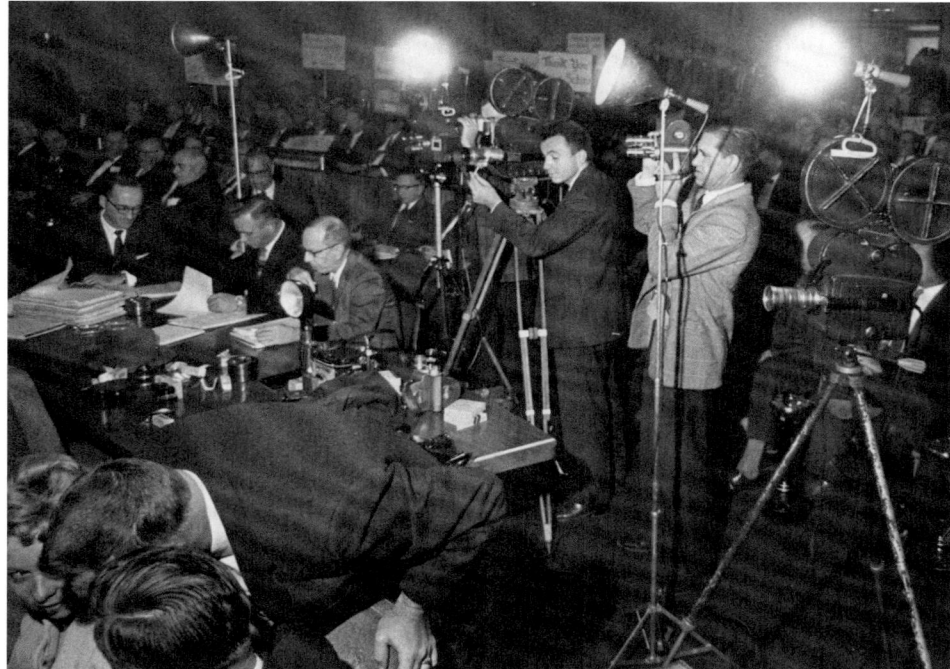

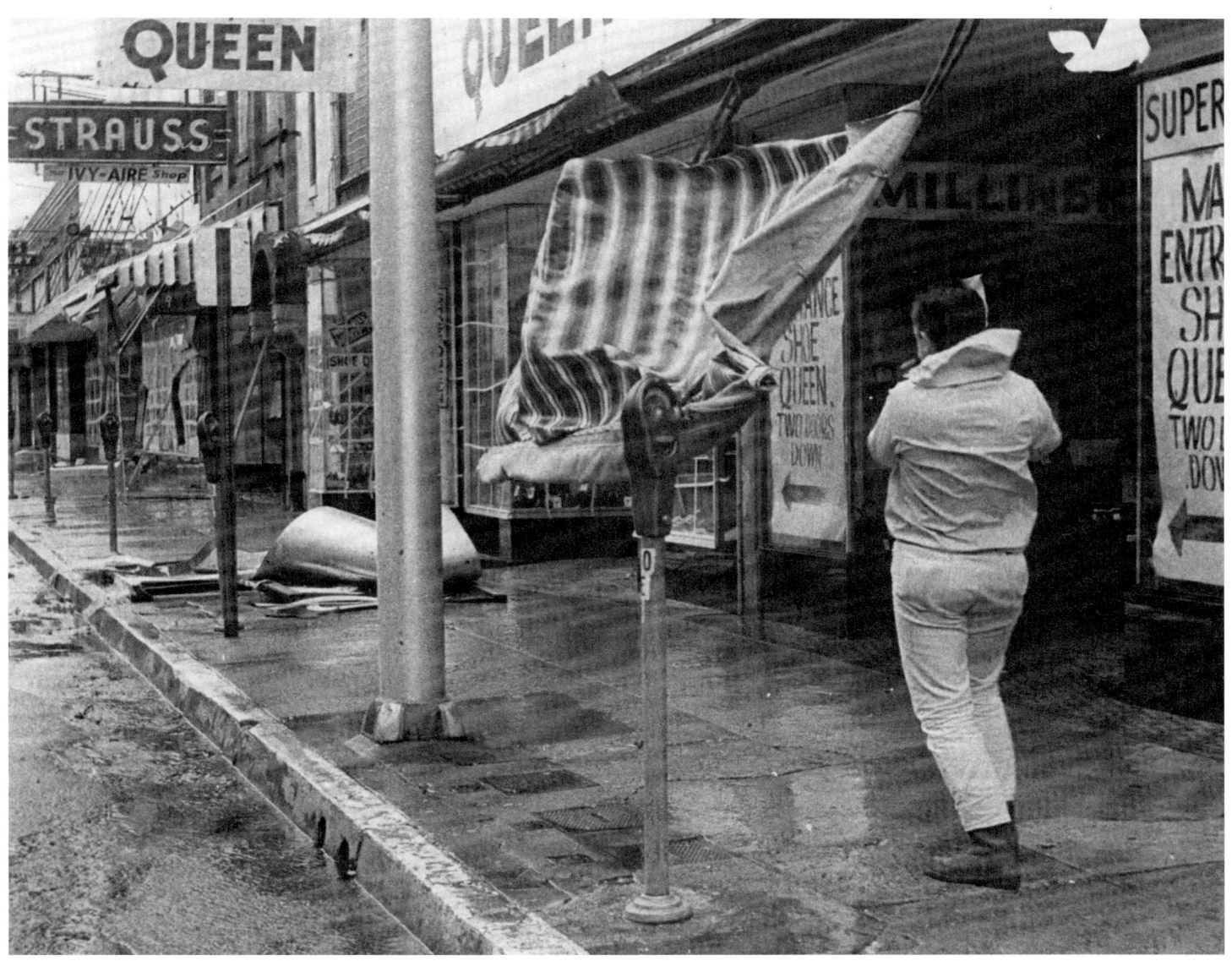

The opening salvo of Hurricane Hilda in New Iberia, 1964. *Photo by WWL/Del Hall Collection.*

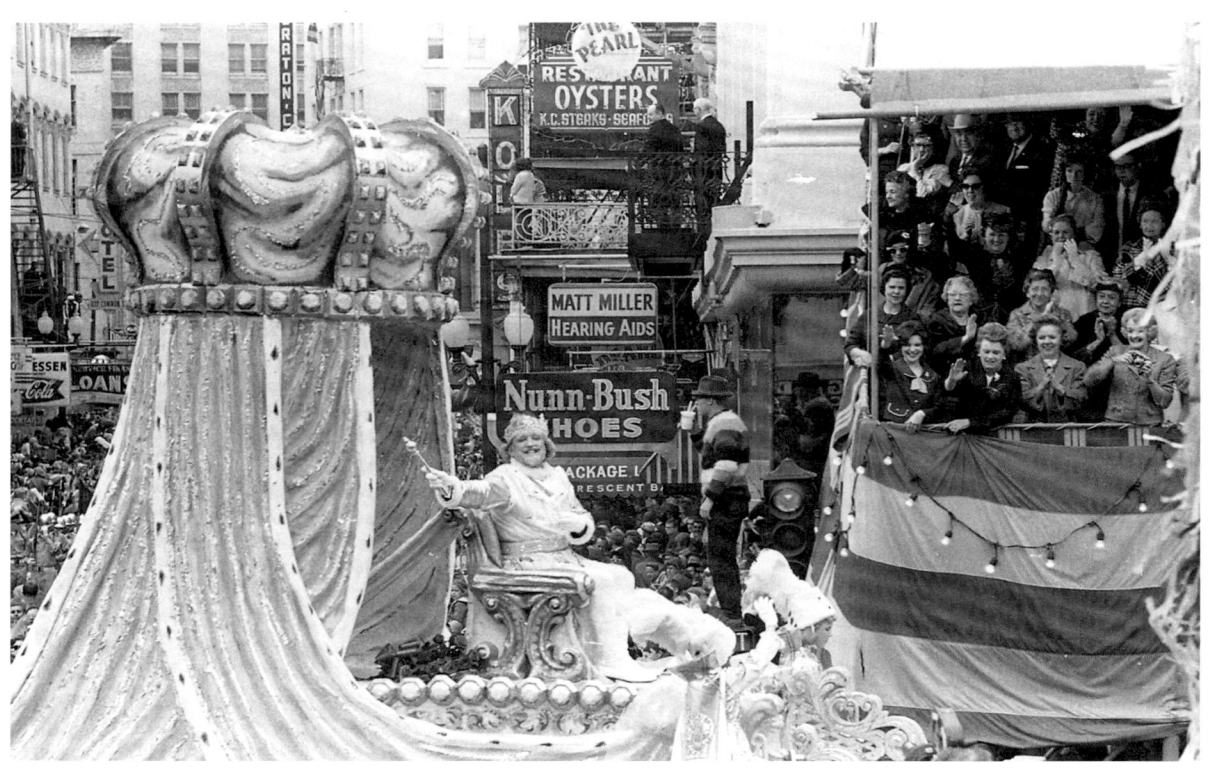

Rex on Canal Street during Mardi Gras, early 1960s. Local "royalty"—the uptown aristocracy—hails Rex from special seating at the Pickwick Club, while the masses revel in the streets below. *Photos by Del Hall.*

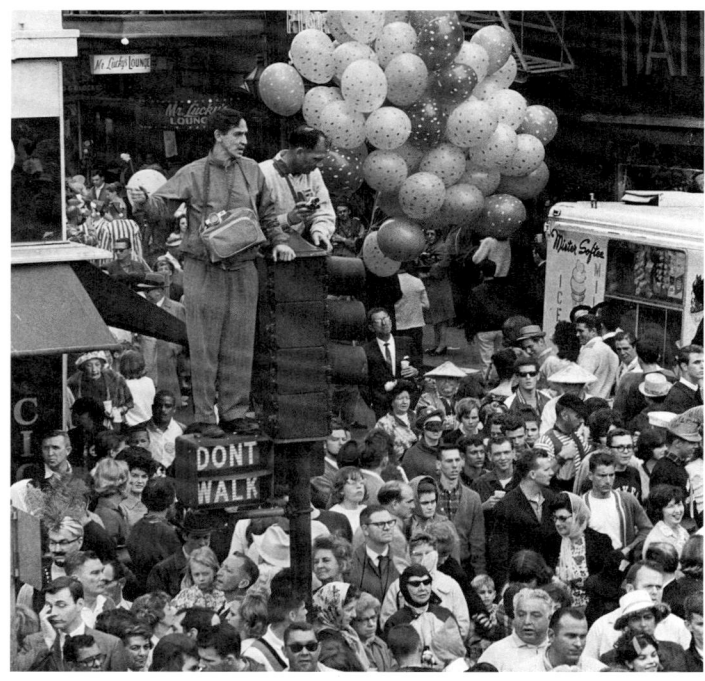

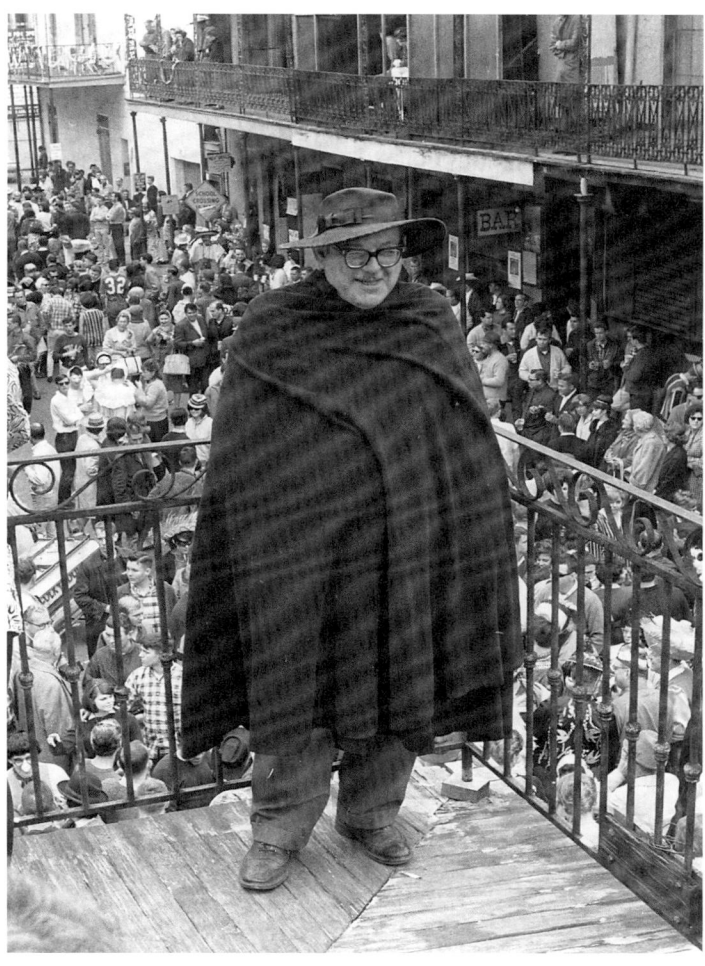

Famed patron of the French Quarter arts, culture, and real estate scene, Larry Borenstein. *Photo by Del Hall.*

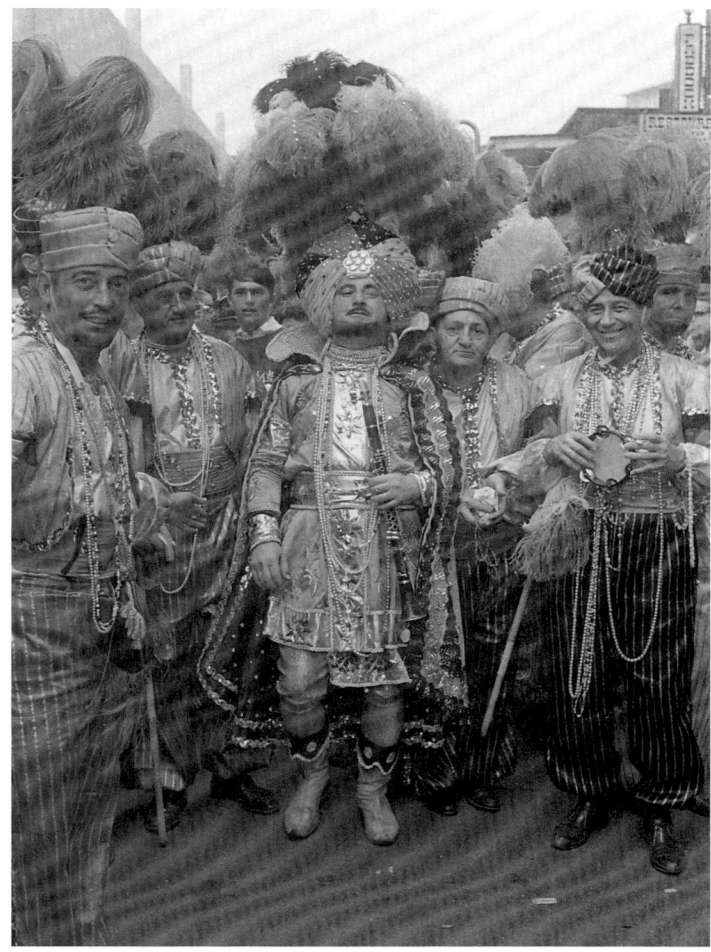

Pete Fountain (center) and his Half-Fast Walking Club on Bourbon Street, Mardi Gras morning. *Photo by Del Hall.*

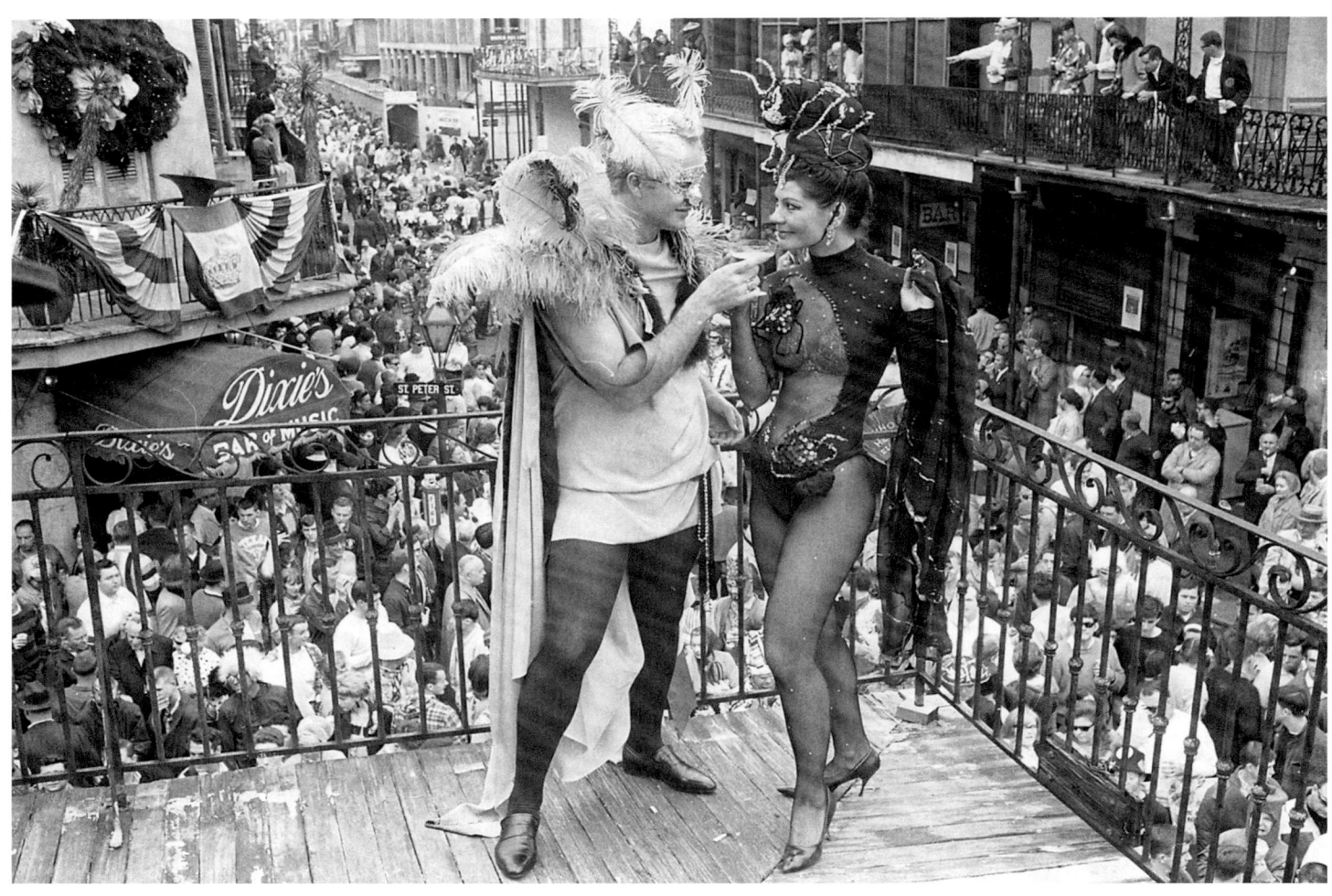

Mardi Gras on a Bourbon Street balcony,
1963. *Photo by Del Hall.*

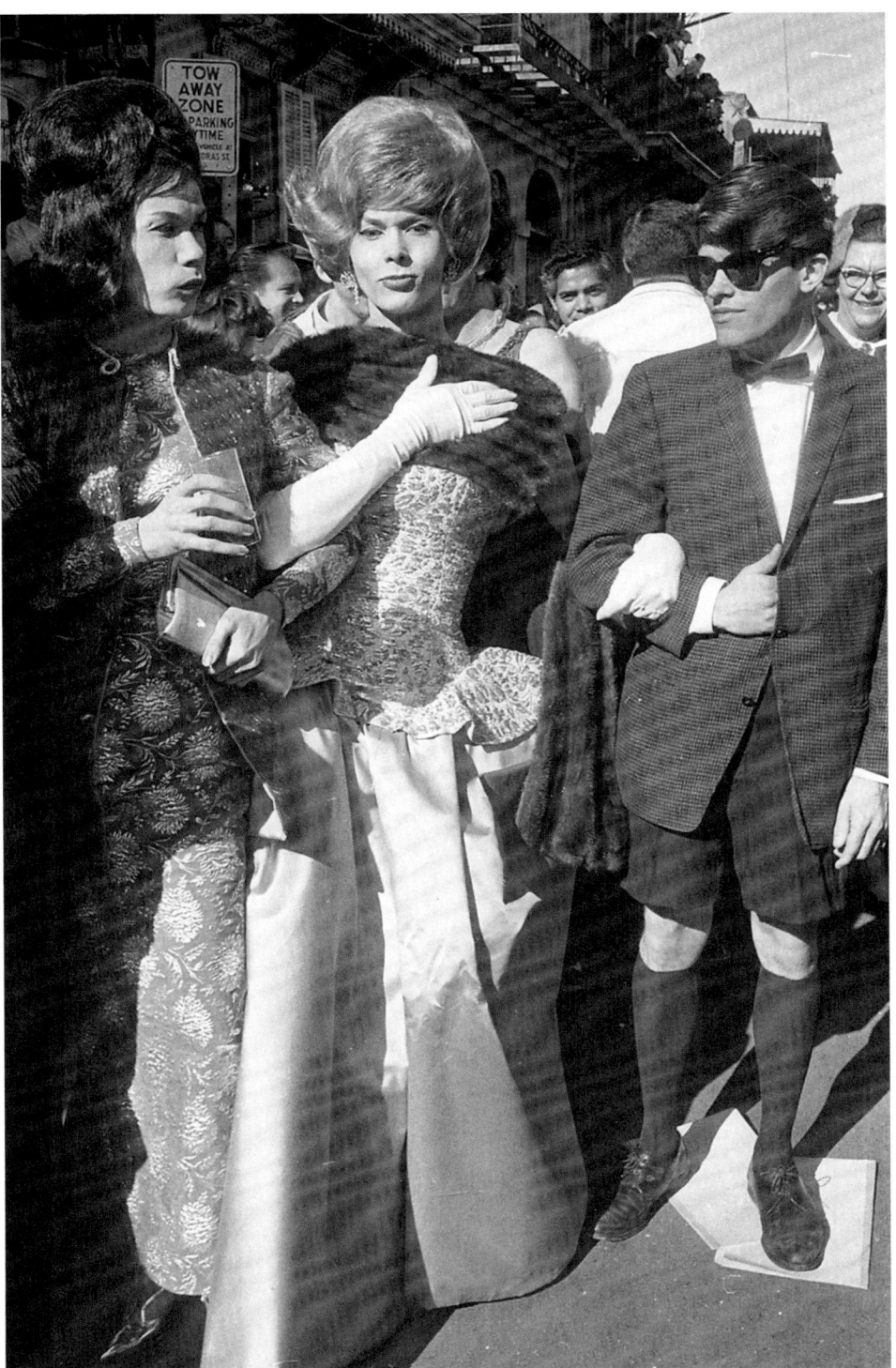

Cross-dressers on Bourbon Street in the early 1960s. *Photo by Del Hall.*

Revelry on Mardi Gras Day. *Photo by Del Hall.*

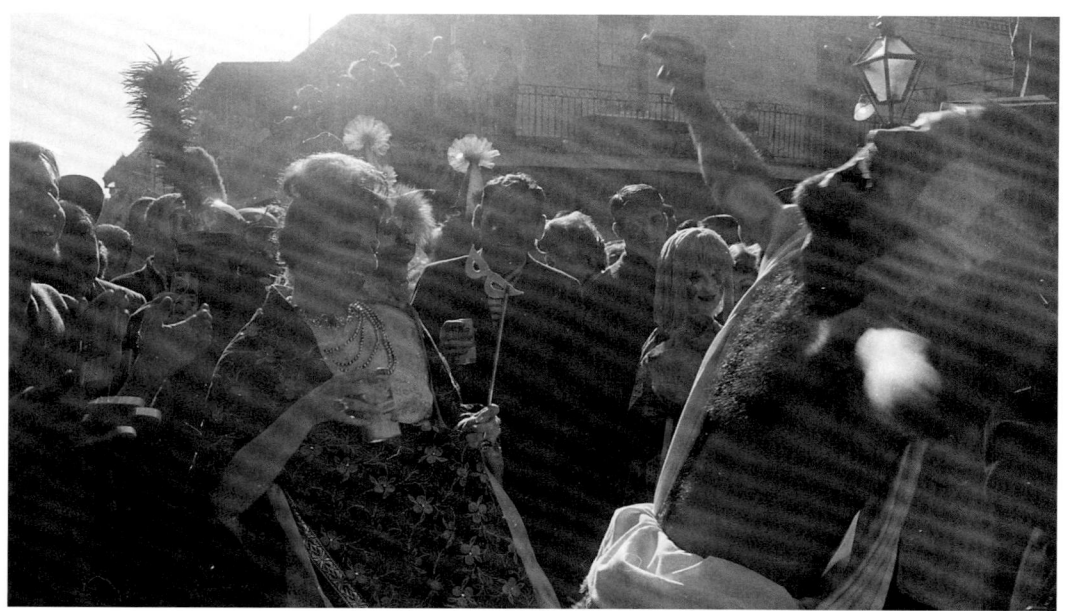

Krewe of Zulu parade. *Photo by Del Hall.*

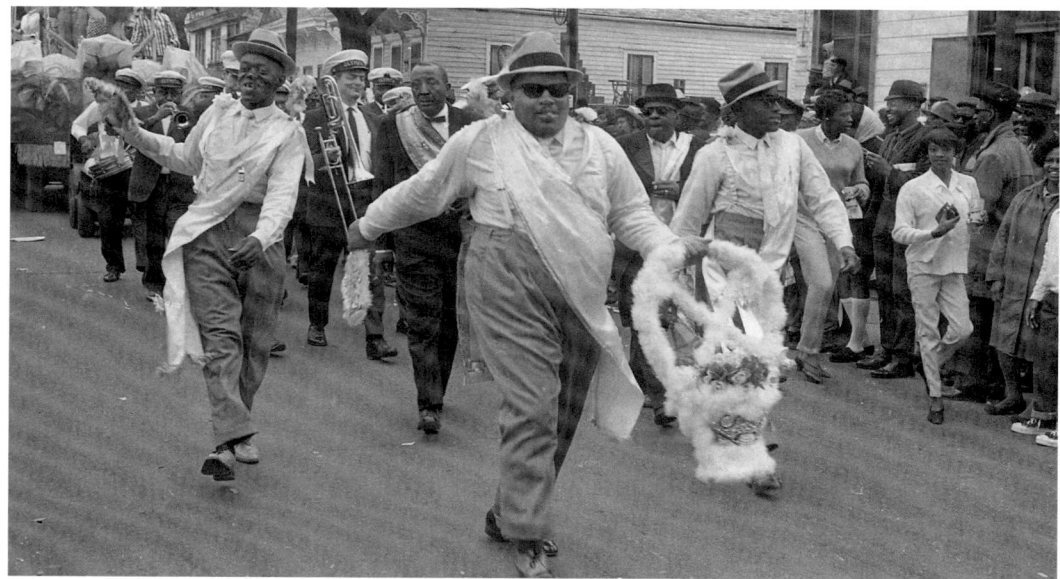

"The Greatest Free Show on Earth"(facing page): At left is Del's coverage of the Krewe of Proteus parade on Canal Street and the ball of the secretive Krewe of Comus, early 1960s; at right, the Krewe of Momus rolls through the French Quarter in the mid-1960s. Large parades were banned from the Quarter starting in 1973, for reasons of public safety. Sights like these have never been seen since. *Frames by Del Hall.*

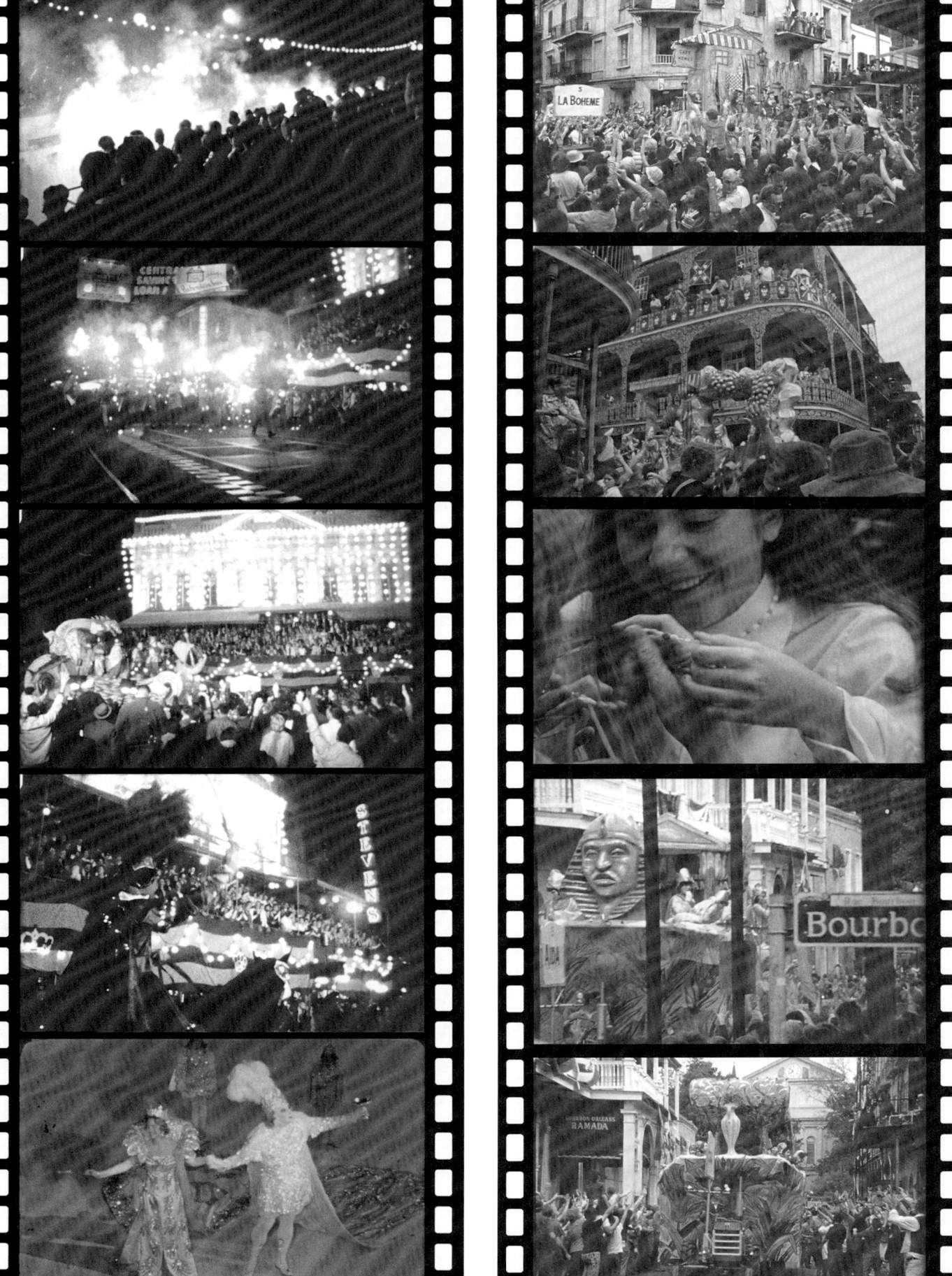

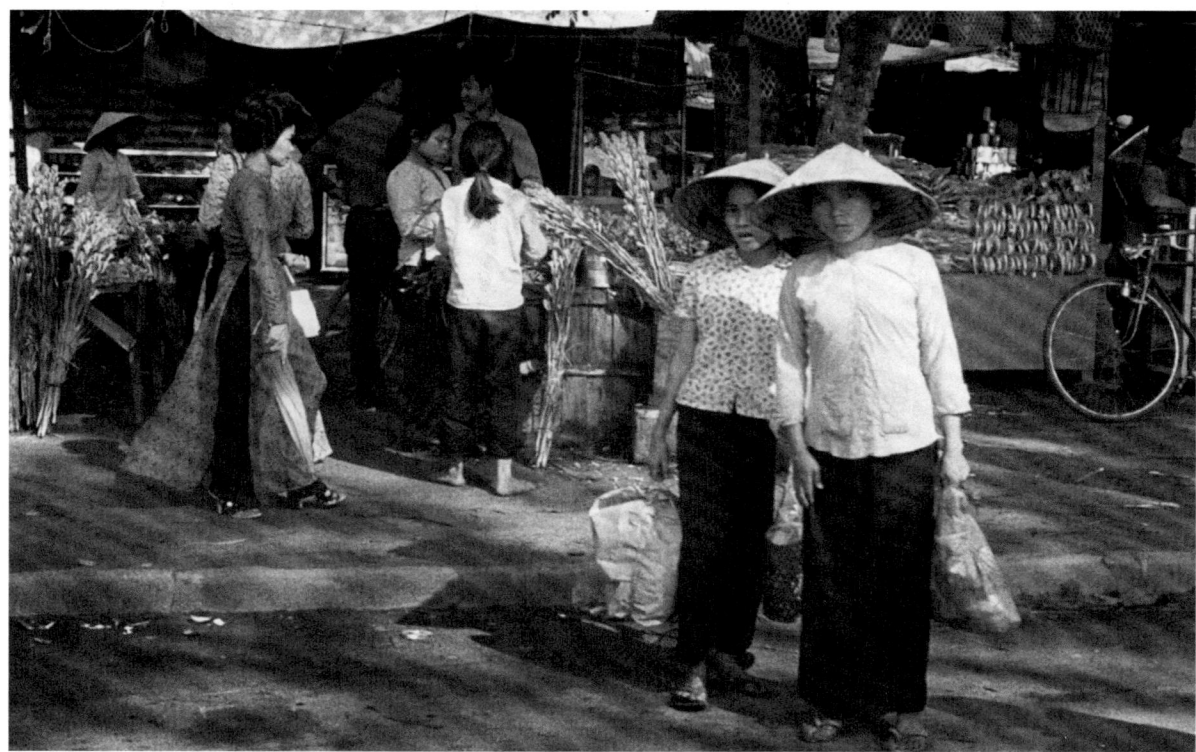

Street scene in Saigon. *Del Hall Collection/WWL.*

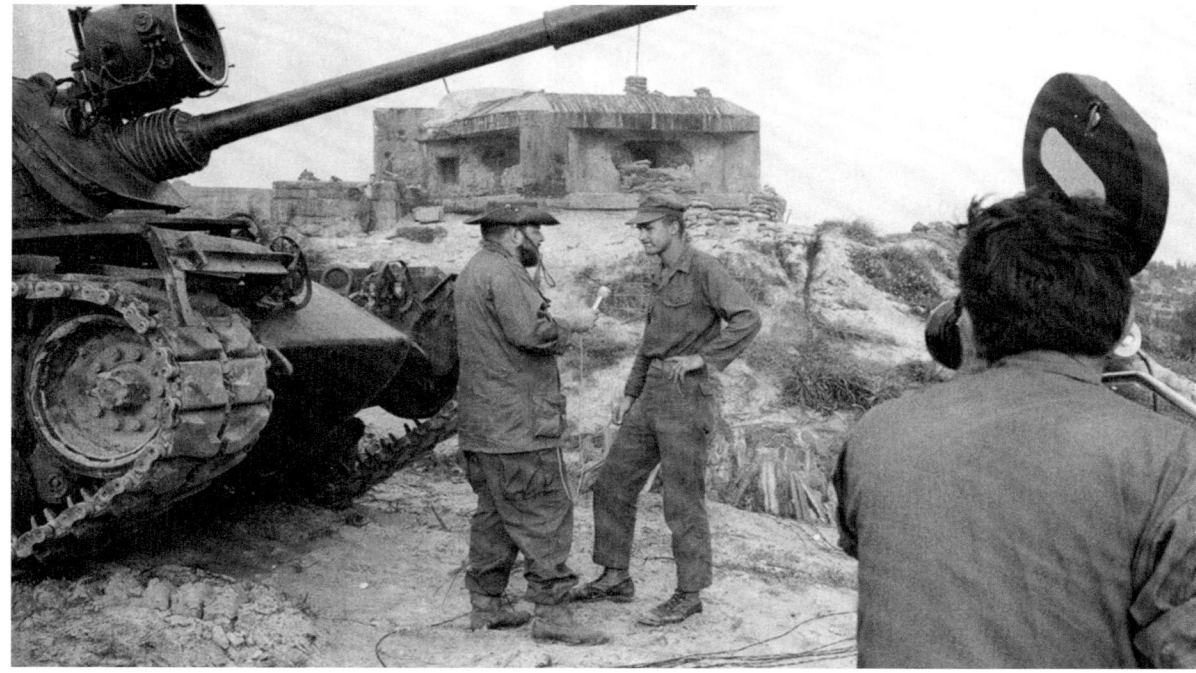

The war in Vietnam. Del and Phil Johnson at work interviewing Louisianians and Mississippians in the field. *Del Hall Collection/WWL.*

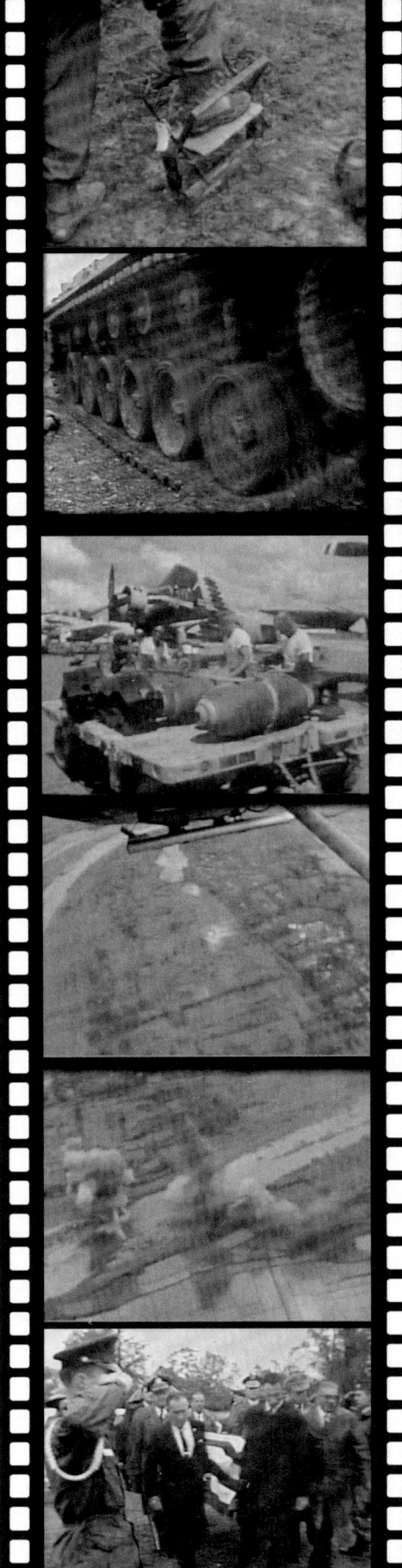

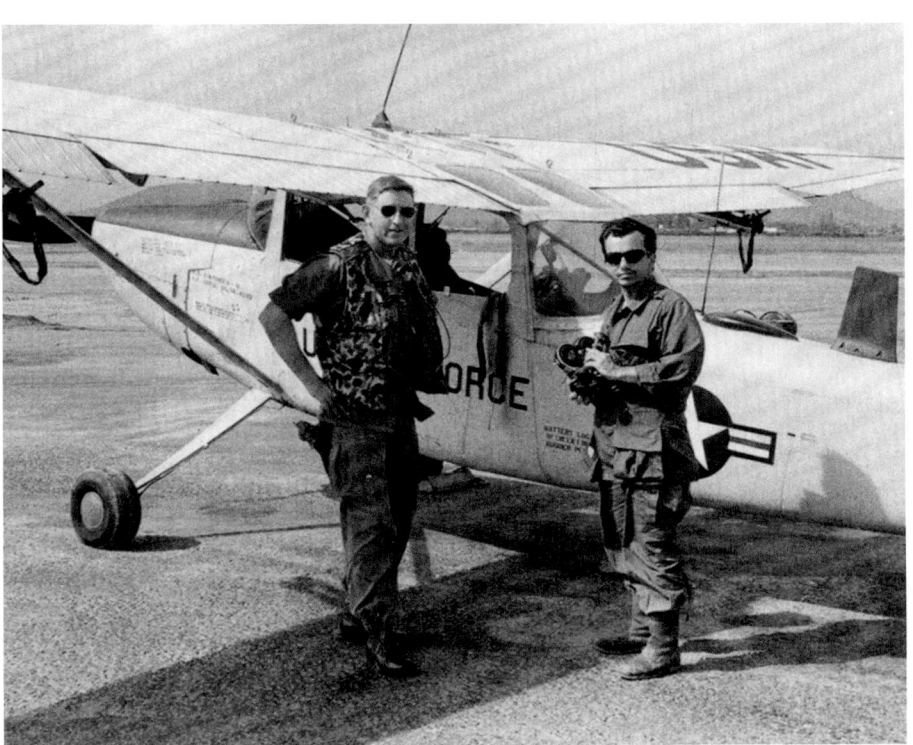

Piper Cub from which Del filmed the live bombardment footage shown in *Viet Nam '65: A Distant Christmas. Del Hall Collection/WWL.*

Frames from *Viet Nam '65: A Distant Christmas,* which opened with the funeral of Louisiana soldier Captain Ronald F. Rod, killed in the mounting conflict (bottom frame). *Film frames from Del Hall Collection/ WWL.*

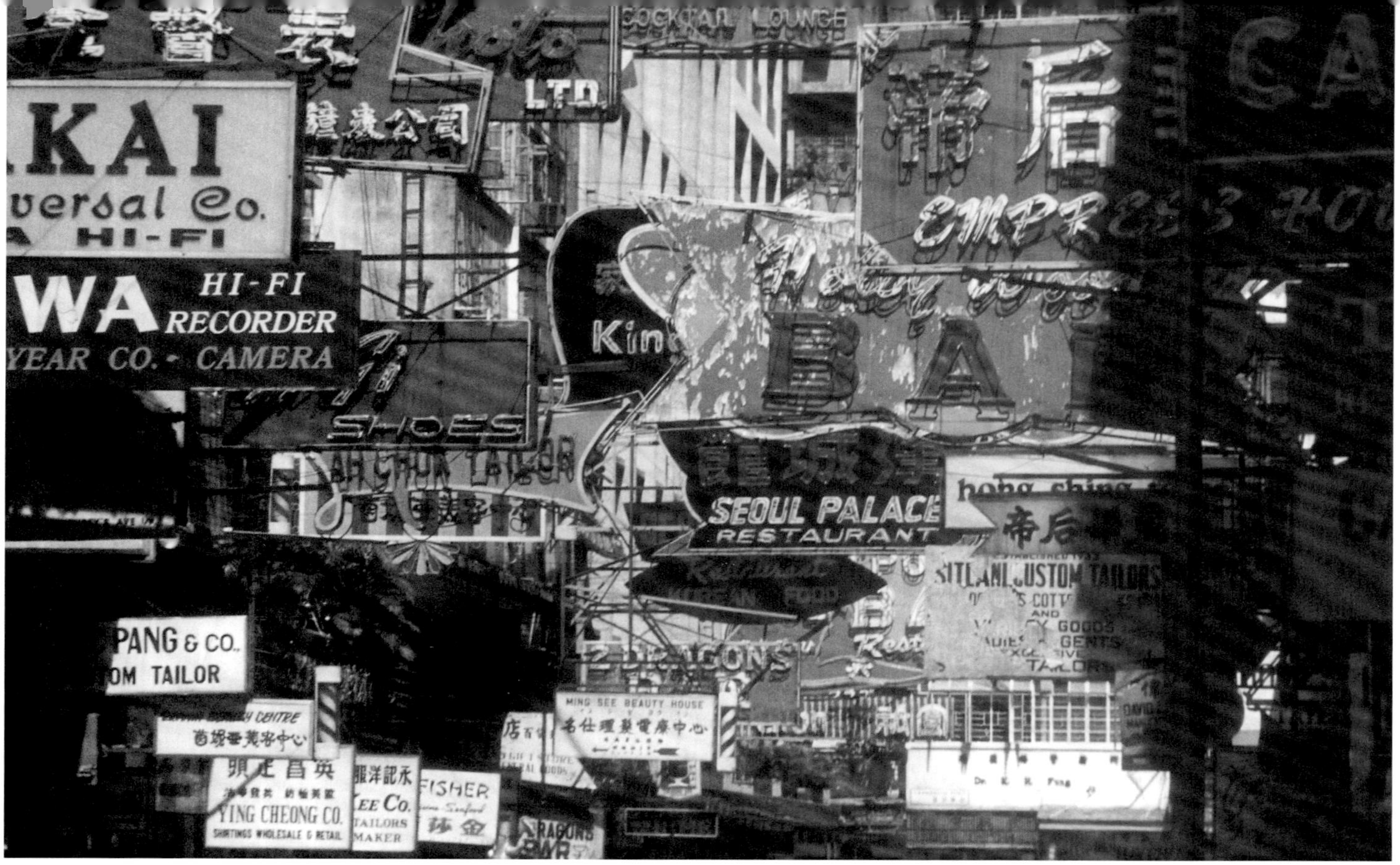

Scenes from Hong Kong in 1965. Right: an ivory craftsman and merchant, at a time when this trade was legal. Middle of facing page: fish drying by harbor filled with "boat people," seen also from the air (below right). *Photos by Del Hall.*

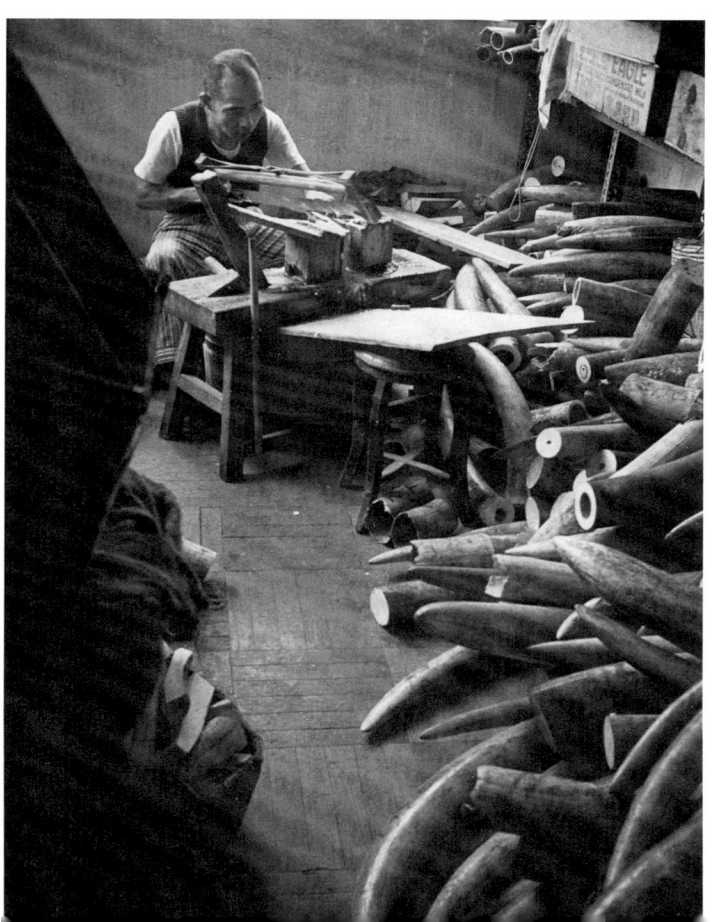

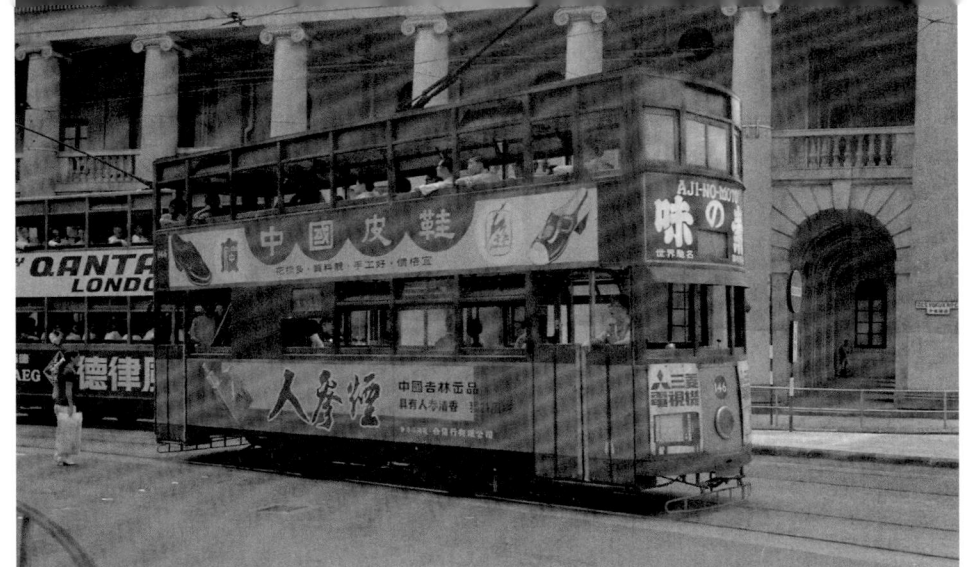

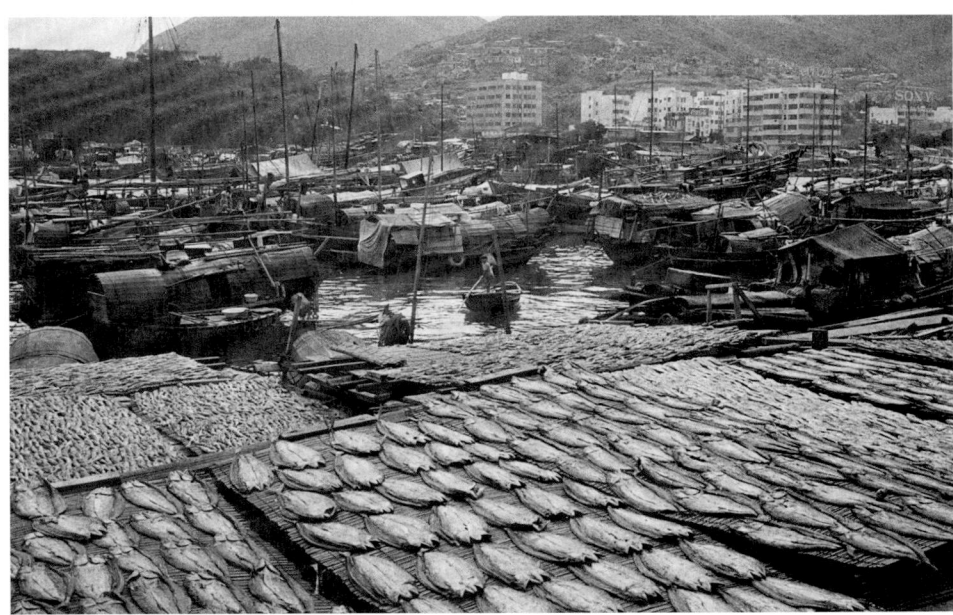

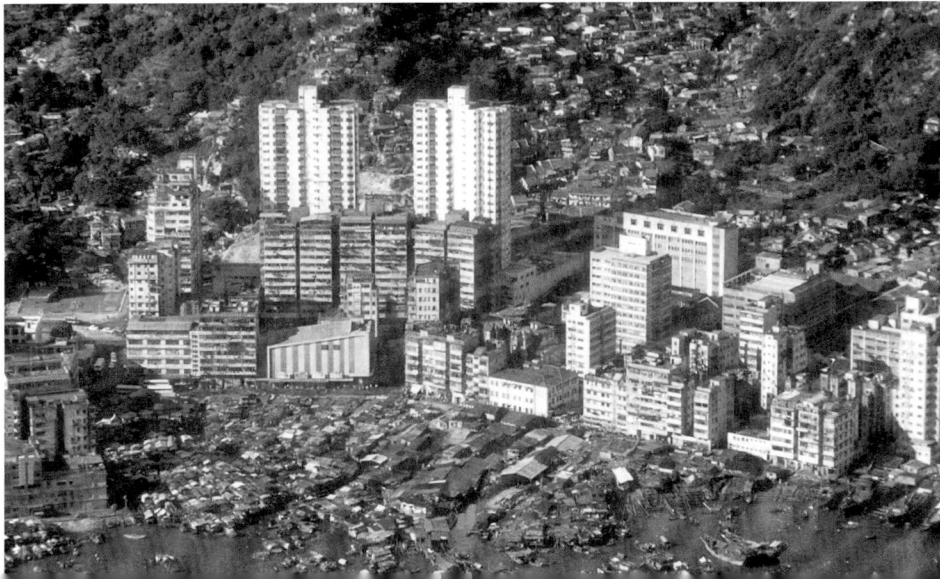

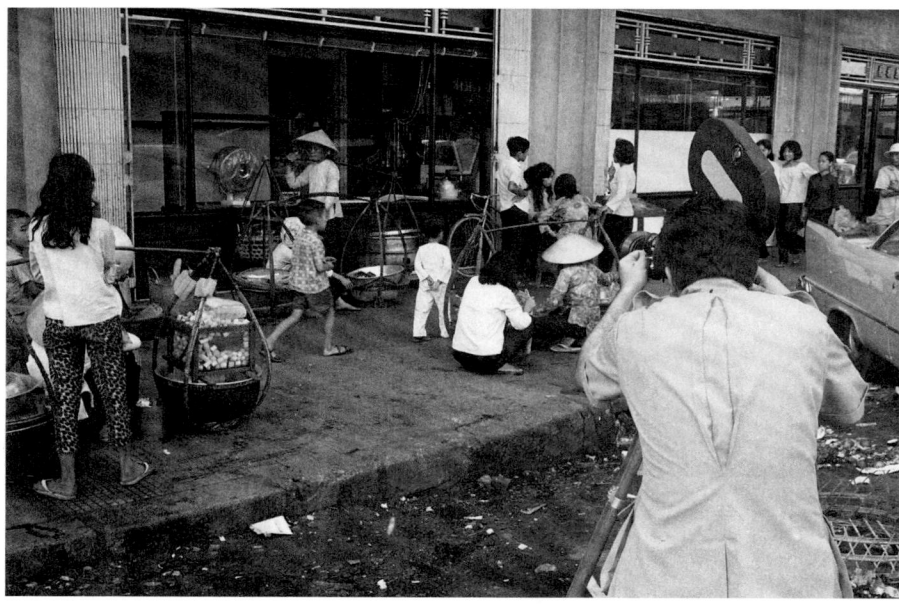

Shooting scenes for WWL's hour-long color documentary on Vietnam included a visit to a booby trap training camp (frames at lower right, and bottom photo facing page). *Photos and frames from Del Hall Collection/WWL.*

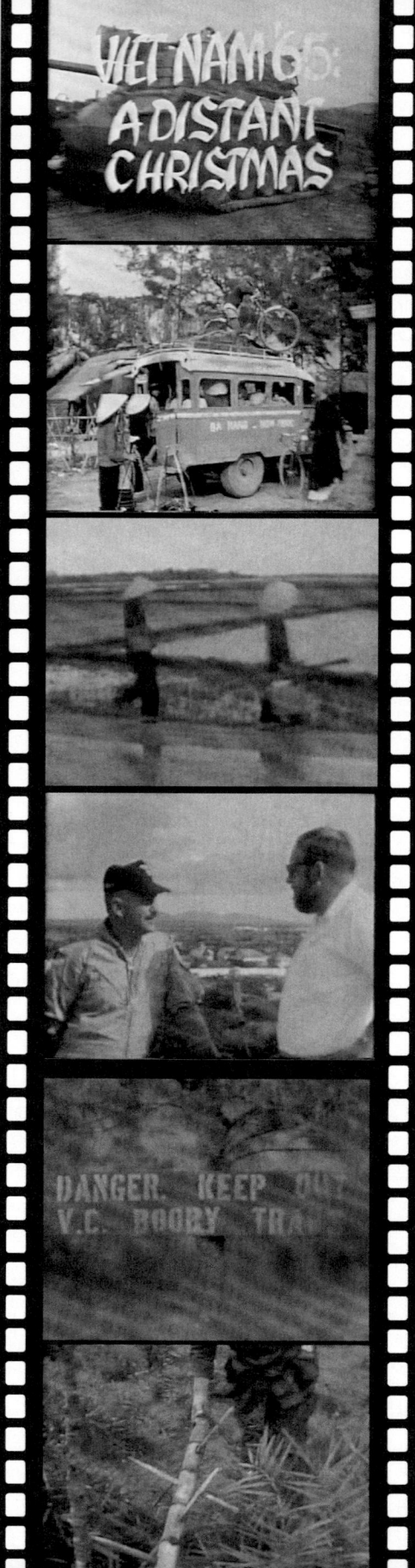

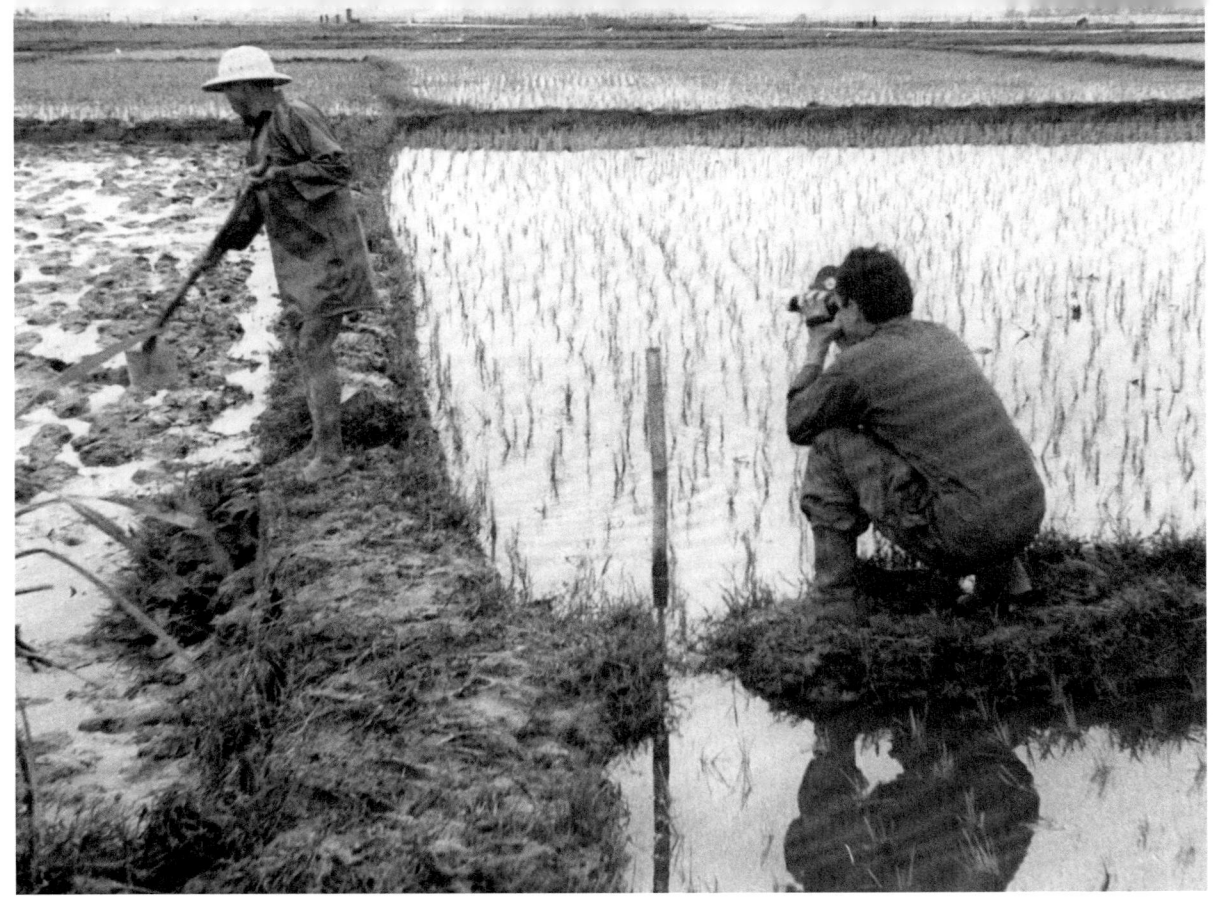

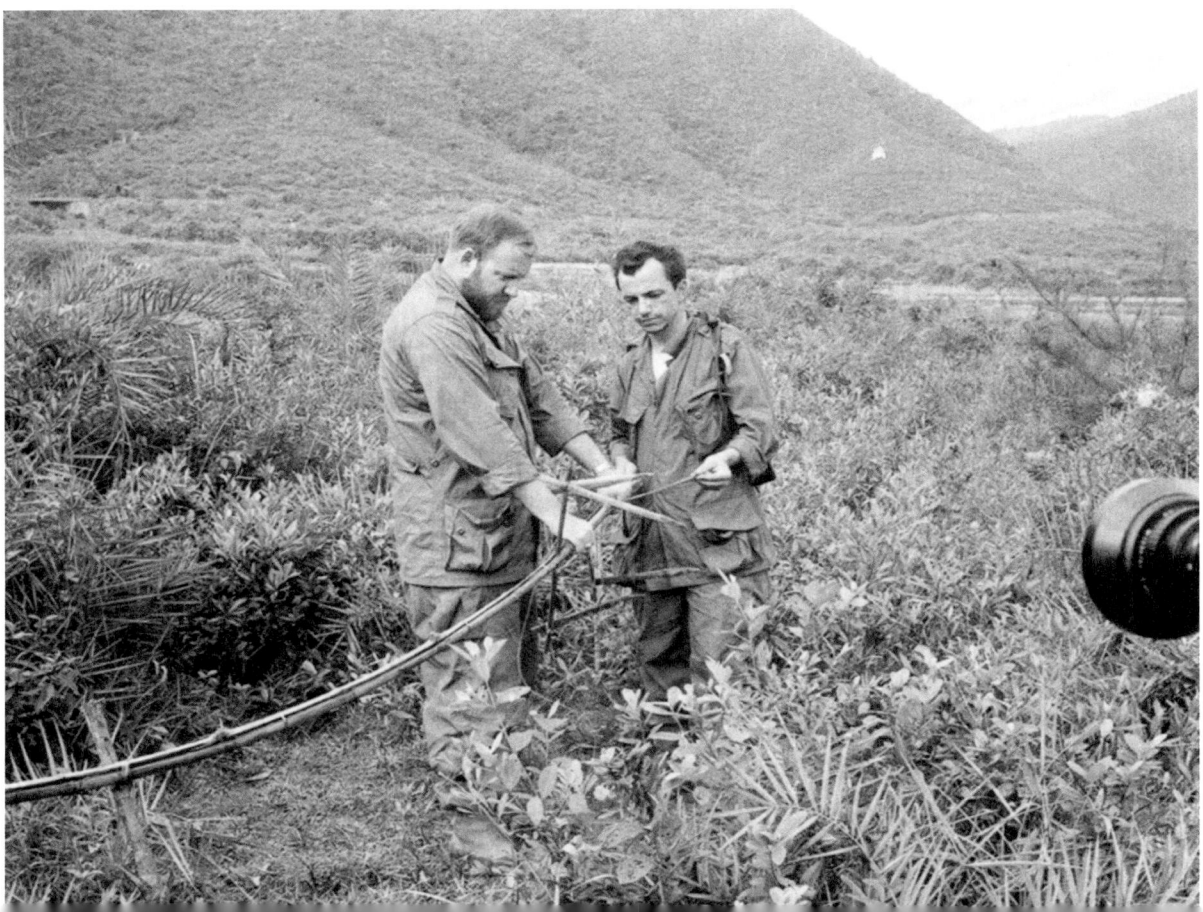

TAKE THREE

King, Cronkite, and Kuralt, 1966–1974

WUMP! THE POLICEMAN'S billy club cracked above his left brow, stunning him momentarily as he fell to his knee. Cradling his all-too-well-marked CBS News camera, Del pushed himself back to his feet, worried more about the blood blinding his eye than another blow. It was 10:30 p.m., August 26, 1968, the first night of the Democratic National Convention in Chicago, and this was something new for him. Not since 1965 did he feel personally threatened by men in uniform. Even then, the Klansman cops of Bogalusa, Louisiana, refrained from bludgeoning him, and the Viet Cong of North Vietnam meant nothing personal.

Not that violent riots and contentious politics were anything new to him. Del was fast becoming expert on both, having covered them nearly weekly since Dan Bloom made good on a promise to get him out of his new Chicago job in the CBS editing room and back on the news beat. His first Midwest Bureau field assignment was an exception, a May 1967 incident involving three country boys lost in a Missouri cave, never to be found. Sad as it was, that story seemed almost bucolic compared to what followed: a series of events that, when pieced together and viewed in hindsight, formed the biggest challenge to American social order since the Civil War. The insistently peaceful movement for civil rights that Del had covered in New Orleans, and that had turned forceful in places like Bogalusa, had lost its patience as it diffused northward and into great industrialized cities. At the same time, the nascent U.S. involvement in Vietnam that Del covered as a human interest story in 1965 had since mushroomed into a bloody and bitterly controversial war involving millions of Americans and a casualty list that would number in the hundreds of thousands. In the editing room at 630 North McClurg Court, Del and Dan were the first people on U.S. soil to view CBS's raw combat footage, and both took with the utmost seriousness the power they wielded in deciding what would air.

War meant the draft, and the draft personalized the conflict for young American men and anyone who counted them among their family and friends. Youth grew alienated from elders and from authority in ways never seen before, adding to the social fissures of race and class and the animus between conservatives and liberals. The nation seemed to be coming apart, and nowhere did the seams tear deeper than in the urban ghettos. Del was busy covering riots in Cincinnati, Dayton, and elsewhere in June 1967, after which Bloom dispatched him to Detroit for what would become the deadliest civic action since the New York City Draft Riots of 1863. Detroit was particularly dangerous because gunmen were not only in the streets but sniping from buildings, adding an element of terror to daily life. The response was nearly as ominous: Army tanks and troop carriers fired live tracer bullets in the direction of the sniper shots, something Del actually witnessed one night while crouched nearby in a doorway—genuine military combat in an American city, among American citizens. Unlike what he would later experience in Chicago, however, the Detroit police did not view the press as antagonistic, and looked out for Del's personal safety. At one point, some cops shot out the streetlights overhead to hide his position from prowling rioters. Yet he always felt better protected by his camera and usually declined physical protection when offered. "I felt like I *belonged* there," he explains. "I wouldn't even wear a helmet," because it might undo the more effective shield that was the camera. "We had covered many riots and fires by this time, but [Detroit] was the largest and most violent in my career."

Northern turmoil brought figures of the southern civil rights movement to places like Ada, Ohio, where on January 11, 1968, Del filmed Martin Luther King Jr. addressing an audience at Ohio Northern University. He'd covered King a number of times earlier, but usually at press conferences, where formality prevails. The Ada event, on the other hand, had the pressing energy of a mounting social movement. Arriving tardy due to car troubles, the reverend began with a joking apology about preferring to be "Martin Luther King late" than "the late Martin Luther King." He ended the speech with a rousing "Free at last, free at last, thank God almighty we're free at last."[1] Both elements of the speech, which turned out to be one of King's last visits to academia, would resonate three months later. Del made a point of introducing himself to King and shaking his hand, as he did with all of his subjects, big and small.

By spring 1968 the campaign for the presidency was in full swing, and Del crisscrossed the Midwest covering the candidates. He was on the campaign trail with Richard M. Nixon and Robert F. Kennedy, and filmed President Lyndon B. Johnson in Chicago one day after he stunned the nation by withdrawing from the race—after which Del also followed LBJ's vice-president and heir apparent, Hubert Humphrey. With the Democratic nomination now wide open, Robert Kennedy rose in stature, capturing Del's attention as he did so many others. Young people adulated him "like a

rock star," Del marvels. "This guy is *going* places, I thought. I was always able to predict a politician's fate by the crowds and the atmosphere."

Sensing Kennedy was now the Democrat to watch, Del covered him closely as he stumped at Notre Dame and Ball State. As the campaign boarded a plane to address a rally in Indianapolis, a startling rumor began to circulate. Shots apparently had been fired at Martin Luther King in Memphis, people said, and reports had him as struck. Upon landing in Indianapolis, Del tracked Kennedy closely as he received an update from supporters on the ground. King had, in fact, died, and in addition to coping with the tragic news, the campaign now braced for possible rioting and grappled with how to handle the rest of the evening. Despite discouragement from advisers and police, Kennedy decided to proceed with the downtown rally. From the back of a flatbed truck, in darkness and with Del's camera rolling, Kennedy announced to the mostly black crowd what he had just learned, to their horrified gasps and wails. He then delivered an eloquent unscripted plea for reconciliation in which, for the first time, he spoke of his own family member's murder "by a white man." It would become his most famous speech.

The candidate was then whisked to a series of televised commitments, leaving his campaign staffers and press corps to regroup. Del used what remained of the traumatic evening to have a quick dinner with Ginger, who happened to be in Indianapolis. The couple ended up having hamburgers with Kennedy's press secretary, famed newsman Pierre Salinger, and CBS News correspondent Ike Pappas, the radio journalist who had asked the last question to Lee Harvey Oswald and reported live his shooting by Jack Ruby. There was much to talk about.

Early next morning, Del set off for Washington with the candidate and campaign staff. As their plane circled for landing, he saw plumes of smoke rising from the gritty neighborhoods surrounding the federal capital—thick, obscuring hundreds of blocks in some areas, and black, meaning the blazes were uncontrolled and still consuming fuel. He remembers thinking, "the nation will never again be the same."

Del was back in Indiana later the next month, this time to

shoot what passed for a relaxing assignment in these times, the Indianapolis 500. Five days later, the country convulsed once again with news that Robert F. Kennedy had been shot in California. He died twenty-six hours later, at a time when he was supposed to have been in Chicago campaigning for the Illinois primary. Del, ever prescient, expected a great political future for Kennedy, but he didn't foresee this. With the nation reeling and the presidential campaign again in a tailspin, Del set out to cover Kennedy's unforgettable funeral train from New York to Washington, a nineteenth-century tradition that would be one of the last of its kind.

There was no time for reflection. Del, oftentimes paired with Mike Wallace and Dan Rather, was right back on a plane to the scene of more riots in Detroit, then on the trail of Vice-President Hubert Humphrey and rivals Eugene McCarthy, Richard Nixon, and George Wallace. By late August, all eyes fell on Chicago, where the Democratic Party was convening to nominate their candidate for the November election.

Dissidents had their eyes on Chicago as well, and for months they brainstormed how to use the convention to confront the body politic and the cultural assumptions behind it. Starting on August 19, leaders such as Abbie Hoffman and Allen Ginsberg organized their Yippie and hippie followers, trained "marshals" among them, and publicized their agenda using Lincoln Park as a staging ground. Youthful exuberance led to bravado and overstatement, which, to authorities' ears, came across as implicit or explicit threats to civic order and public safety. With riots dominating national news for three years on, including at the Republican Convention three weeks earlier, Mayor Richard Daley pointedly intended to maintain law and order as his city stepped on the national stage. To others, he was itching for a fight, and so were many officers, particularly those who resented what they saw as rich young ingrates mocking all that was sacred to the aspirational and patriotic working class. Joining the 15,000 police and Illinois National Guardsmen were Army soldiers, many of them returned or destined for combat in Vietnam, in the largest military deployment on American soil in recent memory. They were well outnumbered by demonstrators, who arrived early from all corners of the country. During the weekend prior to the convention, they would depart their Lincoln Park basecamp and march for two miles, despite that they had been denied permits, to the major Loop hotels where party officials lodged.

Realizing that overnighting in Lincoln Park gave the protestors day-to-day continuity, authorities discussed using the park's little-known 11 p.m. curfew to their advantage. On Sunday night, August 25, they decided to enforce it—swiftly and decisively. "We were living on the twenty-sixth floor of an apartment on Armitage and Clark," explains Ginger, "and I remember looking out the window to see the cops like a Nazi band marching through the park, behind the Lincoln statue," chasing and clubbing dissidents in every direction.[2] Embittered, the protestors made it through the night in ad-hoc arrangements, and regrouped the next morning to march again that afternoon. By Monday evening, they made their way down Division Street, halfway between Lincoln Park and the Loop, with Del filming them every step of the way. "When we got to the corner of Wells and Division," he says, "around the corner the cops came running, for no reason, unless they wanted to break up this parade that did not have a permit." At first there were ten or twelve policemen, though Del remembers up to fifty eventually entering the melee. "As the first cop reached me, he swung his billy club and hit me in the face, right above my eye [and] I went down to one knee." After he caught his breath, Del rose defiantly. "I actually chased the cop that did it, and filmed him, face to face: *You did this.*" Either the stream of blood or the rolling camera restrained the officer from striking again.

Del turned out to be the very first member of the 6,300-strong press corps to be beaten at the '68 convention, but not for long. Moments later, five peers came under similar attacks, including personnel from *Newsweek,* the *Chicago Sun-Times,* and NBC. Del's colleague John Laurence saw the action unfold. He yelled, "We're taking casualties!"—lingo he picked up from his recent tour in Vietnam—and filmed Del's bloodied face, even as Del himself continued filming. Laurence set out to inform the producers in the convention hall of the development. The beating of a journalist, the first such incident, qualified as a news story, and that they were all members of the CBS family probably added to Laurence's determination. He was delayed in his effort because a communications workers' strike had tied up telephone circuits all week, but he eventually succeeded in reaching Walter Cronkite. "Del Hall's wounds were treated at a hospital," Cronkite reported on live national television; "a few stitches were taken, and he's in good condition, we're glad to report." The beating, followed by the famous roughing-up of Dan Rather and Mike Wallace inside the convention hall on subsequent nights, led a peeved Cronkite to comment on air, "About the worst thing you can say to these people here is that you're from the press, apparently. They don't recognize that as any sort of a pass!" Police would end up beating at least twenty-two members of the press, including thirteen who filed official reports of their injuries.[3] Del bears a visible scar of his wound to this day.

Tuesday evening, Del, bandaged, met up with the CBS team in the Conrad Hilton Hotel, where party brass were headquartered and where dissidents by the thousands had converged in adjacent Grant Park. From above in the hotel and later down on Michigan Avenue, he filmed the chanting crowd on one side and edgy authorities on the other. Unexpectedly, a third and rather incongruous element arrived on the scene. It was the Poor People's Campaign, a civil rights and social justice crusade that had been rolling across the nation in mule-drawn covered wagons since King's assassination. The mostly black men, women, and children in the rickety carts now found themselves positioned between hostile authorities and sneering hippies, mostly white, who wanted nothing more than to get at each other's throats. Their mules nervously braying, the Poor People's Campaign "seemed to have no idea of what they were getting themselves into," remarked the authors of a later inquest, as "they were immediately surrounded by this huge crowd, totally engulfing Michigan Avenue [and] much of the park."[4] As Del witnessed it, the police opened a section of barricades to allow the mule train to pass, and on seeing the opportunity, the protestors lunged through the opening and poured forward en masse toward the hotel. What ensued would become the iconic street battle of Chicago '68. Thousands of

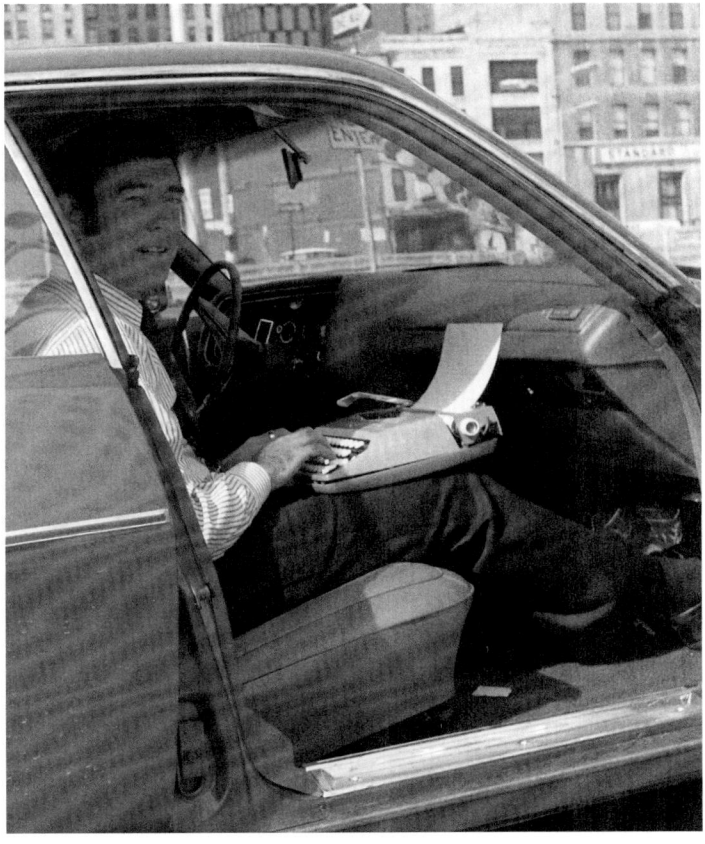

Dan Rather. *Photo by Del Hall/CBS News.*

taunting, debris-throwing dissenters fought hand-to-hand with club-wielding helmeted police throughout Michigan and Balbo avenues and Grant Park, as thousands more chanted, *"The whole world is watching! The whole world is watching!"* National television media interwove live images of the mayhem with candidates' lofty speeches, oftentimes with stinging if unintended irony. The spectacle would help tilt at least one and possibly two presidential elections, and endure for decades in the national psyche.[5]

Del's vantage point got him unparalleled footage of one of the most combative weeks in modern American history. It earned him an Emmy Award nomination for Outstanding Achievement by Individuals in Coverage of Special Events, from the National Academy of Television Arts and Sciences for 1968–1969. It also got him a subpoena to testify in *United States of America versus David T. Dellinger et al.,* better known as the Chicago Seven conspiracy trial. Both sides wanted to hear what Del saw and heard, specifically his interviews with Rennie Davis and Tom Hayden as well as his footage of the "flagpole incident," in which a Grant Park protestor lowered an American flag and waved what appeared to be a Viet Cong banner, triggering a forceful police reaction. As Del was called forth in the September 1969 trial, a snickering Abbie Hoffman draped his arm around Del's shoulder—the least of his antics in the circus-like courtroom—and escorted him to the stand. Del's testimony ostensibly did no favors for the defense until cross-examination by self-described radical lawyer William Kunstler got Del to testify, despite repeated objections, that he himself, a cameraman, had been beaten by the police—further evidence, Kunstler argued, that this had indeed been a police riot and not a conspiracy. After adjournment, Del brought his subpoena to the defendants' table and asked all seven to sign it, which they cheerfully obliged. All were eventually found not guilty of conspiracy, and some were convicted of lesser charges later reversed on appeal. Perhaps the harshest judgment came from Judge Julius Hoffman, who slapped all seven defenders plus both their lawyers with a slew of contempt citations.[6]

The year 1969 proved to be nearly as turbulent as the prior one. Making headlines were the new Republican president Richard M. Nixon (his election aided by a national backlash against the Democrats and their disastrous '68 convention), the continuing struggle in Vietnam, the thrill of the Apollo moon landing, Woodstock less than a month later, and, a day after the concert and fifteen hundred miles south, Hurricane Camille, which threatened New Orleans and flattened the Mississippi Gulf Coast. Del and his colleagues covered none of those stories because an unpopular new bureau policy tasked freelancers with covering national-level news, keeping CBS staffers on short leash for the network's regional needs in the Midwest. Del resented the rule; he wanted to go wherever the biggest stories were. But the policy did tip him off to the potential benefits of freelancing, while also allowing him to engage with CBS's two new

programming jewels: Charles Kuralt's *On the Road,* which gained popularity after first airing on Cronkite's *CBS Evening News* in 1967; and Don Hewitt's news magazine *60 Minutes,* which debuted a month after Chicago and would come to transform television journalism.

Del's first collaboration with Kuralt took him back home to New Orleans for a story on fruit peddlers, a topic redolent of his childhood in the Projects. He brought to this and other *On the Road* stories filming techniques he had honed in *Shades of New Orleans* a decade earlier, which themselves were influenced by the flicks he had watched in the old downtown movie houses.[7] His intimate cinematography, plus that of the series's original cameraman, the equally talented Jimmy Wilson, synthesized perfectly with Kuralt's unaffected enthusiasm and painstaking writing to make *On the Road* an American television classic. The genre has since been endlessly mimicked but never quite equaled.

The trip to New Orleans allowed Del to reconnect with friends and family. By this time his marriage to Greta had ended, in a forthright if not perfectly amicable divorce, and arrangements were made for his fair financial support of the children. Neither he nor Ginger today rationalize the impact of their relationship on the family in Louisiana, although they do speak of a sense of inevitability, given the couple's drifting apart well before Ginger came into the picture. Other aspects of Del's old New Orleans world had also changed. Ella, his mother, a widow since 1963, still worked at Sears, but all grandparents were now deceased, Minnie having died in 1968, ten years after Na-Ma. The old third-floor walk-up on South Rampart now had a parking lot for a neighbor and was itself eyed for demolition, part of a trend that would eventually level three-quarters of the storied old street. Interstates, meanwhile, sliced through swaths of downtown; a gigantic domed stadium was planned for the old back-of-town; the oaks along Claiborne had been felled for an overpass; and a section of old Tremé had been cleared for, of all things, a cultural center. Hippies overran the French Quarter and turned Bourbon Street into a nightly carnival, and a massive flight by middle-class families to the suburbs had left the inner city increasingly poor and black, particularly Del's own childhood home in the Iberville Projects. He renewed old friendships at the WWL studio on North Rampart, and when he excused himself to use the men's room, he noticed another change: the separate bathrooms for "White" and "Colored" were now simply two separate and redundant men's rooms. He pondered which one his former colleagues, white or black, now used. Knowing the folks at WWL, who for better or worse never seemed particularly bent on making statements or taking stands, Del sensed that most probably would have continued the customs they grew up with.

In the new decade, Del—now married to Ginger, who shared his passionate devotion to work over domesticity—became the quintessential peripatetic modern media man. He also, in 1972, made the jump from CBS staffer to ranks of freelancer. The proximate cause was to get away from his sound man, an obsessive-compulsive former bomber pilot who was perfectly skilled and reliable—but was so incorrigibly prejudiced that just about everyone called him Eddie the Bigot.[8] The ultimate cause for quitting CBS was the somewhat better deal that freelancers got. While he continued doing the work he loved for the same bosses, he maintained essentially the same pay and benefits but profited additionally by renting his equipment to CBS, an opportunity for which he invested personally in a rugged lightweight cable-free CP-16 No. 19 camera, the top of the line. Freelancer status also got Del dispatched on national and international as well as regional stories. His assignment sheets from this era attest to a frenetic lifestyle of breaking news and charter jet travel:

To Columbus, Ohio, with Dan Rather to cover a Senate race, followed by a *60 Minutes* story with Mike Wallace.

To South Bend, Indiana, with Adam Clayton Powell, followed by what his itinerary describes as "various peace marches and riot watches."

To cover Israeli foreign minister Abba Eban's visit to the United States—then to Nebraska for a story on Boys Town with Commander Lloyd Bucher, former orphan and captain of the USS *Pueblo* when it was captured by North Koreans in 1968.

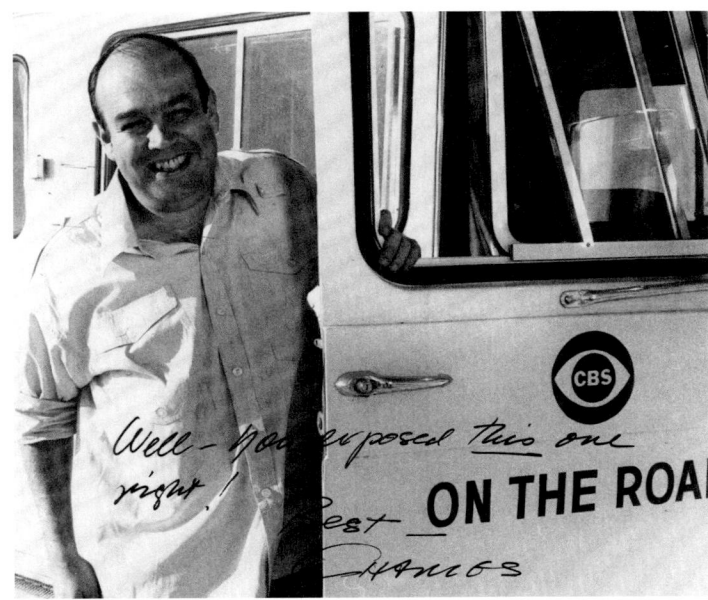

Filming *On the Road* with Charles Kuralt. *Photo by Del Hall/CBS News.*

To Podunk (it really exists, in Missouri) with Charles Kuralt, followed by other *On the Road* segments on tombstones, "Southern Skiing," "The Uranium King," "Mail Pouch," "Skipjacks," Pete Seeger's Hudson River sloop to raise pollution awareness (complete with a banjo solo), Truman's presidential library, the Ash Wednesday ritual of estimating Mardi Gras crowds in New Orleans by weighing garbage, and a once-in-a-lifetime journey down the Mississippi River from St. Louis to the Gulf of Mexico for a story on barges.

To Mexico and Argentina to explain to taxpayers "Why U.S. Aid?" and later to Maryland to cover the trial of H. Rap Brown.

To race riots in North Omaha, started when a white policeman shot a black man in a public housing project—and later to Charlotte, where the busing of black children was met with resistance by white parents.

Back home to Chicago to film the making of Peter Hyams's movie *T. R. Baskin,* featuring two up-and-coming actors named James Caan and Candice Bergen.

To Memphis for an award-winning documentary, *Health*

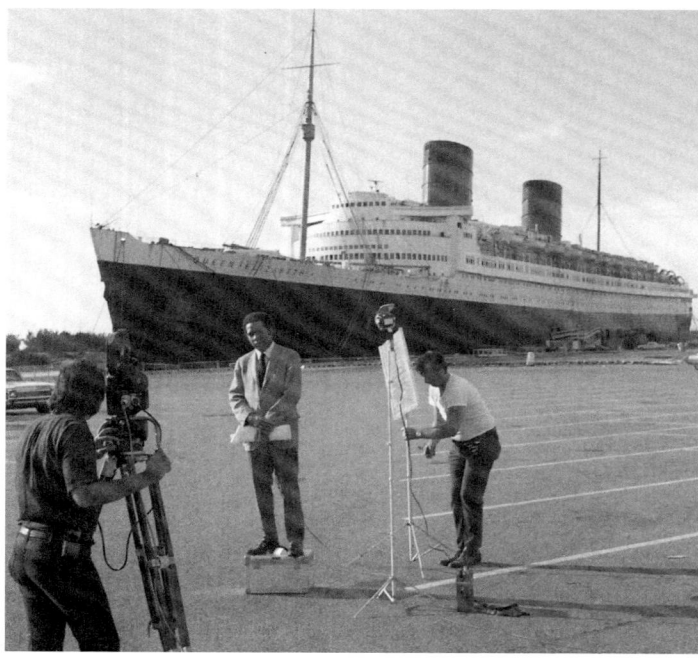

Del films the auction of the *Queen Elizabeth* in Florida. *Photo courtesy CBS.*

in America, then to Kent State in Ohio to cover the riots following National Guard shooting of war protestors.

To Georgia to film Karl Wallenda of the Great Wallendas crossing the Tallulah Gorge, which the legendary high-wire artist later described as "the most dangerous thing I've ever done."

To Mount Rushmore with Ike Pappas, where Del filmed the Indian occupation of what the natives called Crazy Horse Mountain, by hiking up to the summit multiple times and flying around in a helicopter.

To Fort Lauderdale to cover the auction of the World War II troop ship–turned–ocean liner *Queen Elizabeth,* and back to New Orleans for a story on long-serving congressman and Jesuit alum Felix Edward Hébert.

To Tampa to cover President Nixon—then to Greenville, South Carolina, for a fox hunt.

To Illinois to cover a riot—then to Tuscaloosa, Alabama, for a story on gospel singers.

Back home to Chicago for a story on a children's toy designer—and radical underground radio.

To Atlanta for a "Hippie Christmas," to St. Louis to cover scandals in the Federal Housing Administration, then to Houston to film Alan Shepard preparing for the Apollo 14 trip to the moon—all within the last week of 1970.

To the violent and racially charged Attica inmate riot, where he covered the killing of the hostages and the guards' counterattack—then to Black Expo '71 in Chicago, billed as the "largest gathering of black businessmen in history," where a rising star named Jesse Jackson signed his press badge and stole the show.

Jailings. Jailbreaks. The U.S. Open. The Kentucky Derby. The Indianapolis 500. The motorcycle races at Sturgis in the Black Hills of South Dakota. Veterans protesting in Madison, Wisconsin, miners striking in West Virginia, and steelworkers laid off in Youngstown, Ohio.

Del's new status as freelancer put him on the shortlist for major international news. He just missed being dispatched with President Nixon to China in February 1972, but he got a fine consolation prize: to Moscow with the chief executive in May. He and the crew arrived early to do feature stories and, with his own cable-free shoulder-mounted CP-16 camera, proceeded to shoot over 21,000 feet of film on various themes. With an escort he did an *On the Road*–style shoot of the interiors of the Kremlin, the famed ballet at the Bolshoi Theatre, and a full-scale documentary on religion in the Soviet Union, which gave him rare Western access to prayer services in a Muslim mosque, an Orthodox Jewish synagogue, a Baptist church, and an old Russian monastery and convent. At one point he managed to break free and film on his own in Red Square, a foray that *Cinema Perspectives Magazine* described as "probably the first American news camera (and cameraman!) allowed on the square without supervision."[9] Among the oddities he shot was what he described as the "Soviet Universal Drink Machine," a coin-operated dispenser that poured a beverage into a common glass, which the purchaser sipped from and then passed on to the next customer after a cursory wash. Other curiosities: the ubiquity of silver teeth in Russian mouths, ambulances idling on nearly every other street, and the incredible difficulty of making a left turn.

Walter Cronkite and Dan Rather arrived at Moscow prior to the landing of Air Force One, and Del filmed both men doing interviews in the Kremlin and Red Square, in addition to First Lady Pat Nixon's excursions to meet the locals. The next day the summit convened between President Nixon and General Secretary of the Communist Party Leonid Brezhnev. It proved to be a rare thaw in the frosty relationship between the USA and USSR, yielding the signing of the Strategic Arms Limitations Treaty and Anti-Ballistic Missile Treaty at a ceremony Del filmed. Coming just three months after Nixon's triumph in China, the Moscow trip was viewed as a success by all, as was CBS, for its thorough and intimate coverage. Del was particularly content, since he was now a freelancer and completely accountable for everything he did. His lightweight CP-16 served him exceedingly well, allowing him to maneuver nimbly in crowded spots and to work in the Kremlin, where he alone was admitted without a crew, forcing him to carry all his equipment. Dan Rather was so pleased with Del's work he bought him a cigar, and with Walter Cronkite and the CBS team they celebrated with a night out on the town—to the Moscow Circus.

Del always liked Rather; they worked closely when both were stationed at WWL-TV in New Orleans. He came to appreciate Dan when the latter, a legendary Texas storyteller ("It's true, it's true!" was his signature rejoinder), proved also to be a great team player, at once spunky and modest. He was the rare correspondent who would collaborate with his cameraman and film editor toward the final integration of script and footage, rather than writing the script independently and throwing it over the transom into the editing room.

Cronkite was a bit too much of a guarded national institution for someone of Del's rank to get to know personally, but they admired each other professionally and Cronkite adulated Del's camerawork. "To Del Hall," he wrote in a personal inscription, "All the best, to the best."

Before leaving Moscow, Del shopped for gifts for the family and came away with two beautifully crafted Russian shotguns. He packed them in a tripod tube and sent them home on Air Force One with the president, an arrangement unlikely to happen nowadays. They remain in the family to this day, as does the Cronkite inscription and a little bust of Lenin.

Nixon's historic journeys occurred during the heated 1972 presidential campaign. That summer, protestors converged on the Republican National Convention in Miami in a manner reminiscent of, though by no means equal to, the Democrats' chaotic meeting in Chicago four years earlier. Ghosts of that fiasco haunted media outlets as well, not on account of the journalist beatings so much as for stinging accusations that an allegedly left-leaning press had staged some of the violence it aired. Del holds that seemingly suspicious scenes may well have been sets for the movie *Medium Cool,* which director Haskell Wexler shot that same week in his trademark *cinéma vérité* style—perhaps a little too *vérité,* as his *cinéma* at times actually intersected with reality, as at the infamous flagpole incident. Nonetheless, the mere rumor of staging in 1968 was taken so seriously by CBS that producers in 1972 decided to create a documentary detailing how their staff covers a major political event, with an eye toward assuring audiences of their professionalism. Producer John Scharnik tasked cameraman Jim Kartes to cover inside the convention center, while Del and Ike Pappas covered the protestors and police outside. Miami authorities, determined to prevent a repeat of 1968, displayed a more tolerant and flexible front to the demonstrators; Police Chief Rocky Pomerance even allowed them to camp in Flamingo Park, a lesson learned from the ill-fated curfew enforcement at Lincoln Park. Del notes, however, that the crowd in Miami had been infiltrated. "I personally recognized one of the campers sitting outside his tent as a Secret Service agent. We acknowledged each other with a nod, but never said a word. I'm sure he expected me to expose him." The moment represented an ethical quandary that Del and his colleagues routinely confronted. Did he have an obligation to unmask the undercover agent to viewers? Or simply to record the news he witnessed without intervening? He decided not to act on that specific situation, but the team did allude broadly to the undercover presence. They proceeded to film protestors, counter-protestors, and anti-press protestors, as well as nude marchers, an elephant, and wounded Vietnam veteran Ron Kovic, who later gained renown for the Oliver Stone movie *Born on the Fourth of July*. All remained peaceful until the final evening. When Nixon was expected to arrive for his acceptance speech, remembers Del, "everything changed. The cops cleared all the streets around the Center with tear gas. Even Ike [Pappas] and I were not allowed to stay out to continue our coverage. We were threatened and ordered off the streets" as the entourage arrived.

Anatomy of a News Story helped create a discourse about professional ethics between the producers and consumers of news, at a time when television journalism emerged from its adolescence and found itself in the middle of what would later be called a "culture war." Cameramen grappled with ethical dilemmas commensurate to the power of their imagery—which is to say, lots. One strange incident serves as a case study. Late in 1971, an alleged former U-2 pilot-turned-drug-runner-turned-informant teamed with CBS producers to re-create for their cameras how he once smuggled drugs from Mexico. The plan was to fly to Puerto Vallarta, pick up some hay in lieu of marijuana, and fly back at low altitude to evade radar. The risky operation would make for important investigative reporting, not to mention riveting television. CBS surreptitiously dispatched Del and colleagues on the stealth flight, and matters deteriorated almost immediately. Del grew annoyed when the producer refused to disclose the nature of the project, or even inform him of the camera's perspective and point of view, something a good cameraman always needs to know. He became additionally uncomfortable when he was pressed to film certain flight moments and portray them as something else, a form of staging. Dubious situations like that multiplied and exacerbated after they arrived in Mexico, where they filmed staged ambient scenes, such as a mariachi band that was paid to perform—a clear ethical violation. Del grew downright mystified when he was instructed to hide his identity, when the pilot filed phony flight plans, when a steady stream of shady characters came in and out of his hidden-camera shootings, and when it turned out they were not flying back hay but "pressed alfalfa," which looked like pot and was itself of questionable legality. Rancor developed among the crew, and Del became suspicious that this might actually be a genuine drug-smuggling operation. He departed the team and immediately documented everything he had witnessed in a thirty-two-page confidential report to CBS. On the penultimate page he posed twenty pointed questions to his superiors, among them:

Is CBS aware of all of this?

Is it my place to bring all this to CBS's attention?

Why was I never told that pressed alfalfa [was] as illegal as pressed marijuana?

Why was I never told that this film might be used as "simulation"?

Why was a known smuggler [associating] with CBS business executives?

Most important of all: Why did [the producer] refuse to believe me or [the pilot] when told that we now believed our lives were in danger?[10]

Apparently the replacement cameraman had no such qualms, and the undercover investigation continued, sketchy practices and all. *The Mexican Connection* aired later that year and won an Emmy for what CBS would later lionize as "the most dangerous work" in the career of Jay McMullen, the producer with whom Del had his fiercest disagreements.[11] In hindsight, Del came to understand why McMullen was coy about the details, and that no illegal drug running was involved. But he remains steadfast in his accusations of staging, and never, throughout his career, felt comfortable with the aggressive sort of "gotcha" journalism that relies on disguises, false identity, hidden cameras, and entrapment to "make" news. There was plenty of genuine news out there making itself, and over the next few months, he filmed it—now as a freelancer, able to choose rather than obey his assignments—in places like Russia with the world's two most powerful heads of state, in Rome with the leader of one billion Catholics, to a secret CIA base in Laos, and to China, where he interviewed and dined with the Prince Norodom Sihanouk, the deposed and future king of Cambo-

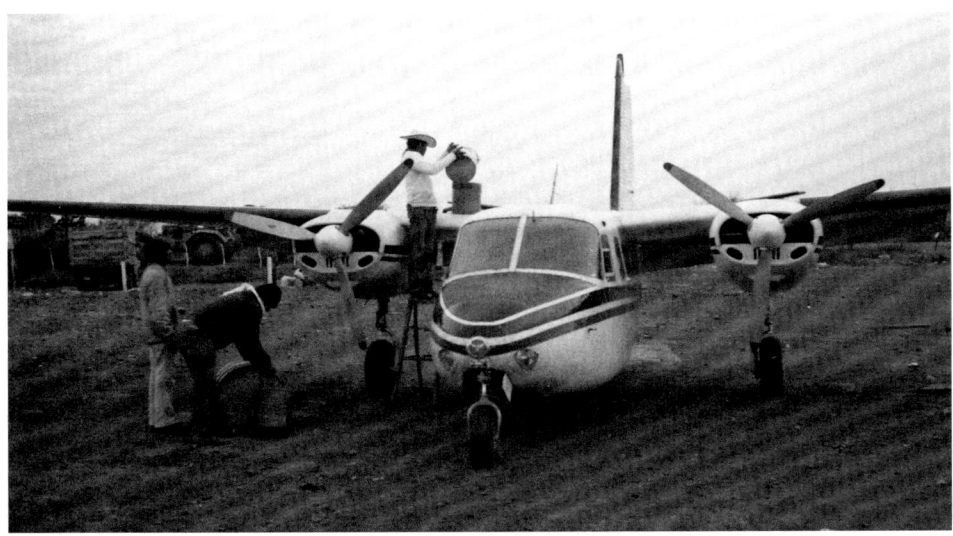

The infamous Puerto Vallarta drug-running story. *Photo by Del Hall/CBS News.*

Back to Kentucky, and to the bleak wintry plains of the Pine Ridge Indian Reservation, where Native Americans laid siege to the South Dakota town of Wounded Knee, site of the 1890 massacre and a symbol of their grievances, in a sad and violent episode that gripped the nation.

Off to stories ranging from civic unrest to sporting excitement in Detroit, Buffalo, Dayton, Bowling Green, Springfield, Washington, D.C. (to a burglarized building known as Watergate), to Rapid City to Cleveland and on and on.

dia (and avid New Orleans jazz fan). He got to film extensive segments of the Great Wall, a rare opportunity for a Westerner at the time, and witnessed poverty and backwardness throughout the hinterlands—and, incongruously, spotted a bottle of Louisiana-made Tabasco in the dining car of the train on which they traveled. He also witnessed the gentility and integrity of the Chinese people. When ABC's Barbara Walters discarded her stockings at a Peking hotel, chambermaids chased her down trying to return them to her.

Next: off to Buenos Aires for Juan Perón's impending return from exile, then to Salta in the far northern reaches of Argentina on a fruitless hunt for the infamous Auschwitz doctor Josef Mengele.

Back home to former president Harry S. Truman's hospitalization and, a month after his passing, to ex-president Lyndon B. Johnson's death in Texas, the day before the ceasefire in Vietnam.

Then off to the Philippines for the first mass release of American prisoners-of-war in Vietnam (where he exchanged invectives with Alfred Eisenstaedt when the famed photographer blocked Del's vantage point at a Manila press conference).

On the Road provided Del a welcome respite from hard news. The field work for the series reminded him that most Americans, even in these troubled times, persevered and prospered to levels that most of humanity could only envy, and still managed to keep themselves down to earth. No better a man than Charles Kuralt could explain that back to Americans, and Del and Ginger got to know the enigmatic traveloguer better than most. Kuralt, a southerner by birth and a journalist by profession, disdained the cutthroat competition and relentless deadlines of the hard-news scene, and created instead a televised version of the local-color column he once penned for a North Carolina newspaper. Kuralt's sense of a good story and ear for beautiful writing, combined with the cinematography of the masterful Jimmy Wilson, Isadore "Izzie" Bleckman, and Del, earned *On the Road* numerous accolades and made Kuralt's convivial enthusiasm a national treasure. Ginger describes the man as kindly and genuine, just as he came across on television, but also shy, peculiar, and distant—to the point that Bleckman, who worked closely with him for years, never quite knew if Kuralt personally liked him. Kuralt selected all the stories for *On the Road* himself, loved his subjects, tortured over his writing, and, like Rather, would collaborate with the cameraman (rather than dictate to him) toward making words and images work together perfectly. A chain smoker and a marvelously unhealthy epicurean, Kuralt would also not hesitate to drive the whole crew fifty miles to try out a diner and meet local folks in their familiar places. (The Halls once took him to a back-of-town dive in New Orleans to try its reputed "world's greatest hushpuppies." When they inquired as to why none were available that evening, Kuralt delighted in the cook's solemn reply: "Our hushpuppy man done gone home.") Ginger says Kuralt was "very proud of America, that he knew every state, that he was a part of this big American mix." But she also has the sense that he loved and understood America in the aggregate, as a noble concept and thrilling experiment, more so than any one American individual. An indefatigable reporter, Kuralt once surprised Ginger by confiding in her that while her husband was the best cameraman he had ever worked with, he also said Del often made him work harder than he wanted.

Del shot one of his favorite *On the Road* segments on July 20, 1969, the day America landed men on the moon. Kuralt recognized that, while the news story was hundreds of thousands of miles away, the backstory was in the cities and towns that put those men on that rocket. So he dispatched his crew from coast to coast and had them film vignettes of American life—at rodeos, coal mines, home comings, casinos—at the very moment of the great national accomplishment. Kuralt himself flew to Maine for the sunrise and Hawaii for the sunset. Del's charge was a Sara Lee cheesecake factory in Northbrook, Illinois, and on July 20, he scoped out positions and set up practice shoots, keeping his eye on the clock. Alas, all the technology seemed to be working on the moon but not in the Sara Lee factory: his lighting had thrown off a sensor and allowed dozens of fresh cheesecakes to glide down the conveyor belt with mislocated Maraschino cherries. He fixed the problem, and "the rhythm of the cher-ries, the machinery, and the movement of the attendant's face all worked together perfectly." The charming and hypnotic piece won him praise throughout CBS and became a viewer favorite as well when *A Day in the Life of the USA* aired in September 1969. Having been an eyewitness to so much history, Del missed Apollo 11 for cheesecakes with Maraschino cherries.

One of Del's favorite shoots with Kuralt was in the upstate New York village of Millers Mills, whose industry of ice harvesting from the days before refrigeration continued in a modern-day festival. The *On the Road* coverage made the obscure event nationally famous, and it continues today. His colleagues thought Del's best *On the Road* work was in Georgia, where he filmed a former hippie who emerged lost from the sixties, tried being a monk, and eventually found himself as a blacksmith and iron-working artist helping restore historic Savannah. "I used every trick in the book for this one," Del says of his camerawork; "flames reflecting off his glasses, color gels, close-up lens, the works." Charles Kuralt later testified that Del "shot the story from every conceivable angle[,] highlight[ing] it in an artistic manner . . . to evoke the feeling of an old blacksmith shop."[12] After the piece aired on Cronkite's *CBS Evening News* on March 25, 1974, his colleagues submitted *Clanking Savannah Blacksmith* to the National Academy of Television Arts and Sciences. The academy awarded Del an Emmy for Best Cinematography for News and Documentary Programming. The year was 1974, and he was now recognized as being the best of a profession he helped invent. He recalled the nuns at St. Joseph in New Orleans thirty years earlier, with their dark flowing habits and old-fashioned wimples. The habits were gone, the school and even the neighborhood had been bulldozed, and the sisters were probably dead. But their lesson lived on. "Good, better, best," they would recite. "Never let it rest. 'Til your good is better, and your better's best."

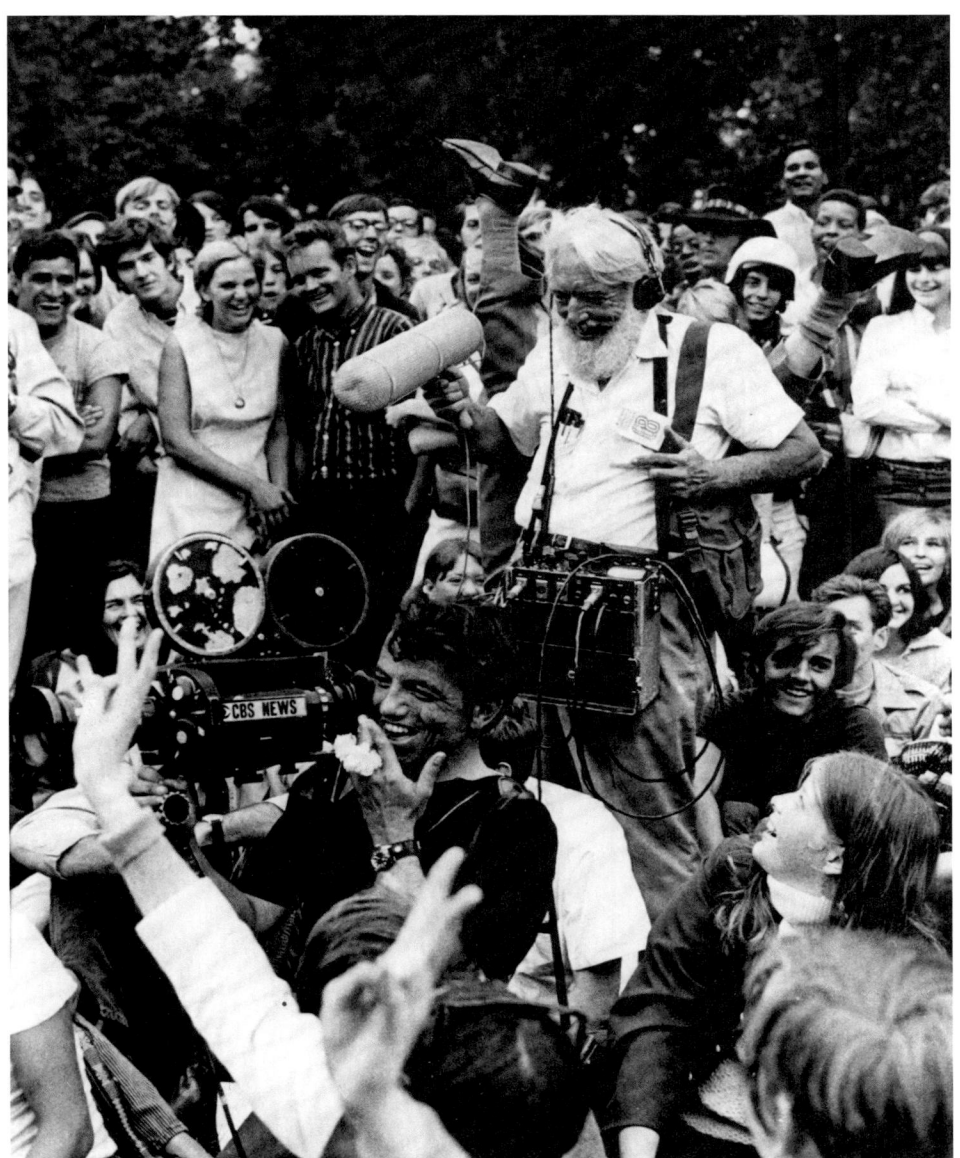

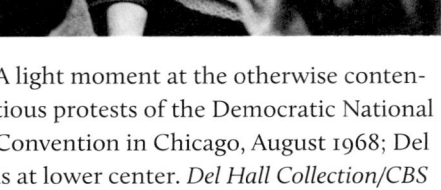

A light moment at the otherwise contentious protests of the Democratic National Convention in Chicago, August 1968; Del is at lower center. *Del Hall Collection/CBS News.*

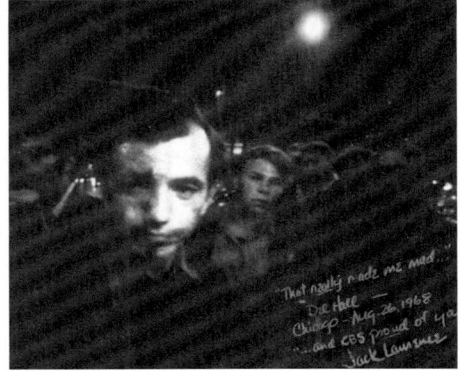

Del bleeding from a policeman's blows, which made him the first journalist beaten at the '68 convention and landed him on Walter Cronkite's national news program. *Frame shot and signed by John Laurence/CBS News.*

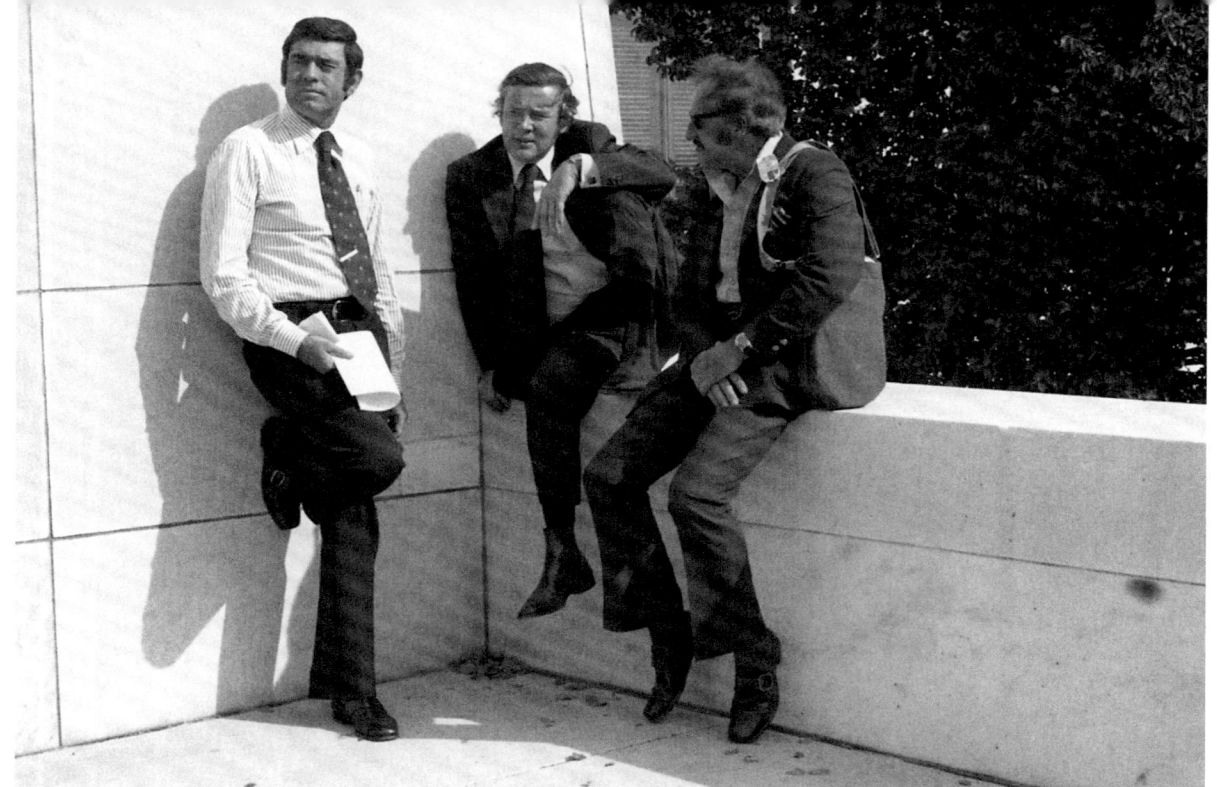

Dan Rather (left) and colleagues. *Photo by Del Hall/ CBS News.*

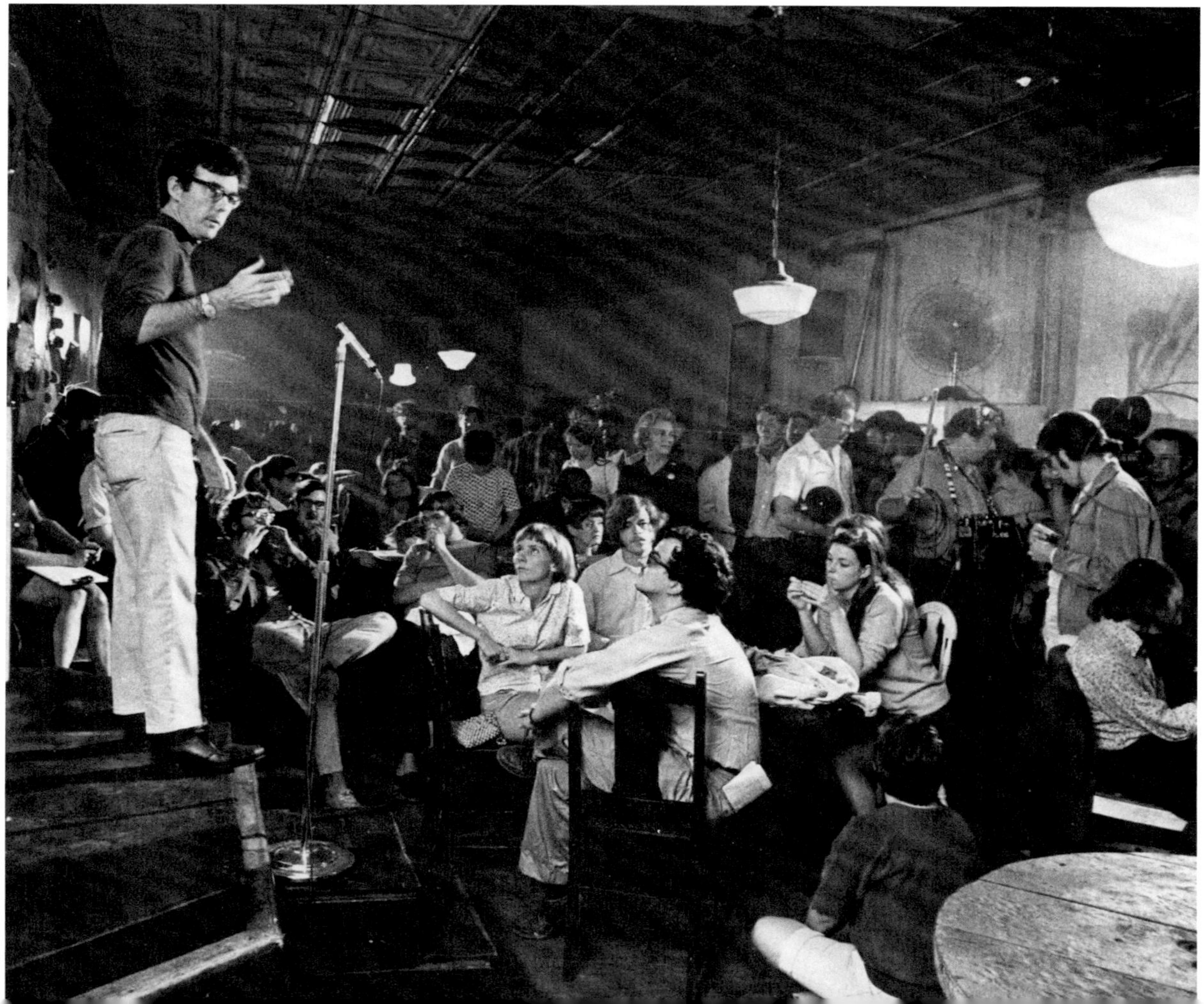

Rennie Davis rallying protestors in Chicago. *Photo by Del Hall.*

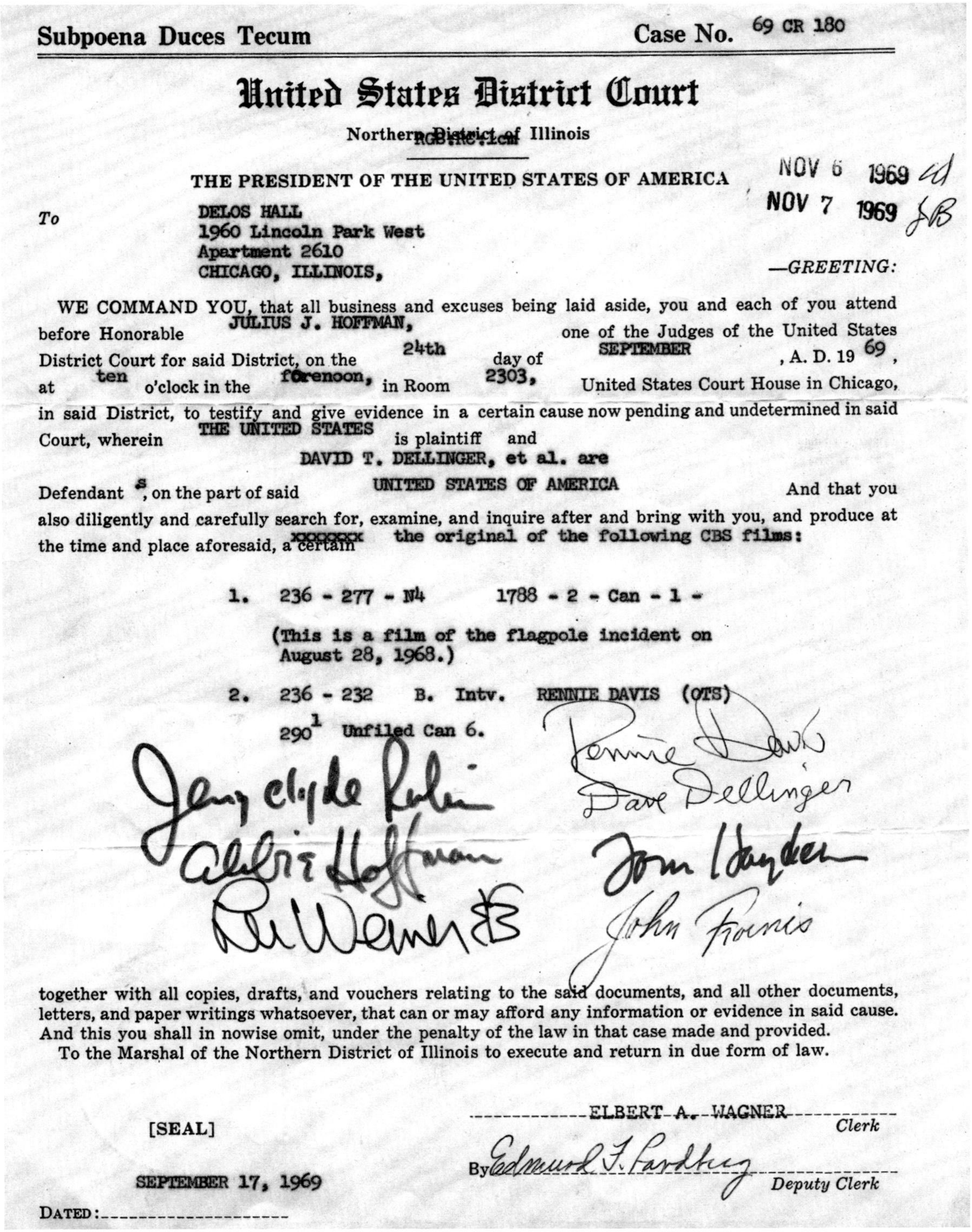

Subpoena Duces Tecum   Case No. 69 CR 180

United States District Court

Northern District of Illinois

THE PRESIDENT OF THE UNITED STATES OF AMERICA   NOV 6 1969

NOV 7 1969

To   DELOS HALL
1960 Lincoln Park West
Apartment 2610
CHICAGO, ILLINOIS,   —GREETING:

WE COMMAND YOU, that all business and excuses being laid aside, you and each of you attend before Honorable JULIUS J. HOFFMAN, one of the Judges of the United States District Court for said District, on the 24th day of SEPTEMBER, A. D. 19 69, at ten o'clock in the forenoon, in Room 2303, United States Court House in Chicago, in said District, to testify and give evidence in a certain cause now pending and undetermined in said Court, wherein THE UNITED STATES is plaintiff and DAVID T. DELLINGER, et al. are Defendant s, on the part of said UNITED STATES OF AMERICA And that you also diligently and carefully search for, examine, and inquire after and bring with you, and produce at the time and place aforesaid, a certain the original of the following CBS films:

1.   236 - 277 - N4   1788 - 2 - Can - 1 -

(This is a film of the flagpole incident on August 28, 1968.)

2.   236 - 232   B. Intv.   RENNIE DAVIS (OTS)
290^1 Unfiled Can 6.

together with all copies, drafts, and vouchers relating to the said documents, and all other documents, letters, and paper writings whatsoever, that can or may afford any information or evidence in said cause. And this you shall in nowise omit, under the penalty of the law in that case made and provided.

To the Marshal of the Northern District of Illinois to execute and return in due form of law.

[SEAL]   ------------ ELBERT A. WAGNER ------------
                                                            Clerk

SEPTEMBER 17, 1969   By Edmund F. Pardberg
                                                            Deputy Clerk

DATED: ----------------------

Del's subpoena to testify at the Chicago Seven conspiracy trial, signed by all the defendants. Photo by Del Hall.

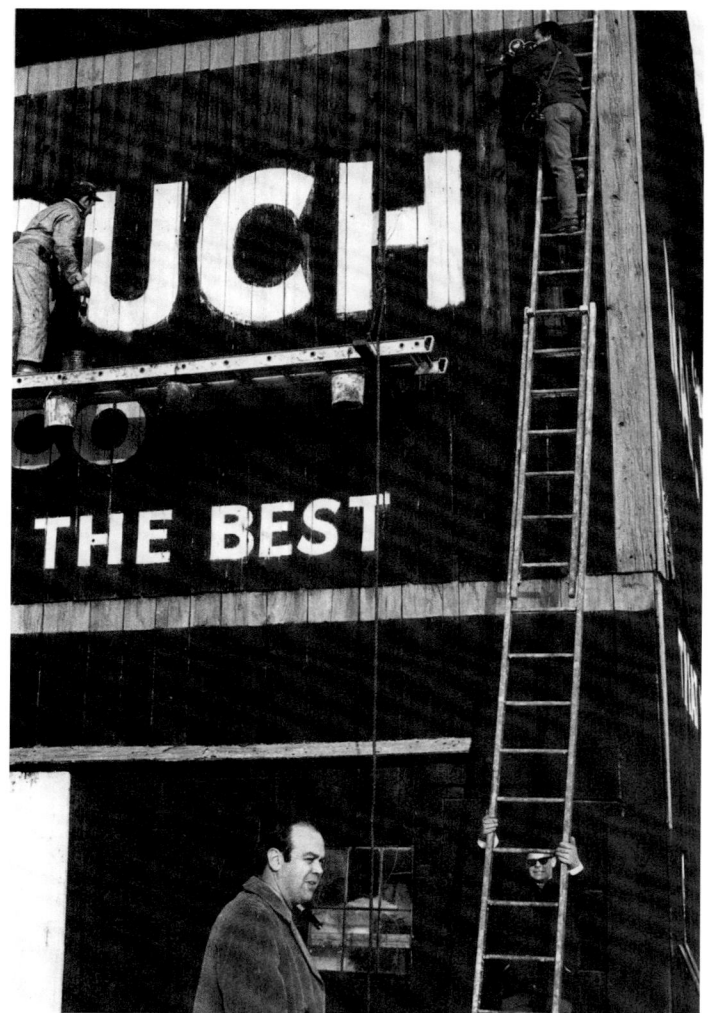
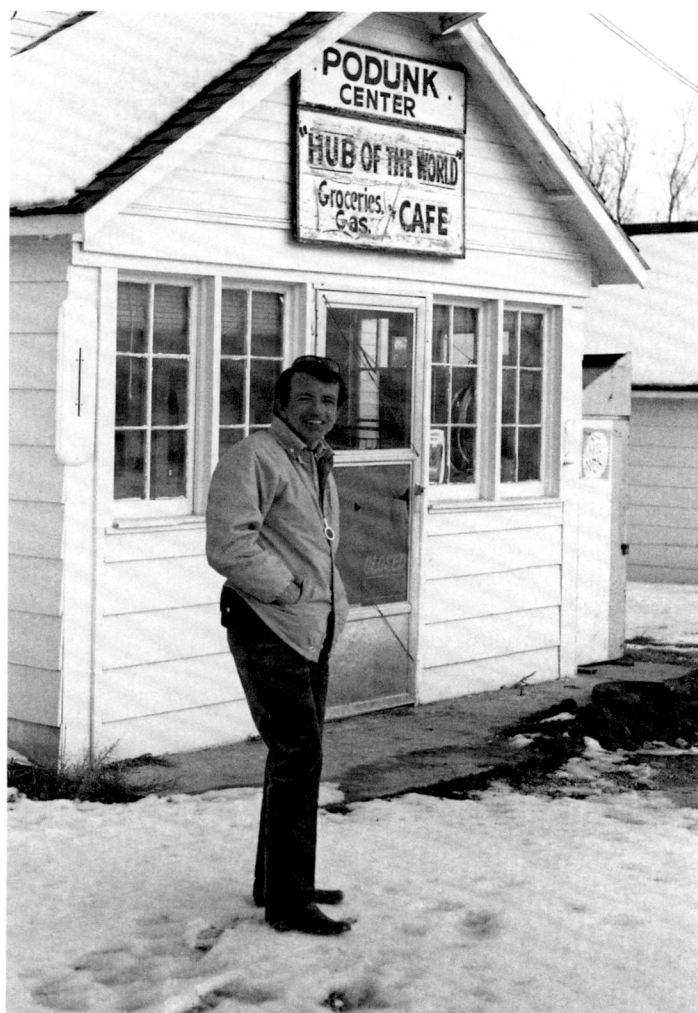

Filming *On the Road* with Charles Kuralt.
Left: Del films from top of ladder while
Kuralt walks by below. Right: Del poses in
front of the Podunk Café. *Del Hall Collection/CBS News.*

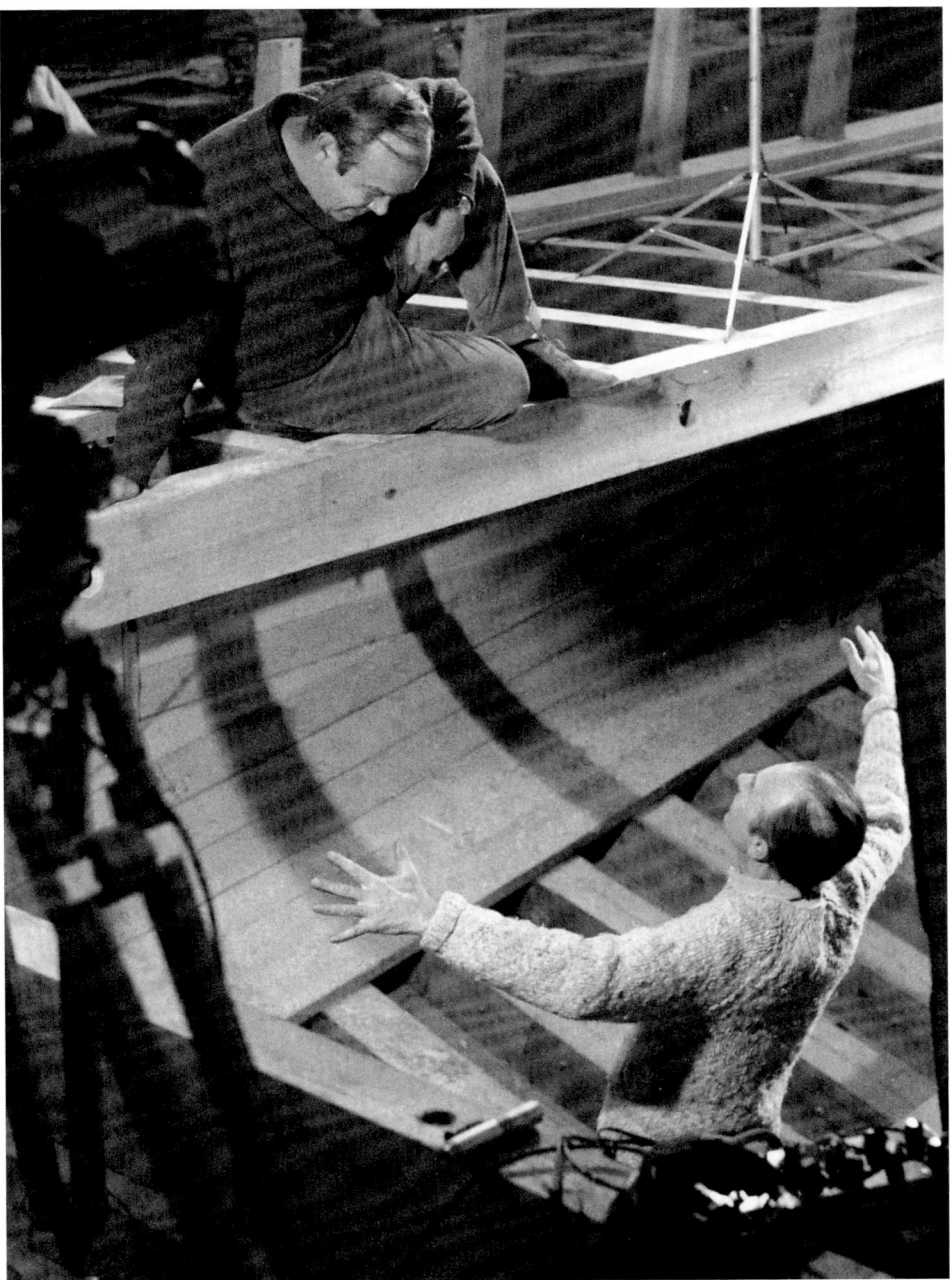

Pete Seeger shows Kuralt his Hudson River sloop. *Photo by Del Hall/CBS News.*

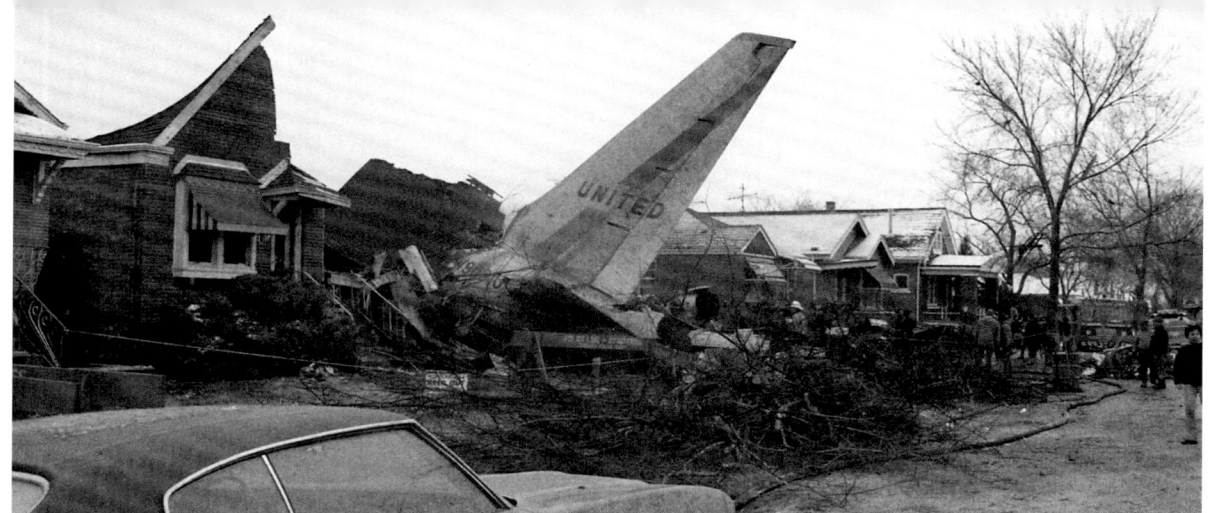

Three views of the United Flight 553 crash in Chicago in 1972. *Photos by Del Hall/CBS News.*

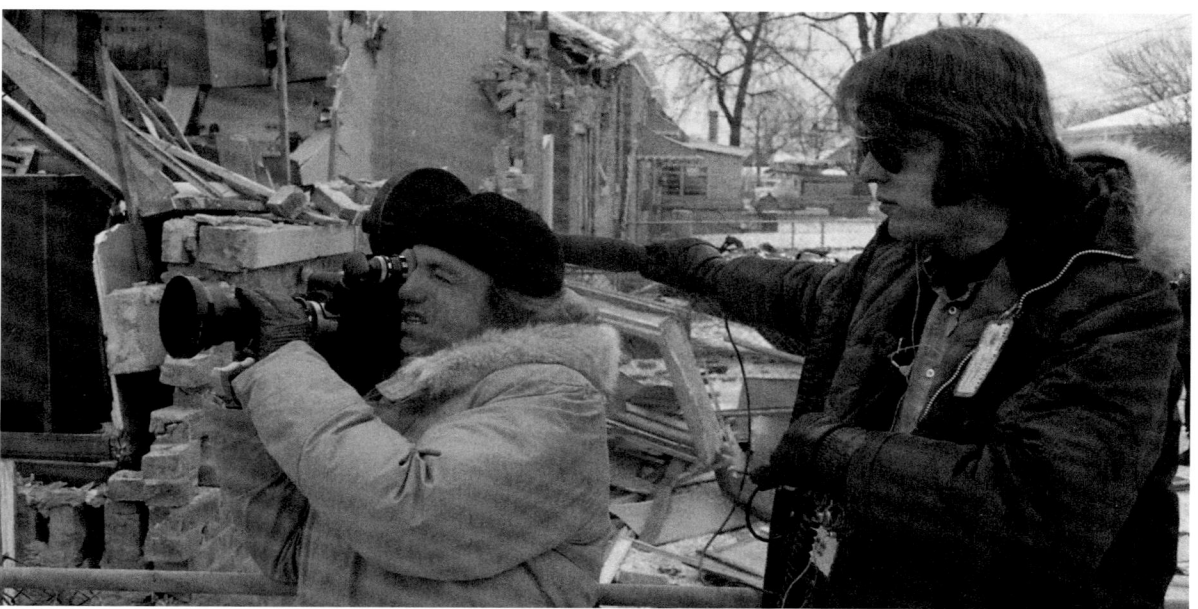

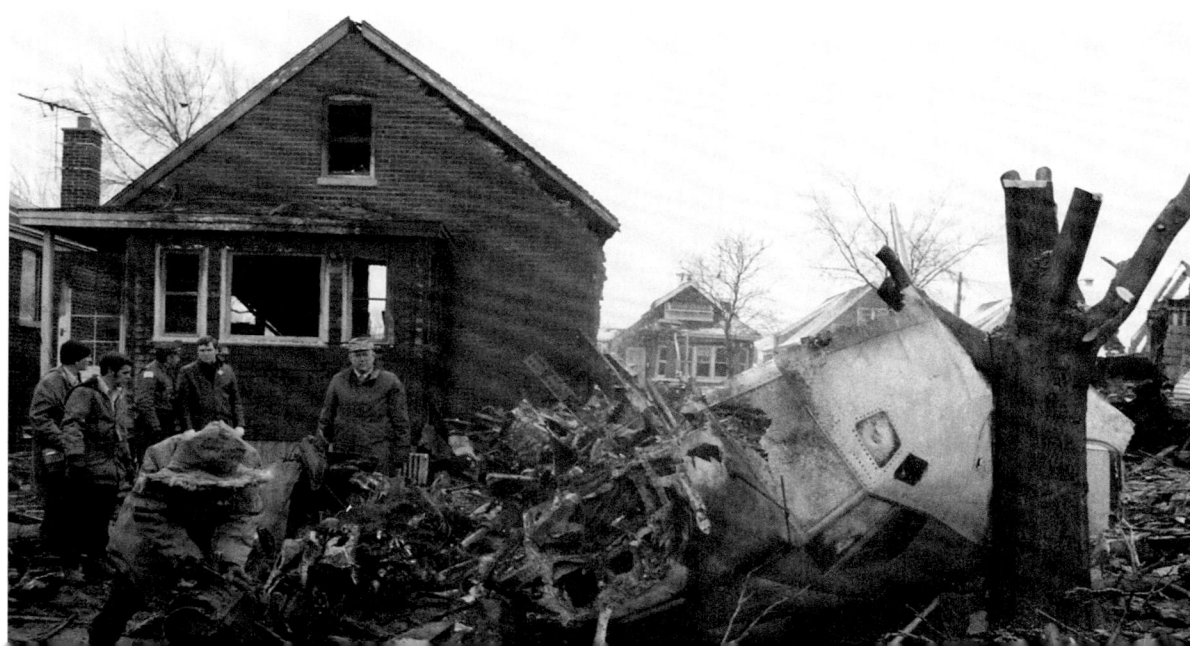

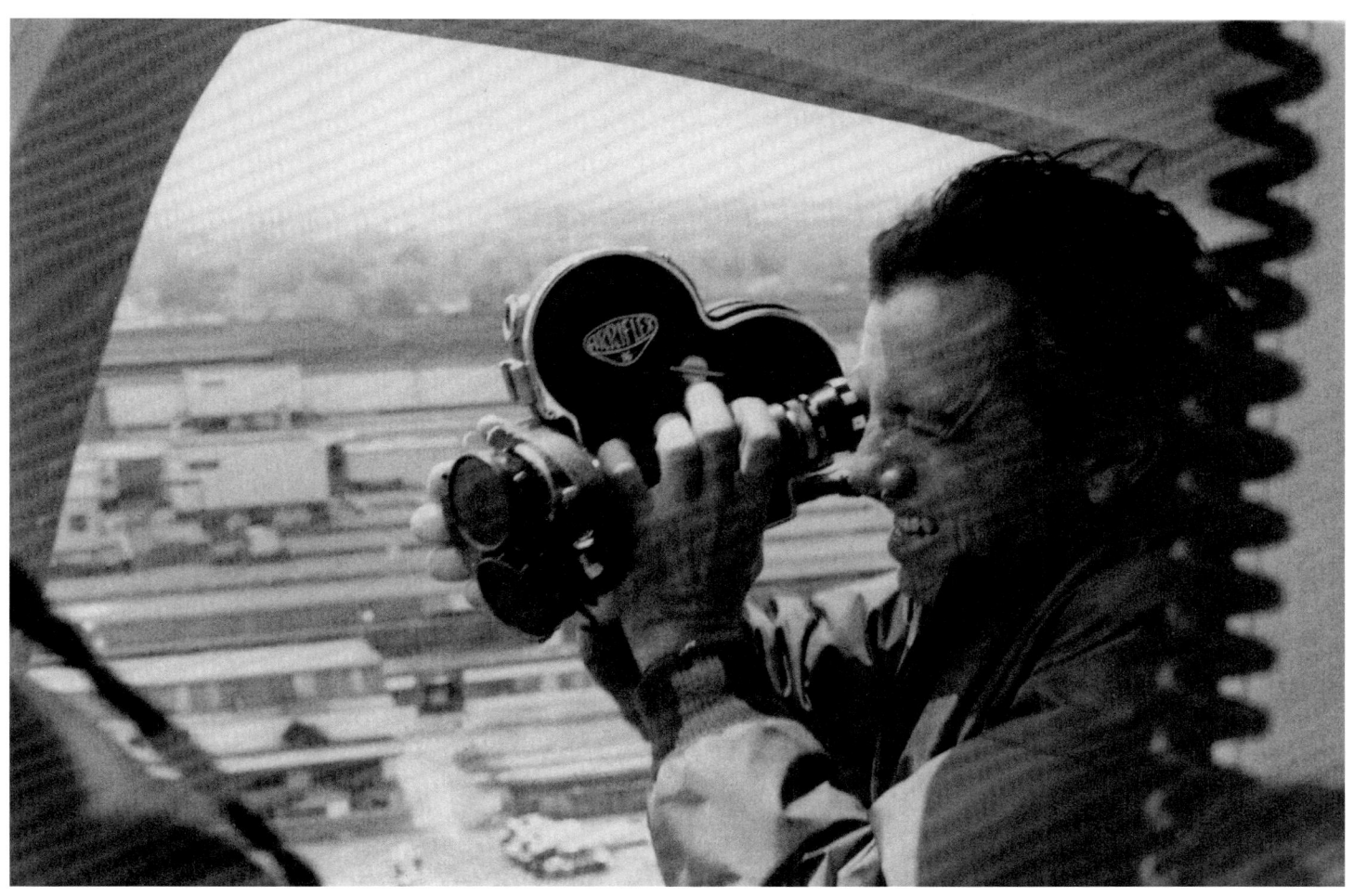

Covering the
Indianapolis 500,
a springtime
ritual. *Del Hall
Collection/CBS
News.*

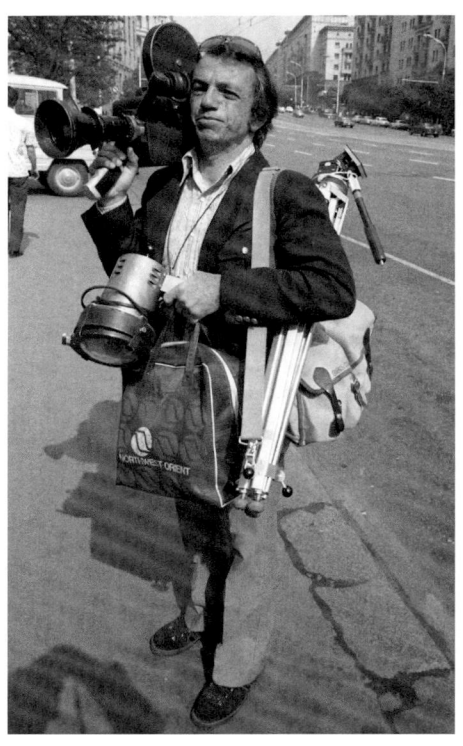

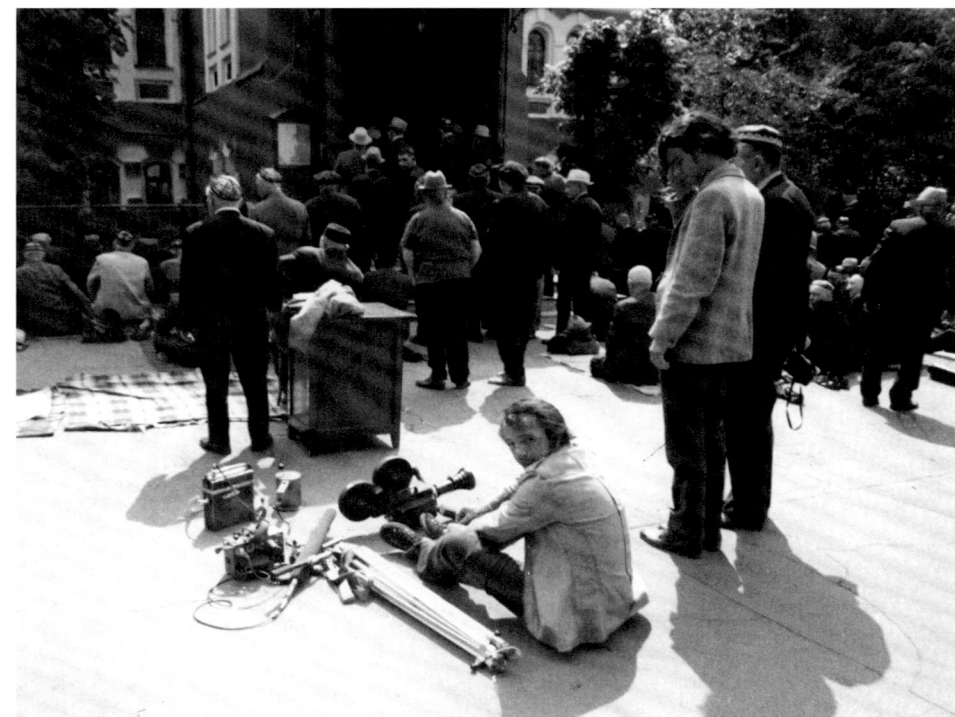

Bearing a cable-free, shoulder-mounted CP-16 camera, Del covered sights rarely seen by Westerners in circa-1972 Moscow, including religious services and the "Soviet Universal Drink Machine." *Del Hall Collection/CBS News.*

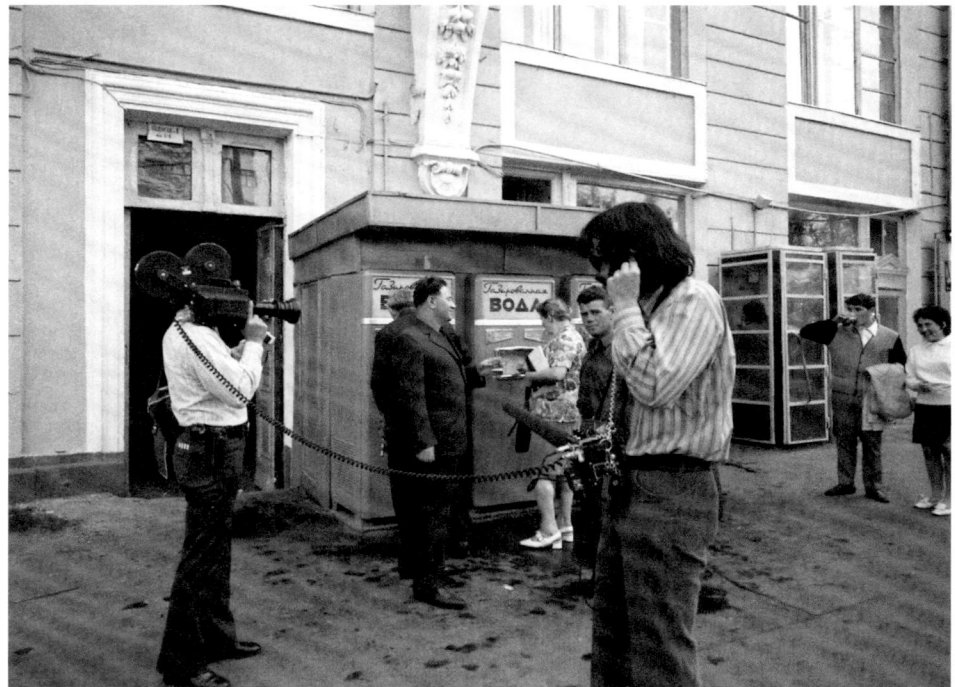

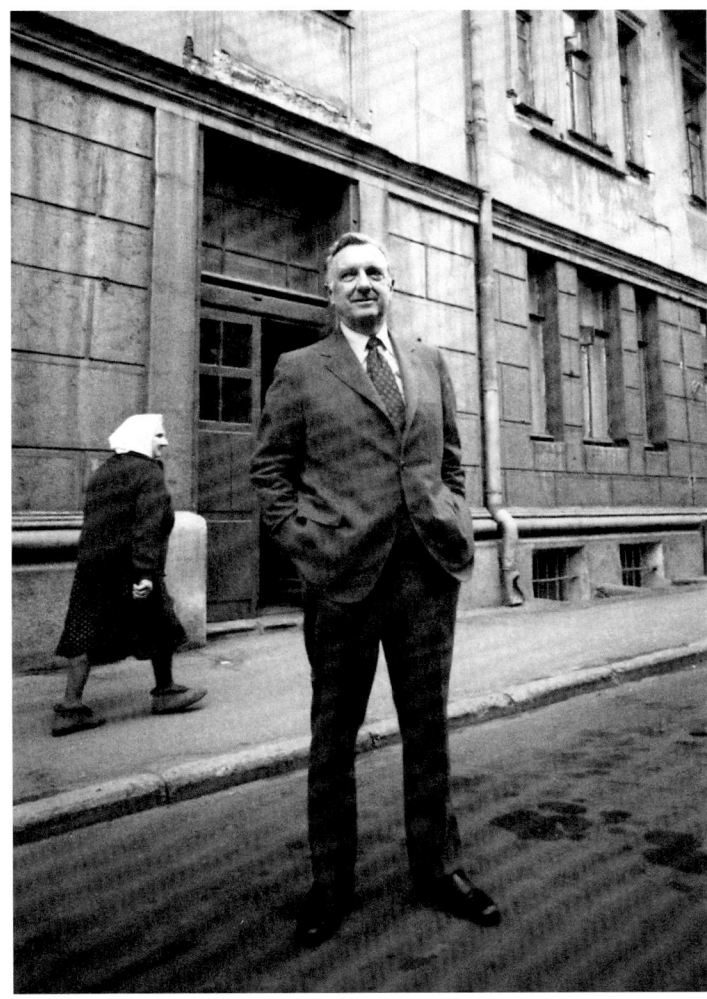
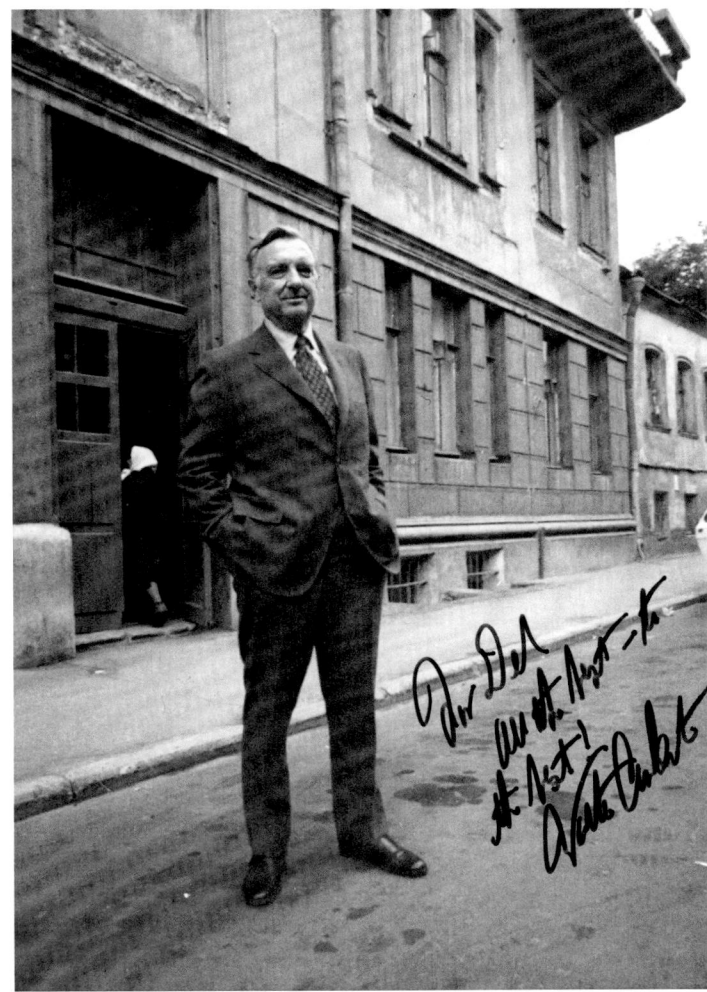

The most trusted man in America, and among the most influential in the world—but not to one elderly Moscovite, who didn't know Walter Cronkite from Adam. Here, Cronkite poses for Del's camera in front of the apartment where he lived in the late 1940s as a young reporter stationed in Moscow. *Photos by Del Hall.*

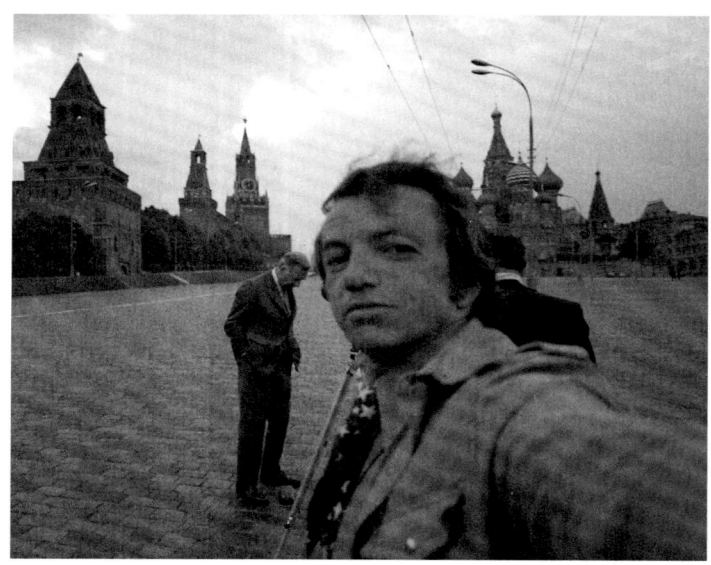

Del with Cronkite in Red Square. *Del Hall Collection/CBS News.*

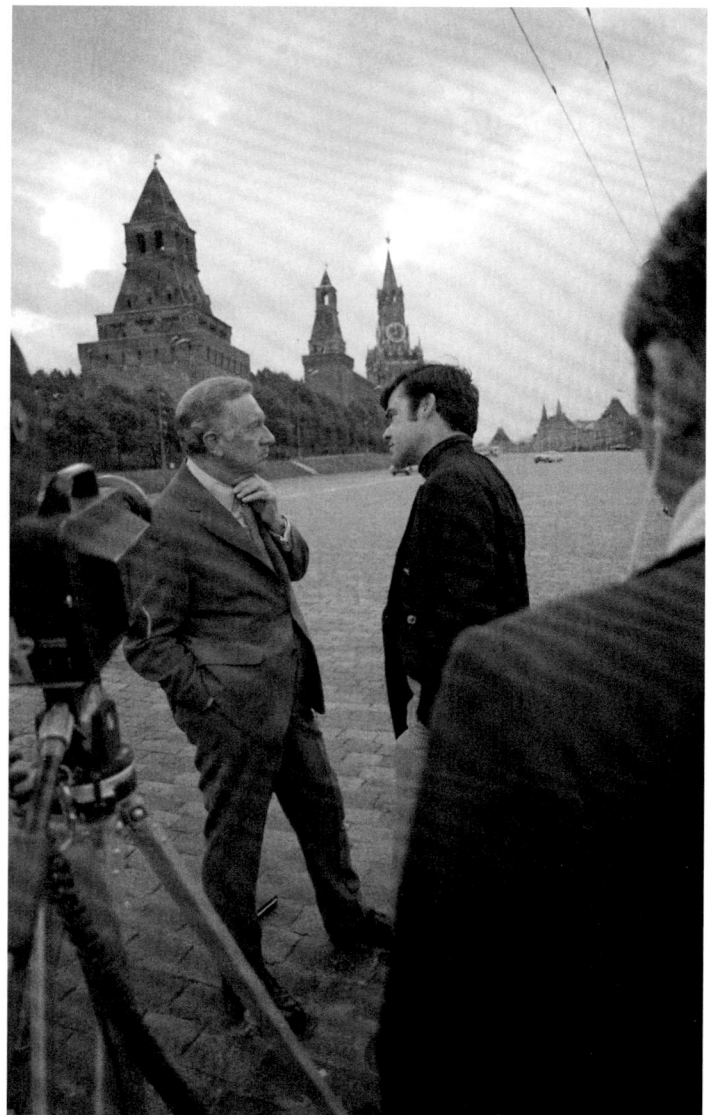

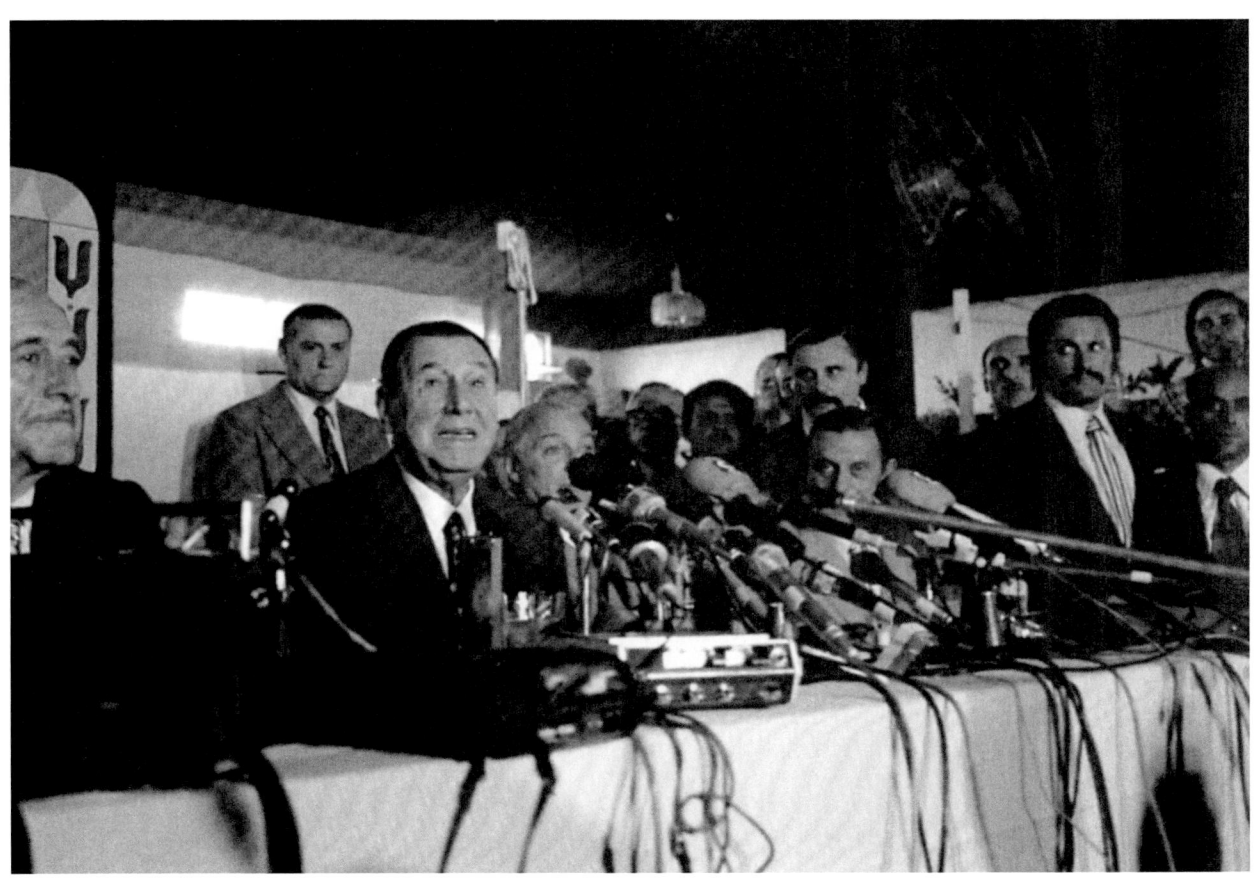

Juan Perón's return to Buenos Aires. *Photo by Del Hall/CBS News.*

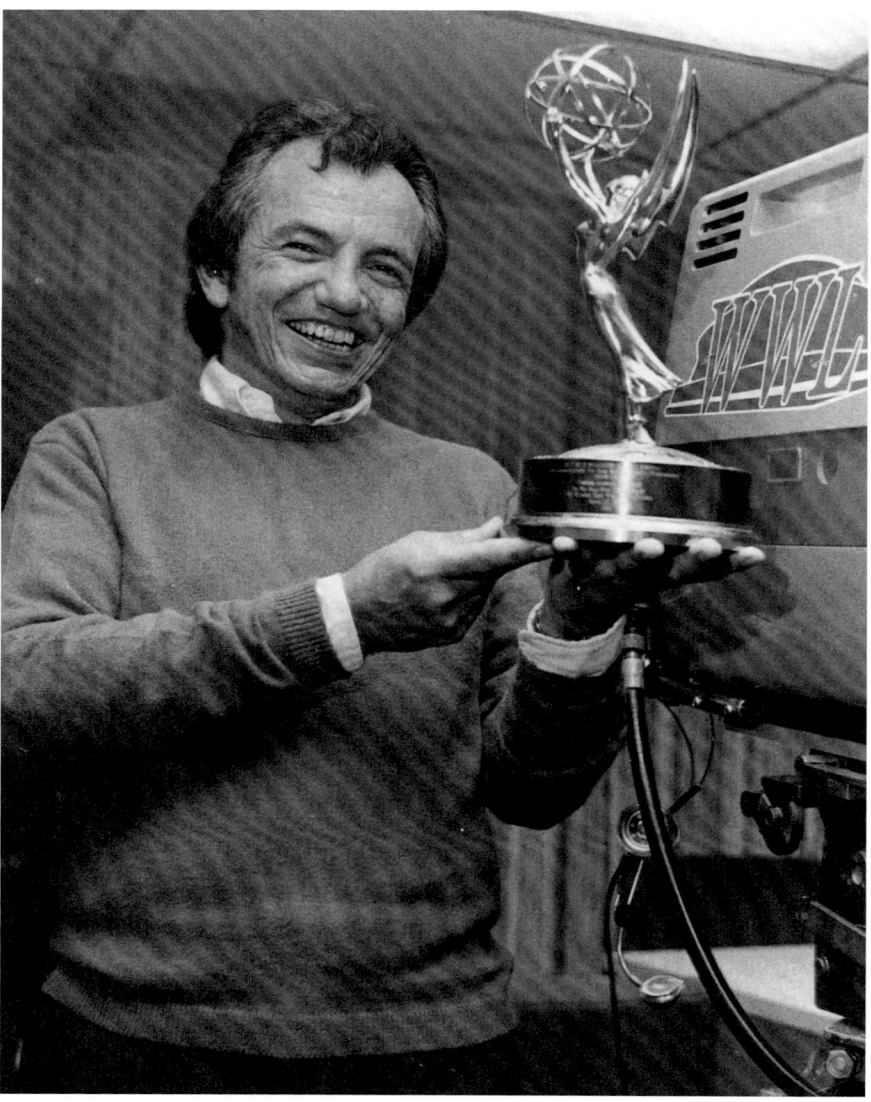

Del's camerawork for *Clanking Savannah
Blacksmith*, an *On the Road* segment with
Charles Kuralt, won him an Emmy Award.
Photo by CBS; frames by Del Hall.

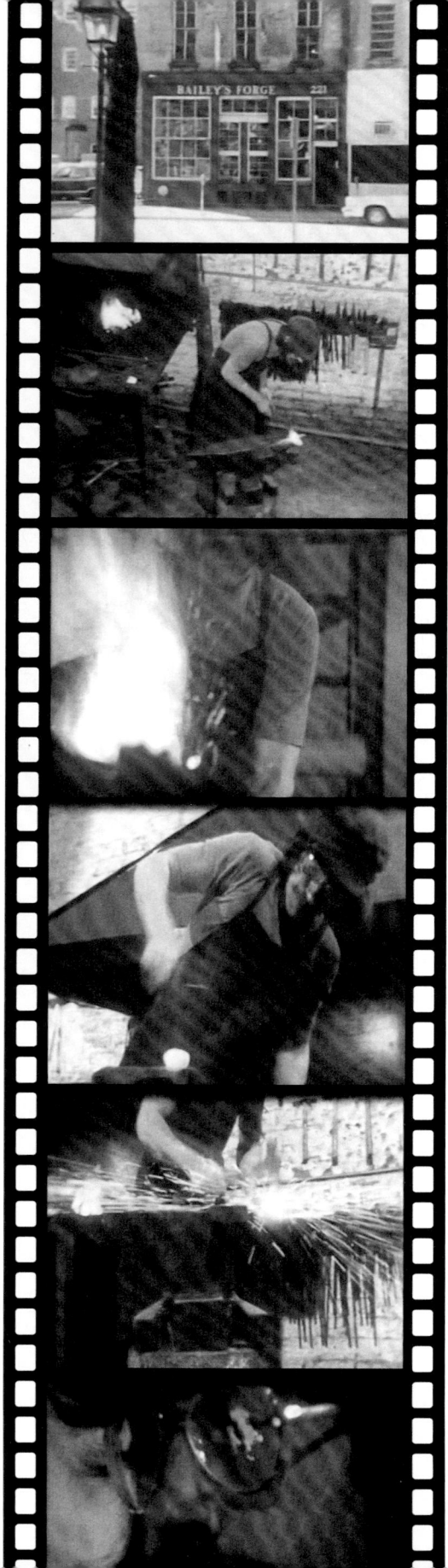

TAKE FOUR

Near Death and New Life, 1974–1987

A T FIRST IT felt like the Zephyr—the roller-coaster at Pontchartrain Beach, where he took dates in the '50s: that accelerating plunge to the right, right, right. Only this time, no rail whisked him back to rectitude. The last thing he remembered was the helicopter pilot saying, "I got a problem here. Can we go back?" Del and his partner looked at each other. *Why is he asking us?*

Del was no stranger to flight. His work had taken him 'round the world multiple times in every type of commercial and charter aircraft, not to mention bombers, cargo planes, seaplanes, spotter planes, blimps, balloons, cherry-picker buckets, and helicopters galore. August 22, 1974, was just another daily adventure, this time to cover the America's Cup elimination trials in Newport, Rhode Island, with Charles Osgood, the CBS correspondent known for *The Osgood File* and later for *CBS News Sunday Morning.*

The best way to cover a yacht race is by air, so the team hired a helicopter and, because they would be over water, had to switch to one with pontoons—a Bell 47J-2A. Pilot John Wallace removed the right door to accommodate the gyroscopic camera, next to which Del would sit. The third seat remained available, and the soundman expressed interest in coming along for the ride. "Why not let Bobby go?" Del suggested, as he wolfed down a ham sandwich. Bobby Oddo, a freelance electrician and, at age 26, an eager young newbie to televisions news, rarely got to fly. The soundman acquiesced, and Bobby happily climbed in with Del. Wallace, meanwhile, had gotten word from the organizers that air traffic would be circling counterclockwise over the trials, so he proceeded to remove the left door and decided not to reattach the one on the right. Del switched his camera to the left and swapped seats with Oddo. Osgood, meanwhile, remained at the airport, catching up on some writing while guarding the doors. The soundman snapped some photos of the crew just before takeoff, a custom among television guys that was part archival, part collegial, and part superstitious.

What no one knew was that a tiny castellated nut had somehow come loose from the blade mechanism. A helicopter banks by rotating its blades and returns upright by unrotating them; the dislodging of the nut, which probably exacerbated after they took off, meant that a turn to the right could not be reversed. At first this was not an issue, because the counterclockwise flight plan had them mostly banking left. But when Wallace needed to adjust his route, the problem came to light. Nine miles out over Narragansett Bay, the chopper slowly spiraled in wide rightward banks, coming closer and closer to the water over a period of 30 to 45 seconds. As Wallace nervously suggested that they return to land, the craft twisted wickedly to the right, Zephyr-like, and crashed sideways into the water. Hard Atlantic white-caps thrust through the wide-open right doorframe—and

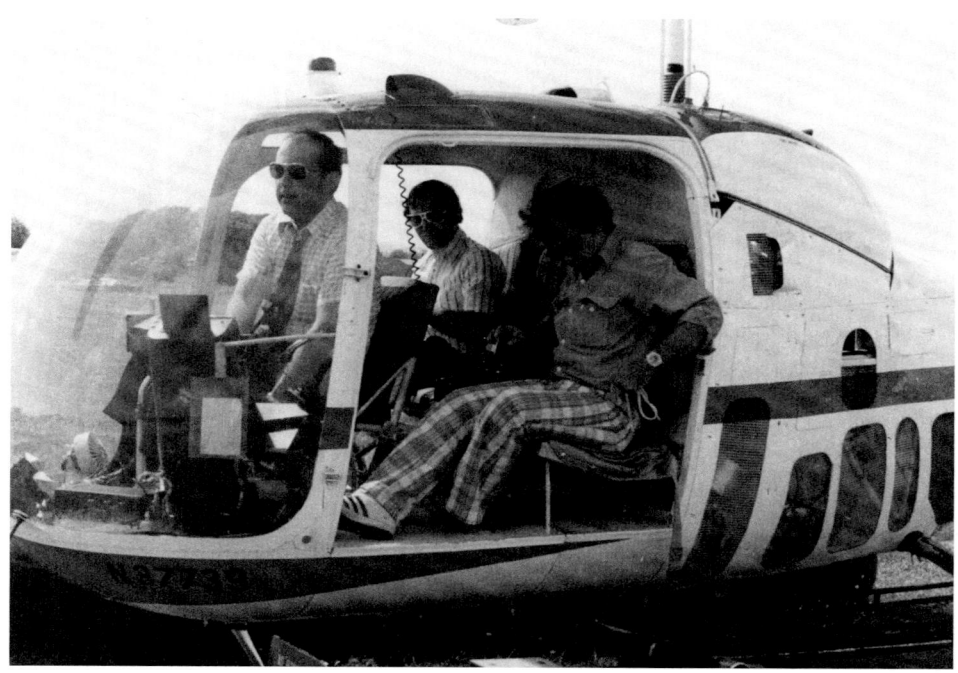

Preparing to cover the America's Cup trials over Narragansett Bay in Rhode Island, for which a pontoon helicopter was required for safety reasons. *Del Hall Collection/CBS News.*

Del had been underwater for most of that time, during which he vomited up his ham sandwich lunch and inhaled it back into his lungs along with oily sea water. He managed not to drown in part because his cameraman's instincts told him to *hold your breath when the action starts.* But the foreign objects in his lungs now threatened his life with infection and pneumonia. Then there was his right leg, which the heavy gyroscopic camera mount hammered top into bottom, shattering his knee. His right eye socket, also crushed, threatened his vision—and that was his shooting eye.

Ginger, in Chicago, got the dreaded news from CBS via her mother's phone call late that afternoon. "The good news is, Del's alive," she said. Ginger braced herself, and when the bad news came, she dissolved in tears. Gathering herself, she contacted one Dr. Joseph Blumen at the Newport Hospital, and the first thing he asked was, "Are you pregnant?" Startled, and then realizing that the doctor did not want to provoke a miscarriage, she answered no and prepared herself to learn that Del had died. She felt almost relieved to hear Dr. Blumen instead explain the extent of his injuries. Del was in the intensive care unit, and his prospects were not bright. "You need to get here fast," the doctor told Ginger. "But don't come alone."

directly into Bobby Oddo. The helicopter then swung upside down, held afloat only by its pontoons, and trapped all three men underwater.

Coast Guard lieutenant David Hosmer, who had been tracking the erratic flight, raced to the scene and plunged into the water to extricate the men. Fuel blinding his eyes, he reached Del first, only to find his seatbelt impossibly secure. Somehow he pulled Del's limp body out, got him to the surface, and laid him on the pontoon. Next he retrieved Oddo, and by the time he extracted Wallace, Hosmer found himself in trouble, exhausted and overcome by the chilly, choppy polluted sea. By this time, pleasure boats pulled close and respectfully ceased their partying, and an Australian librarian (who was nursing a hangover and therefore had not been drinking) jumped in to save Hosmer, itself a risky endeavor. The entire accident, which threatened the lives of five men, was over in five minutes.

CBS chartered a Learjet to pick up Ginger in Chicago and then to stop in Indianapolis for her mother, who quickly overcame her fear of flying for what was her first flight. They landed in Newport just before dawn. First sight of Del was wrenching: his head was swollen like a watermelon, his body bruised black and blue, his right eye bandaged, tracheotomy in the throat, and a tangle of dressing and braces around his knee. He did, however, open his left eye, and he remembers today being completely lost in time and space, "like a *Mission*

Impossible episode." Ginger gently informed him of what had happened and, having made a pact never to sugarcoat or lie, spared him no details—except one. She told him John and Bobby were in another hospital.

John Wallace, the pilot, had in fact survived and was recuperating elsewhere. But Bobby had been killed, by drowning if not from a broken neck, the result of having swapped seats with Del and bearing the brunt of the impact. "I do believe that Ginger made the right decision," Del says. "I believe if they told me that [Bobby was dead], it would have been my end. I would have just given up."

If only he had not invited Bobby on the flight. But then the soundman would have died. There were other "if's" that tortured him. If Lieutenant Hosmer had reached Del after he got to one or the other two men, both Bobby and Del would probably be dead. And had they gotten a standard helicopter that worked rather than one with safety pontoons that didn't work, all three would have had a perfect day.

Del went from capturing news to making news. Media covering the America's Cup caught the accident and rescue on camera and reported it on national news. Even earlier, word of a crash had circulated throughout the CBS family, and when Del's buddy Phil Johnson heard it in New Orleans, he had a sense that Del was among those involved. He called the Newport Hospital using an old *States-Item* trick—claiming to be Del's doctor—and heard directly from Dr. Blumen the nature of his injuries. A true friend and southern gentleman, Johnson took it upon himself to visit Del's mother Ella and tell her in person what had happened.

Dan Rather was equally gracious, calling the hospital daily and even writing letters to Del and Ginger, as did a host of friends and colleagues, including a rising star named Connie Chung. CBS covered all expenses and paid full salary throughout his recovery because, fortuitously, Del had decided shortly before the accident to rejoin CBS as an official employee after two years of freelancing.

His prospects remained bleak for weeks, but by September, he reached the point where he could begin to make sense of all that had happened. "You were in purgatory for several days," Dr. Blumen said with a smile. Del's catechism lessons failed him. "What does that mean, purgatory?" The doctor clarified: "You could have died any second." A former Vietnam combat medic, the doctor knew what impending death looked like. Del paused. "Well," he inquired hopefully, "do you think I can go to the Emmys?"

The number 22 arises with curious frequency in Del Hall's life. His first wife Greta was born on the 22nd; they married on the 22nd and became parents on the 22nd. Many years later Greta died on the 22nd, as did his mother and his grandmother. He buried his father on the same 22nd on which JFK was assassinated, and on August 22, 1974, he himself nearly lost his life, after having sailed the same waters that morning in a boat numbered 22. Twenty-two months later, he was finally able to return to work.

That amount of lost time in the world of television news is the equivalent of an epoch in geology. During Del's convalescence, the war in Vietnam had ended, in defeat. Watergate, which climaxed two weeks prior to Del's accident, was by 1976 a bad memory, and a hit movie. An accidental president was in the White House, and would soon be replaced by a new one from a different party. Riots and demonstrations had given way to discothèques and self-absorption. People spoke of "the sixties" as if to seal off the sensibilities of that era from the hedonism of "the seventies."

The CBS Midwest Bureau in Chicago, for its part, was full of new faces, and whatever professional and social tenure Del had earned up to 1974 had dissipated by 1976. Other cameramen had taken his assignments and were not about to relinquish them, leaving him behind to edit their shots. To the Young Turks, Del was some forty-something who hobbled with a cane into a windowless editing room at 9 a.m. and departed at 5 p.m. "No more roaming the world photographing kings and queens, presidents, governors, political hopefuls, [and] business tycoons," read a statement submitted as part of Del's lawsuit against the Bell Helicopter Company. Del testified in a legal document that the accident caused him problems that "are more than just physical. . . . I have lost pride in myself, and my identity and self-respect as a top CBS cameraman. I have also suffered significant financial losses [and] at least three years of productivity and happiness."[1] Much of that time was spent almost literally in the wilderness; he and Ginger at one point bought a camper and drove around the United States and Mexico, in the hope that travel would abet his recovery. It didn't, and they ended up camping in his sister Sharon's front lawn in Metairie. "It was horrible," Ginger winces. "Horrible."

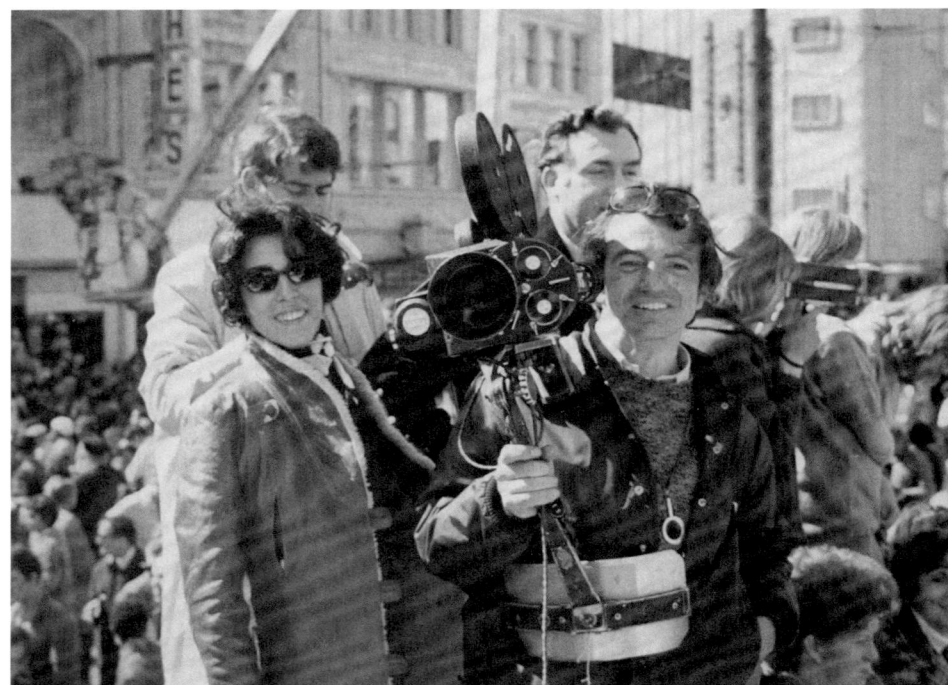

The Halls covering Mardi Gras in New Orleans. *Del Hall Collection.*

Returning to CBS also meant a change in technology. A new media format, magnetic videotape, began to circulate in the early 1970s, piquing the interest of producers. But old-fashioned film still prevailed among most networks, local and national, and the unique skills of shooting, handling, processing, and editing it kept the position of cameraman specialized and difficult to enter.

By 1976, however, videotape had made gains on film, and its ease of handling and shooting lowered the bar of entry. More "videographers" entered the field, qualified or not. Del saw firsthand the inevitable results, and grated at being relegated to edit the sort of lousy footage he'd have excoriated years ago. But he also had a knack for foreseeing the terrain ahead, and suffered a minimal amount of mawkishness about what lay behind. He realized that videotape, with its immediate viewability, was the future, and he endeavored to make the best of a bad situation by learning everything he could about it. Indeed, the last roll of film Del ever shot on assignment lies today somewhere at the bottom of the Atlantic Ocean.

As Del built up his video skills in the editing room, Ginger made her own advances into the news field, learning how to load a particularly complex French film camera system. When word circulated that the bureau needed an assistant to the cameraman, Del suggested they consider Ginger.

At any other time, such a hire would have been nixed by institutional sexism at the network, or by the union, which was all male. But CBS in the late 1970s had been striving for diversity, in terms of both race and gender, and the network pressured its unions to do the same. Ginger got the job of "assistant cameraman"—actually the sound person—for *60 Minutes,* which continued to shoot film even as the rest of television news adopted video. Teamed with Del, an electrician, and a lighting man, Ginger became one of the first female crew members for a program of this stature. "Wives of cameramen oftentimes became the first wave of women hires," Ginger explains.

The extra income made things easier for the Halls, as did a favorable settlement on the Bell Helicopter lawsuit. Del's physical condition had also improved after extensive therapy, to the point that his superiors in New York felt he was ready to return to the field. They offered him a cameraman position for *60 Minutes,* an offer most people in his position would have jumped on. But Del was confident that returning to the film medium would be a step in the wrong direction—so much so that he had already purchased his own professional video camera and editing system. "When you're ready for videotape," he told the producers, "I'll be ready for you." Shortly thereafter, they switched to videotape, and Del accepted the position.

Now he needed to assemble his crew. He and his friend Janet Roach, who happened to be the producer of the ill-fated America's Cup story, batted around some ideas and then decamped for dinner with Ginger. It took Roach's third-party perspective to make an obvious suggestion. "Del," Janet asked, "why don't you take Ginger as your sound person?" "It was like a light went on in both of our heads," Ginger tells. Of course! But there were some concerns. Cameramen could be tough on their crews, they both knew, and few are the happily married couples who also work together. There was only one way to find out. On January 1, 1980, Del and Ginger Hall officially teamed up as a two-person cameraman/sound crew freelancing for CBS. Del invested in a Sony BVP-300 three-tube broadcast camera, with a separate BVU-50 3/4" U-matic recorder and an external time code generator hanging on the side. "I would carry the camera," Del explained, "and Ginger carried the recorder, spare batteries, extra tapes, and at least one mic." Loaded down with sundry paraphernalia, they held everything together with yellow onion bags made in New Orleans, which, with their light weight, strength, and expandability, proved just perfect for gear-laden multi-modal travel.

An optimistic new decade had begun, and it would all be caught on videotape.

Cable television. CNN. MTV. Fox. Late-night. *Nightline.* VCRs. Satellite dishes. The fifteen-minute national broadcasts of the early 1960s had augmented by the 1980s to a relentless round-the-clock cycle, with new players and devices raring to enter the fray. Media attention seemed to grow exponentially despite that newsworthy events only grew arithmetically. Presidential campaigns started earlier and grew uglier; fame and celebrity came to dominate the public discourse; and, starting in 1982, falling oil prices helped catalyze an economic boom that would last the remainder of the decade. Del and Ginger in this period got nearly all their work courtesy two of the most respected programs on television, *60 Minutes* and *CBS Sunday Morning.* "We worked as hard as we could as long as we could" in the new world of media.

The nature of war changed by the 1980s as well. The major front-based conflicts of the past had fragmented into dozens of smaller sporadic guerrilla battles, many of them proxies for the Cold War or corollaries of colonialism. Some erupted rather unexpectedly, in remote places, and the oddest of all was in the South Atlantic atolls called the Malvinas by the Argentines and the Falklands by the British. Both countries laid claim to the tiny archipelago, and when Argentina's military dictatorship, intent on distracting its ill-served citizenry with ill-conceived nationalism, moved to consummate its claim to the islands, Prime Minister Margaret Thatcher sent warships to defend the legitimacy of Britain's remaining empire. Some wags called the military engagement "a splendid little war," isolated, self-contained, and seemingly custom-made for the 1980s. Others called it "the journalists' war."

Del and Ginger were in the CBS office in New York when the chief news producer stopped them in the hallway. "Want to go to London? Maybe for months?" The couple got visas in Times Square, raced back to Chicago to pack, and landed at Heathrow all of three days later. With Del as cameraman and Ginger on sound, they covered the Ministry of Defense building near Downing Street, where official war reports were issued and press conferences were held. Their sporadic nature meant that crews had to stick close and endure hours of waiting. For sustenance a catering truck was brought in, but was soon re-dispatched—not for war purposes, but to feed Barbra Streisand's crew filming her movie *Yentl.* It was that sort of decade. So the crews outside the Ministry of Defense ate instead at the Red Lion Pub, where, among other things, they discovered "bangers and mash."

London became the center of world attention, and when at one point President Ronald Reagan and Pope John Paul II arrived to visit Prime Minister Thatcher, Del was pulled off

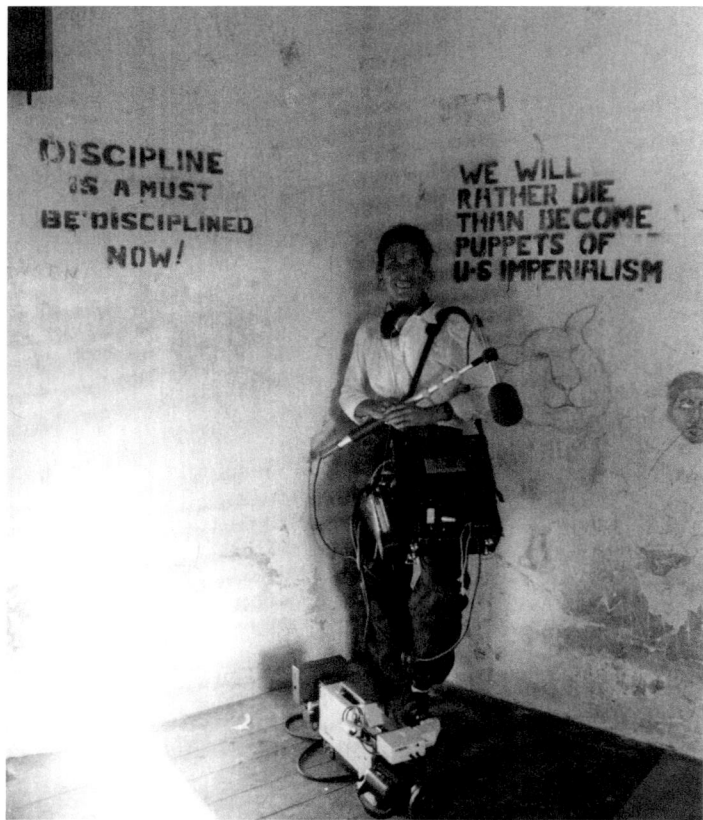

Ginger in the ruins of Maurice Bishop's compound in Grenada.
Del Hall Collection.

the ministry coverage to edit multiple stories on the pope. A local cameraman filled in for him, and one day when he ventured to the Red Lion, out came the Minister of Defense with a major update. Ginger frantically jumped into action, figuring out how to shoot the complex camera system in real time while also handling sound. The local cameraman never returned, and Ginger's footage aired on the national news. It was that sort of business.

As England handily defeated Argentina in the South Atlantic—in a series of sea battles with little geopolitical significance except for the thousand who perished—American military eyes were tracking Grenada, a tiny island in the Caribbean whose socialist prime minister, Maurice Bishop, had

been overthrown by hardline Marxists. Noting the construction of a suspiciously large runway, the Reagan administration worried that Cubans and Soviets were collaborating with Grenadians of both regimes to create a base for aiding Communist insurgencies in Central America. In October 1983, U.S. troops invaded. When Americans first learned of the location of the surprise action, the standard response was, "Where?" Now, it was the biggest story in the country, although the actual fighting went all but uncovered because of a highly controversial press blackout imposed by administration officials still bitter about Vietnam.

After the ban was lifted, the Halls were dispatched to assess what had happened. CBS stationed Del in Barbados, where video footage would be flown in for him to edit and pass on to New York, while Ginger would be in the field paired with a cameraman and a reporter. Del was not thrilled with the arrangement, although he did not mind the first-class accommodations in Barbados ("everyone on the island," he marvels, "seemed to play steel drums"). Neither was Ginger, especially when the cameraman, whose family had suffered a recent tragedy, indulged in extreme alcoholism, and the reporter proved to be incompetent. The threesome nonetheless flew into the former combat zone in a Black Hawk helicopter and found the local population recovering from the trauma with plenty of stories to tell. They videotaped wrecked buildings and burned-out conveyances littering the landscape, and showed wide-eyed children parroting Airborne paratroopers by draping their heads and shoulders in camouflaging. They did a story on villagers lining up at U.S. military tents seeking reimbursement for livestock killed in the strafing (everyone seemed to have been rancher with six or a dozen head of cattle, Ginger grins). They also filed a story on the role of U.S. military women, who were initially deployed for hospital and other noncombat duty in Grenada and later recalled because it was technically a war zone. In the interim, it marked the first time in American history when substantial numbers of women in uniform could be seen with loaded weaponry in a near-wartime situation.

By now the alcoholic had failed utterly in his ability to do his job, leaving Ginger once again stranded without a cameraman, and stuck in a hillside motel with wide-open windows and Cuban soldiers rumored to be in the vicinity. CBS thus flew in Del from Barbados to do the camera work. (When told that this was Del's first helicopter flight since his near-fatal crash of 1974, the pilot asked, "He's not going to go berserk on me, is he?") Now on their own reconnaissance, Del and Ginger shot remarkable footage of Bishop's bombed-out compound and the centuries-old fort that had been used as the government's prison for dissidents. All buildings were wide open, ruinous, and covered in defiant as well as triumphant graffiti, the epitaphs of one of so many violent flashpoints throughout the tropical world in the 1980s. The Halls returned to Chicago by Christmas and resumed working nearly round the clock for *CBS Morning News* and *60 Minutes.*

Camera crews get to know journalists in ways few viewers do, and Del and Ginger particularly admired those of *60 Minutes.* Del had been with the program since so early in its history that he remembered when its inventor and producer, Don Hewitt, would himself appear on camera. Hewitt not only established the news magazine but "helped invent television . . . a brilliant man." Del's respect for Dan Rather dated back to the early 1960s and was matched by that which he held for Mike Wallace. Unlike most other journalists who became their own brands, Wallace would linger on public sets and answer oftentimes pointed queries from local people who felt his investigative reporting would unfairly harm their community. "*Convince* me, *convince* me," he would challenge the challengers, determined to hear out every alternative interpretation before devising and filing his own. "He wouldn't run or evade them," the Halls pointed out. He would integrate their views into the story to the degree he judged them to be reasonable and accurate. One time Del asked Wallace, who gained fame for his confrontational interviews, why ne'er-do-wells would agree to go before the camera. Wallace paused pensively. "Because they think they can beat us," he replied. "They *think* they can *beat* us."

Ed Bradley was their favorite, and the three maintained a close friendship to the day he died. A true gentleman, Del and Ginger call him, and a superb journalist with a certain

set of tactics. Bradley would, for example, intentionally ensconce himself while the crew wired up the subject for an interview, eschewing all small talk or sizing-up prior to the rolling of the camera. He would absolutely prohibit a previewing of the questions. Even more important, he followed up on answers, pressing on ambiguities and pointing out inconsistencies. That spontaneity and perseverance wiped away all forms of glibness and brought forth the truth. Bradley was also a romantic of the old school (he once hired a set designer to deck out his apartment for a special date) and had a mischievous sense of humor to boot. As the first African American to be hired into a major journalistic position at CBS, he solemnly announced one day that he had changed his name to Mohammad Al-Asim Mohammad and had new business cards to distribute. Colleagues smiled nervously and nodded politely—and became the butt of the joke when it turned out "Mohammad" was pulling their leg. Bradley also deeply loved New Orleans and its music and food, and the three wined and dined there whenever the chance arose.

One time, CBS producer David Saltman—a brilliant and idiosyncratic character endearingly nicknamed the Great Saltini—assigned Del and Ginger to cover a Bradley-inspired piece on New Orleans music legends. They happily obliged and soon found themselves floating down the Mississippi River on the *President* riverboat in the Louisiana twilight. Fats Domino and Dr. John played their best, long and hard, to the Halls' cameras and an appreciative audience that included Ellis Marsalis and his sons, who themselves would be viewed as legendary in the coming years. "I reeled from the sheer absolute joy," Ginger remembers, thinking "we were the luckiest people in the entire world." Even when things did not go so well, they did so splendidly. Fats, it turned out, played so passionately that night that he had to postpone his next-day JazzFest gig on the festival's second weekend. Because his scheduled appearance on the big stage had been envisioned as the culmination of the televised piece, the Great Saltini paid Del and Ginger to remain in New Orleans for another seven days—nice work if you can get it. Hoping to capture vignettes on Fats's domestic life, such as cooking his signature red beans and rice in his Lower Ninth Ward home, they telephoned the famously shy star repeatedly, and he would answer and chat politely. But any prodding to agree to a meeting time was met by a blithely noncommittal "Ooohhh noooo, I don't *bee-lieve*"; "Ummm, lemmessee. . . . noooo, I don't *bee-live.* Call me *tumar-oo,*" enunciated in a melodic singsong that was pure Fats—and pure New Orleans. They never did record the cooking session, but came home instead with a delicious memory.

By this time, Sony had come out with its new line of Betacam recorders and tapes, rendering obsolete Del's BVP-300. Lighter and smaller, the Betacam captured higher-quality imagery and recorded it on a smaller tape cassette, making the Halls' job so much easier that, while filming a Sony corporate event, Ginger testified to its superior design to company president Akio Morita and he happily autographed their camera in return.

So equipped as freelancers, the Halls could take on any work they wanted, within or beyond CBS. One niche market developed for making behind-the-scenes documentaries of big-name movies, particularly those being filmed in Chicago. They covered a number of John Hughes projects, including *Sixteen Candles* in 1984 and *Pretty in Pink* in 1986. Hughes, they discovered, was omnipresent but evasive of the camera ("he was afraid I would catch him smoking," Del says), and actress Molly Ringwald turned out to be almost indistinguishable from the brat-pack characters she played. ("I told her the back of her coat collar was riding up from her shirt, like it was on a hanger." She sighed, rolled her eyes, and patiently explained that this was "the style." Laughs Del, "I didn't argue, and we did the interview with her sitting cross-legged on the high school floor, between lockers.") That year Del and Ginger also shot the making of *The Color of Money,* a remake of *The Hustler* filmed at the end of the Navy Pier in Lake Michigan. In addition to conversations between director Martin Scorsese and star Paul Newman, they documented how the billiard scenes were created, complete with "the professional pool players, technical advisers, and strategically placed balls that would all magically fly into separate pockets." Recalls Del to his chagrin, "As I was shooting those breaks, I backed up and almost knocked someone

over. I turned around and saw it was Scorsese. I said, 'Oh no, not you.'"

Occasionally the Halls would freelance for another network. ABC once hired them to shoot an exposé for their own news magazine. The subject was an allegedly corrupt congressman, and the setting was a midwestern city notorious for organized—and disorganized—crime. What Del and Ginger remember of the story had less to do with its details and more to do with the foibles of journalism. After the correspondents had confronted a number of FBI suspects with evidence of illegal gambling, they were granted an interview with the mayor of the city. With lights on and camera rolling, the chief correspondent dramatically disclosed to the mayor that he himself was under investigation by the FBI. His eyes widened and his mouth dropped open. "Oh my God!" he gasped incredulously. The crew looked at each other blankly. This was not the typical response elicited at such a moment. Afterwards, the producer asked the correspondent where she got that information. "Huh?" she retorted. "I got it from you!" It proved to be flat-out erroneous, the product of sloppy note-taking or confused names. The episode served as a reminder that the press maintains certain advantages over its subjects, and in the process of reportage, it commits comparable mistakes just as often.

The story also provided a lesson in journalistic candor. The same producer had asked the Halls to set up a hidden camera in a neighborhood bar known to operate an illegal poker machine. Del never liked hidden cameras; they smacked of the most self-righteous sort of entrapment, and brought to mind the fiasco of Puerto Vallarta a decade earlier. Besides, this was not a bunch of mobsters screwing over little people; this was a mom-and-pop tavern making a few extra bucks providing entertainment that was legal elsewhere. "Why don't we just ask them if we can shoot?" Del asked. The producer couldn't think of a good reason not to. "Knock yourselves out," he relented. Del then turned to his wife and said, as he recalls today with an impish grin, "Ginger, you go!" Now in charge of his own moral high road, he drove Ginger and the producer up to the bar for their experiment in candor. It was nighttime, and he approached with unnecessary stealth—until he accidentally set off the car alarm. Chuckling and shaking her head, Ginger got out and strode in confidently, identified herself to the owners, and politely asked if they could videotape the illegal poker machine for a news report. Can you assure us you won't reveal our identity? the owners asked. Ginger admitted she did not know this producer well enough to guarantee it, so she returned to the car and got his word. Satisfied, the owners agreed, and the crew came home with high-quality footage sans sneakiness and deceit. The scene helped make the final story, foibles and all, a success. Afterwards, the producer called back and said, "I learned a lesson from Del. . . . I thought I had to be stealth and all, but there's a better way to do it. Just be honest!" Adds Del mischievously, "And send Ginger!"

Freelancing had served the couple well for over seven years. On the job for more than three hundred days per year, they enjoyed the challenges thoroughly, looked forward to each adventure, and saw three streams of income flow into their household, one for each of them and third for renting out their equipment. None of the feared problems crept into their marriage; in fact, the shared work benefited the relationship and the two complemented each other perfectly. It was now 1987, and the doldrums of the late 1970s were well behind them. There was just one problem: upon arriving home each night, work followed them. It remained there overnight, awaited them the next morning, and found them on Saturday evenings and Sunday afternoons, constantly. They decided to rent an office downtown and separate home and work. The move would pave the way for the formation of their own production company. It would be called Del Hall Video.

Coast Guard lieutenant David Hosmer leads the rescue effort after the pontoon helicopter carrying Del and his companions crashes and overturns. Del is shown here being pulled out of the water, perilously near death. Pilot John Wallace survived; tragically, electrician Bobby Oddo died on impact. *Photos courtesy Associated Press/Del Hall Collection.*

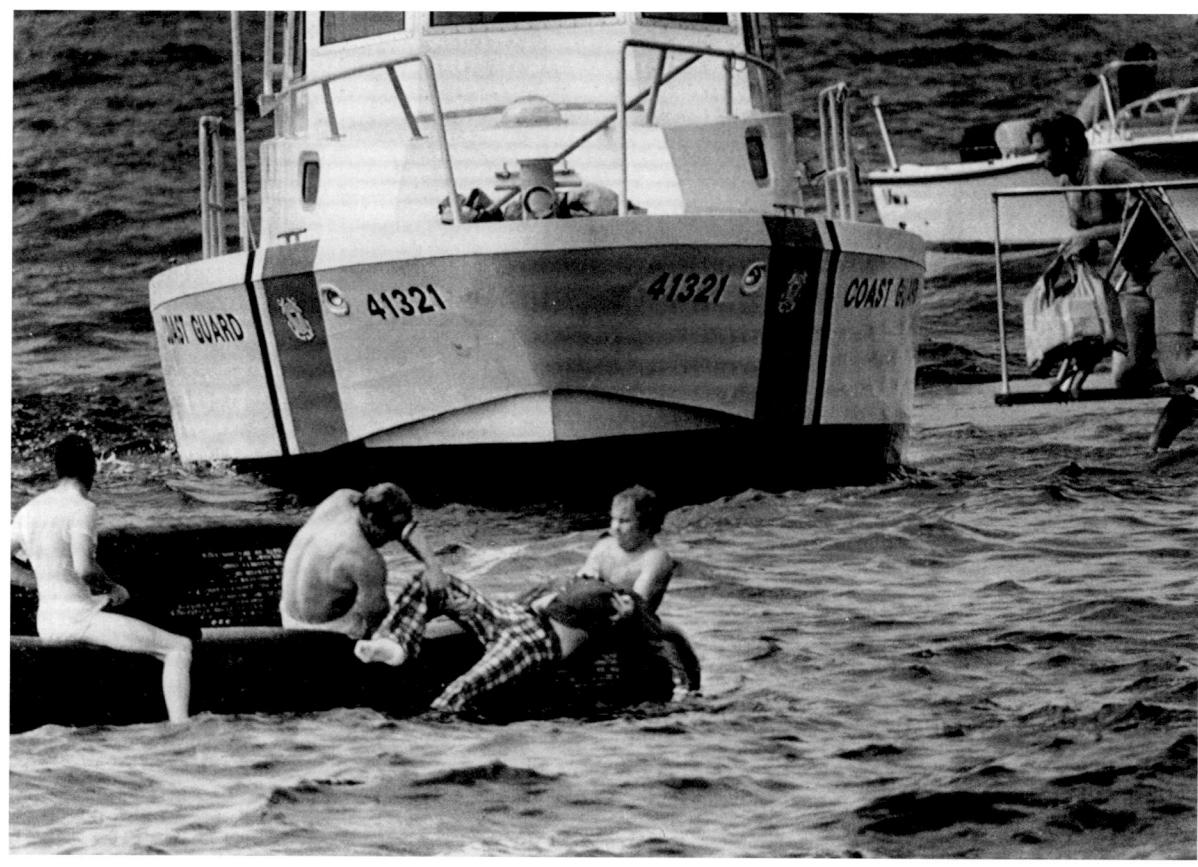

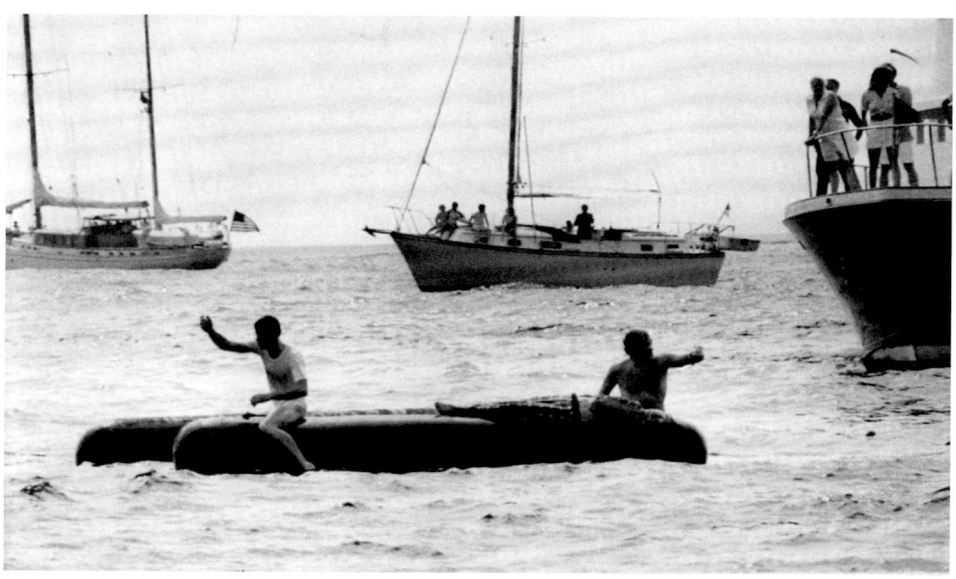

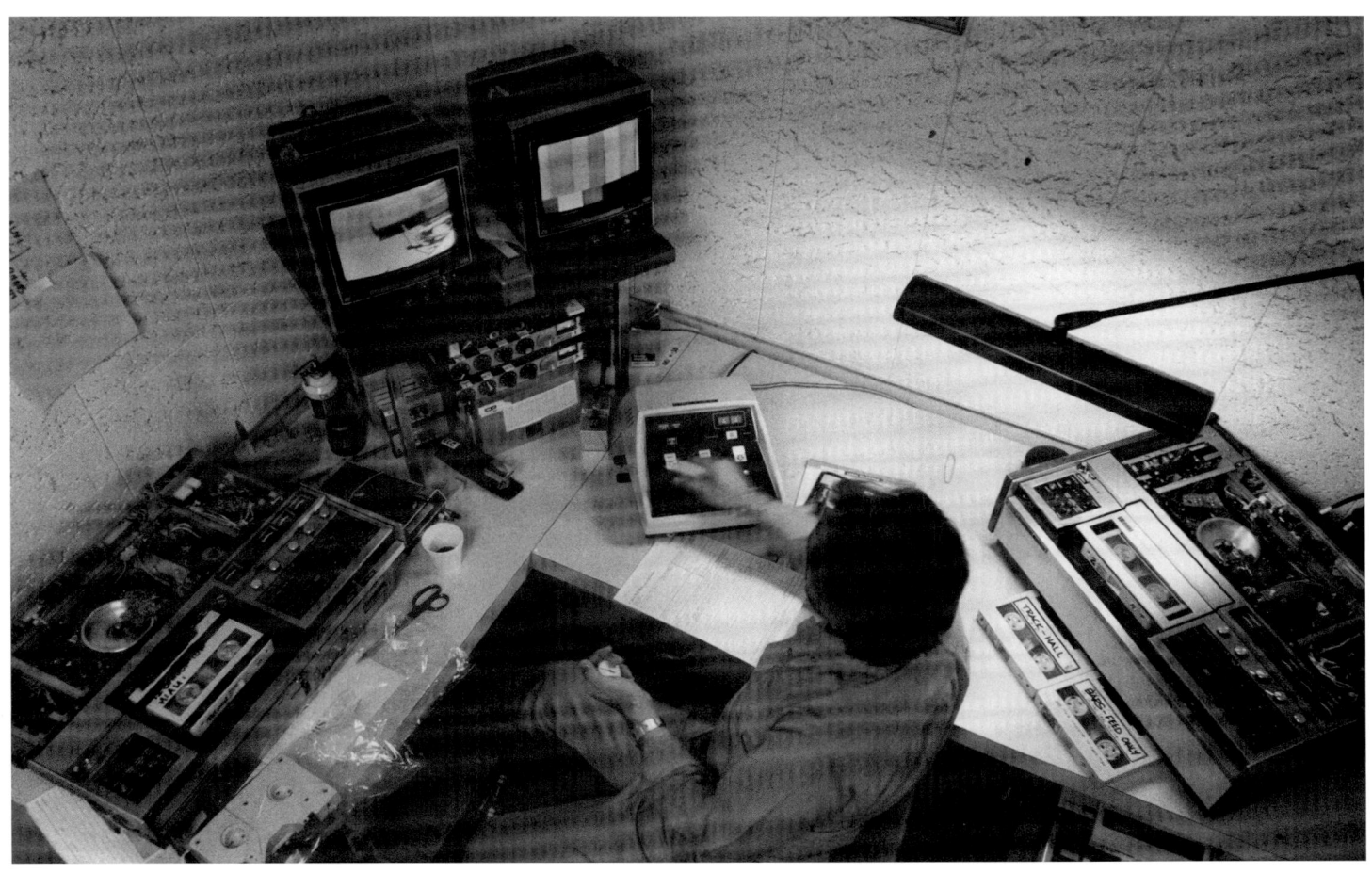

After two dismal years of recuperation, Del found himself in a CBS editing room, far from the whirlwind of network cameramen covering world news. It was high time for a reinvention. *Del Hall Collection.*

By 1980, Del and Ginger were free-lancing for CBS News. Here Ginger prepares for an interview with Yankee great Yogi Berra. *Photo by Del Hall/CBS.*

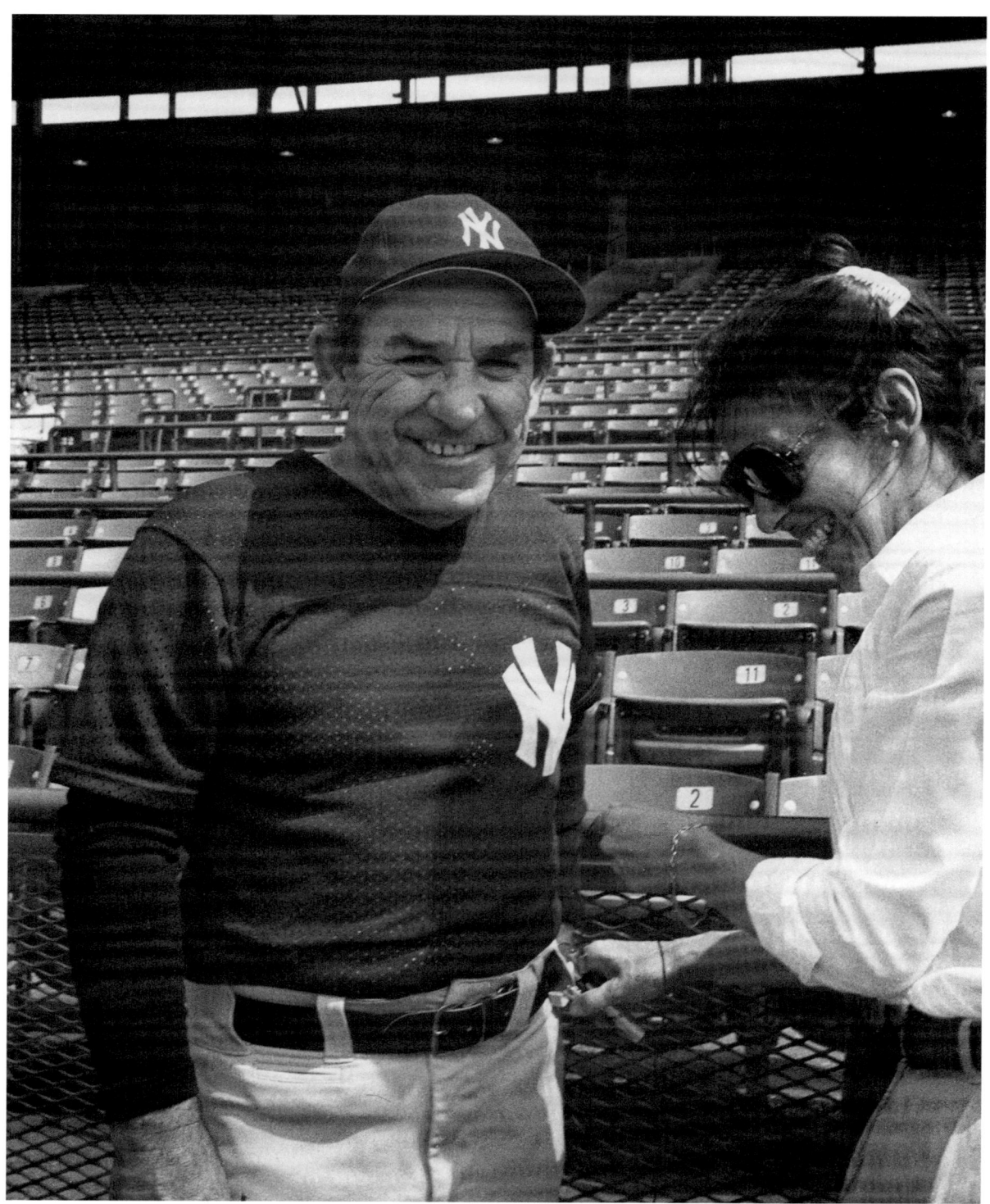

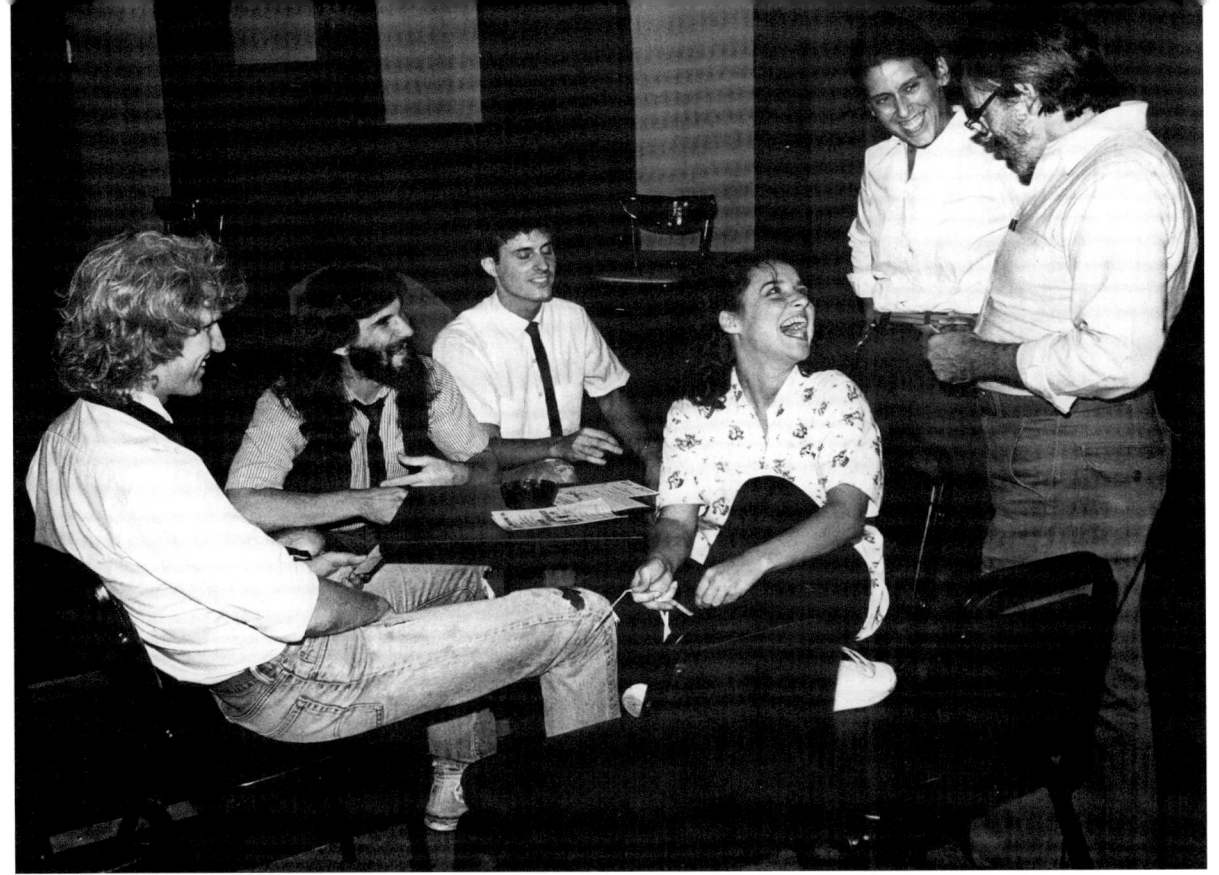

Del and Ginger at work with Julia Louis-Dreyfus, Brad Hall, and colleagues. *Del Hall Collection/Del Hall Video.*

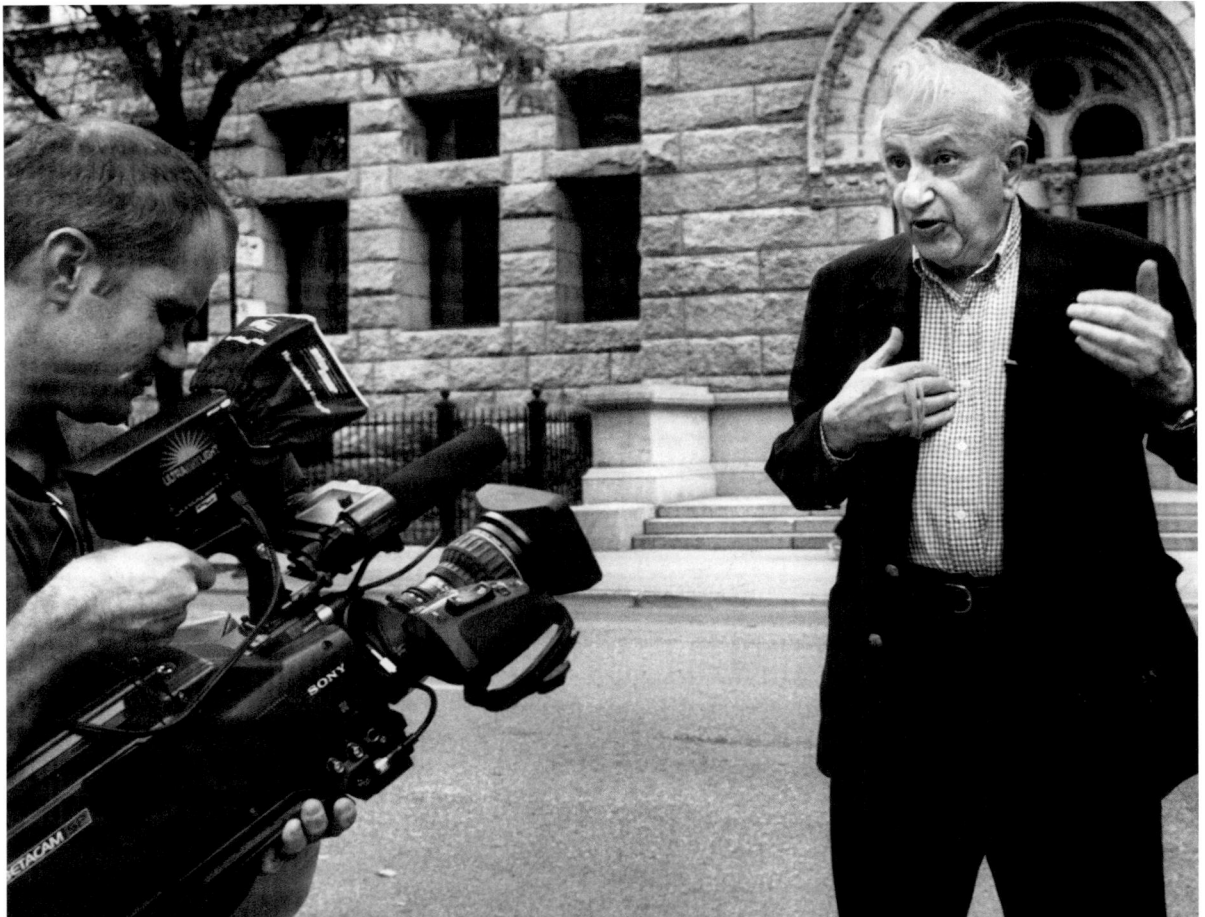

Pulitzer Prize–winning author and historian Studs Terkel. *Del Hall Collection/Del Hall Video.*

Del and Ginger
with Jesse Jackson,
Julian Bond, and
an unidentified
staffer. *Del Hall
Collection/Del Hall
Video.*

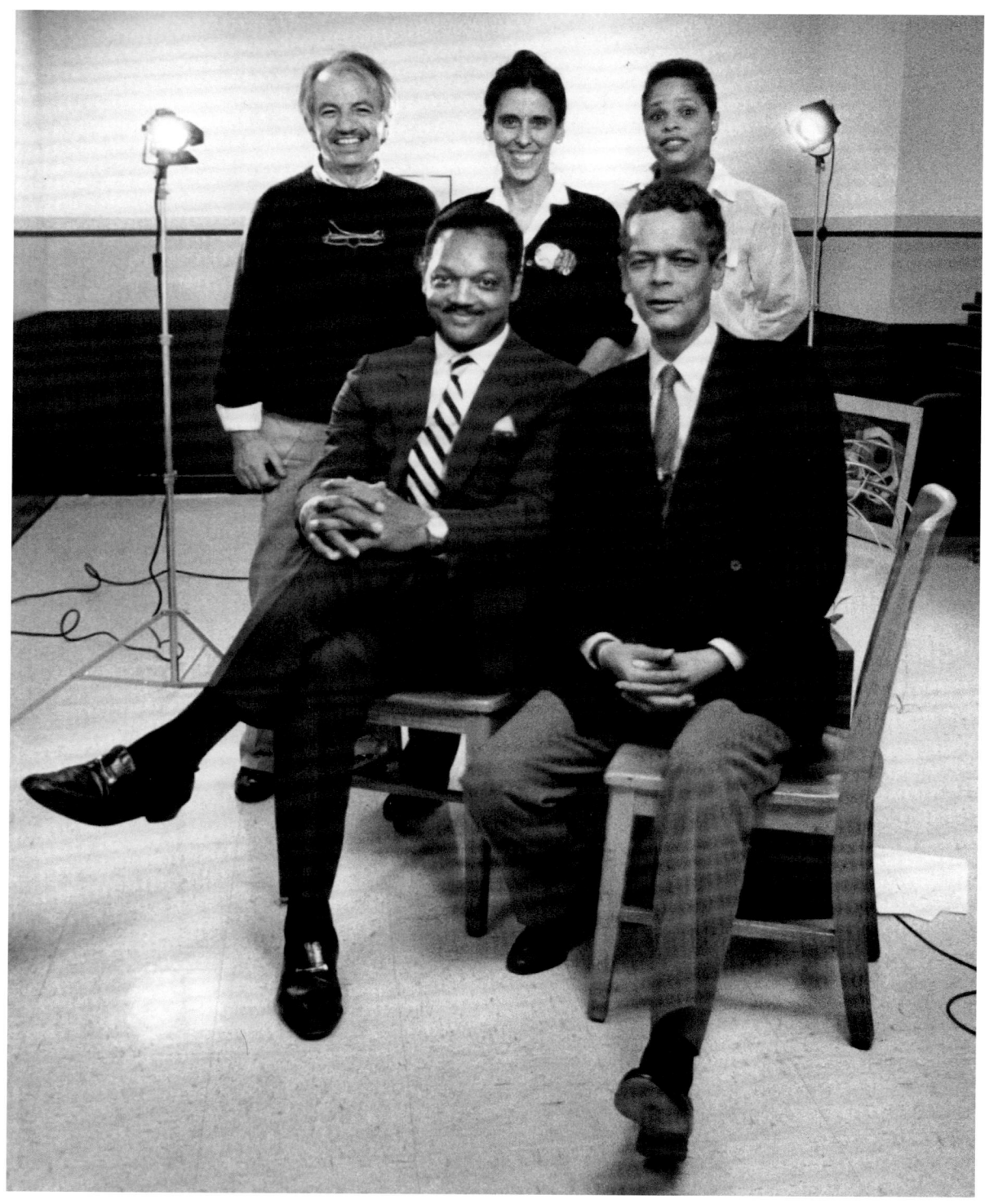

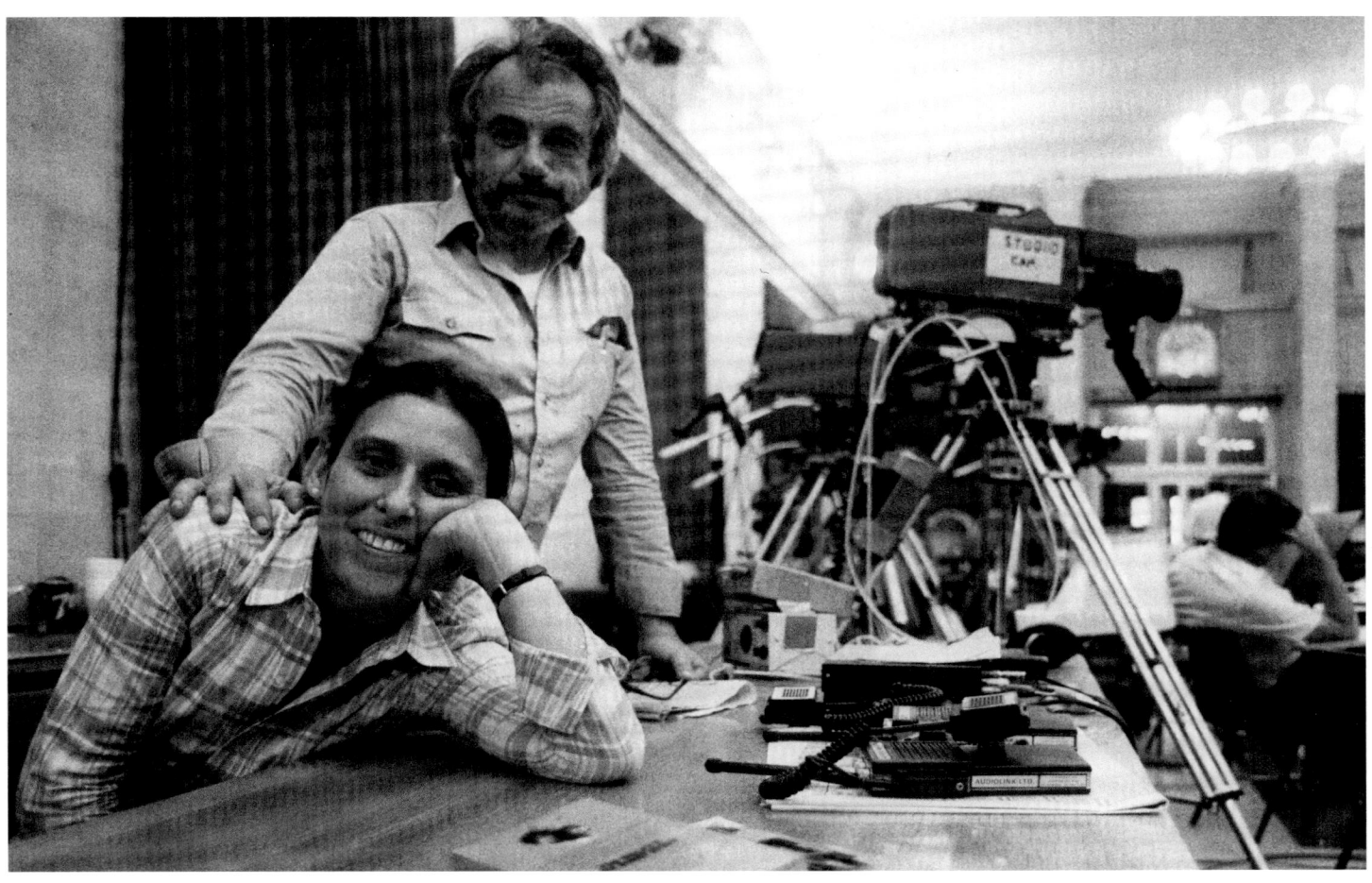

Del and Ginger take a break from covering England's Ministry of Defense during its war against the Argentines in the Falkland Islands. *Del Hall Collection.*

After the press was allowed in, Del and Ginger shot footage of the aftermath of the U.S. invasion of Grenada in October 1983. *Del Hall Collection.*

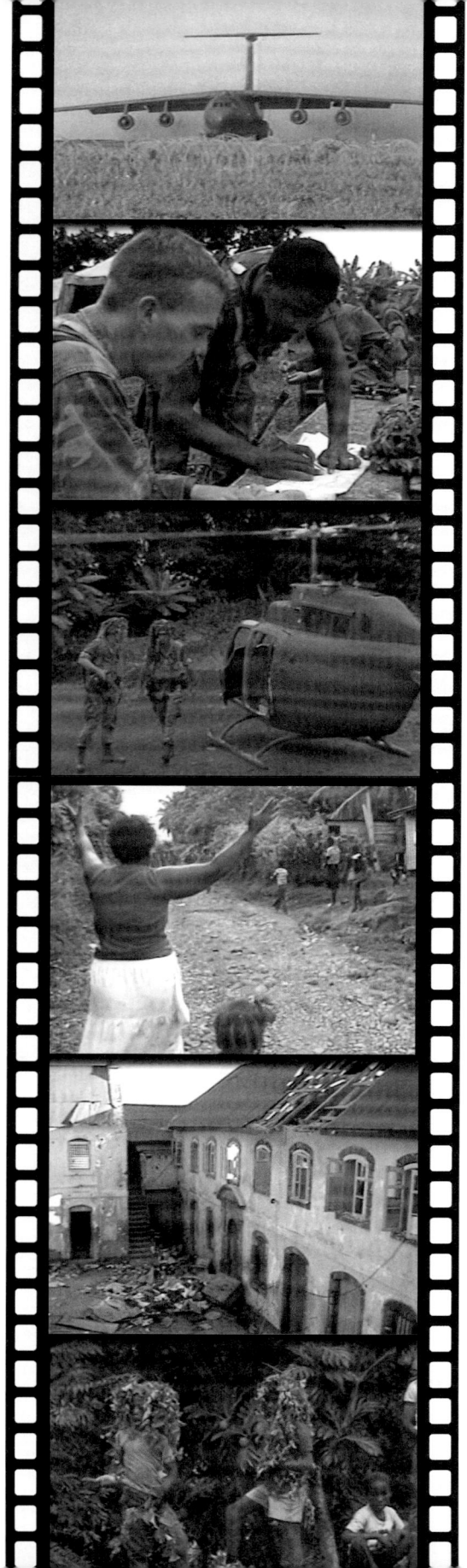

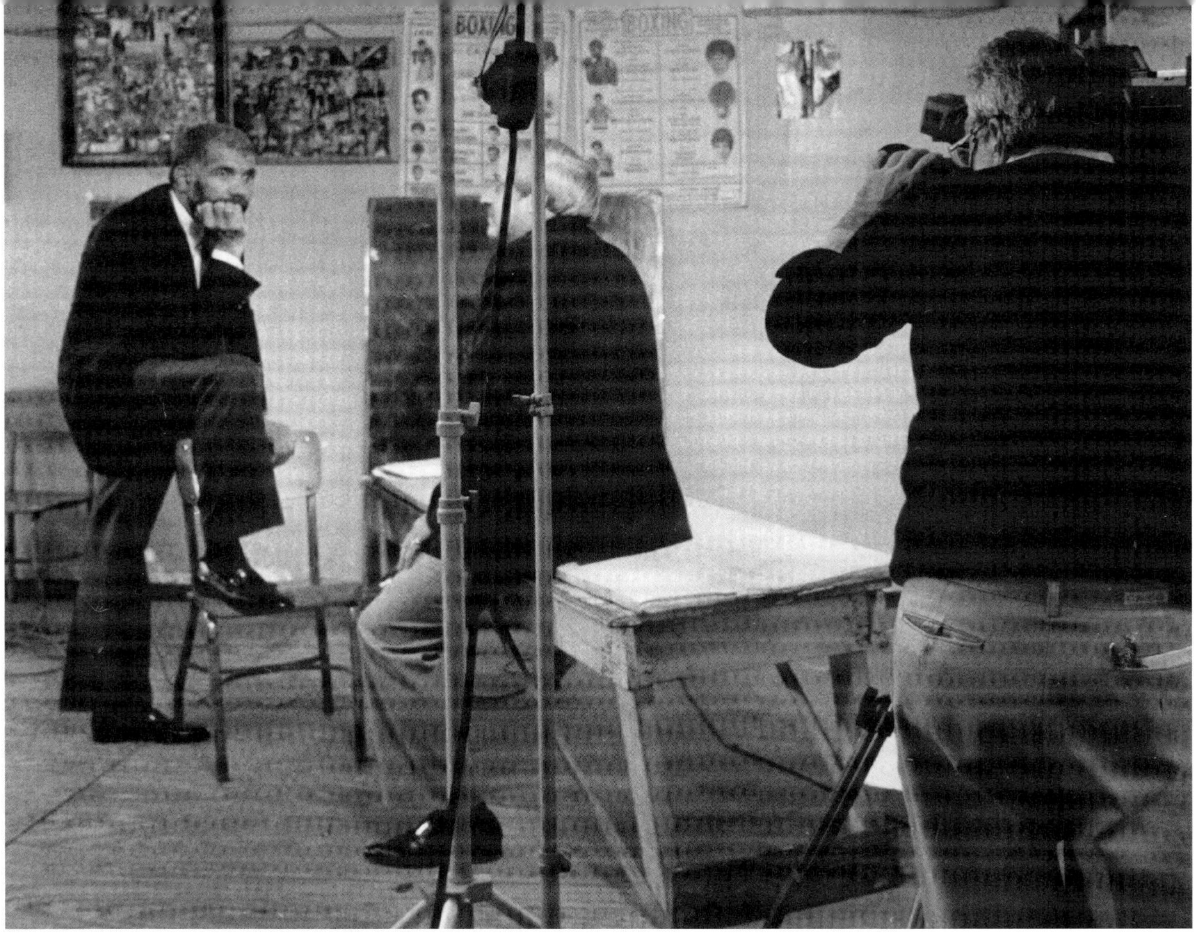

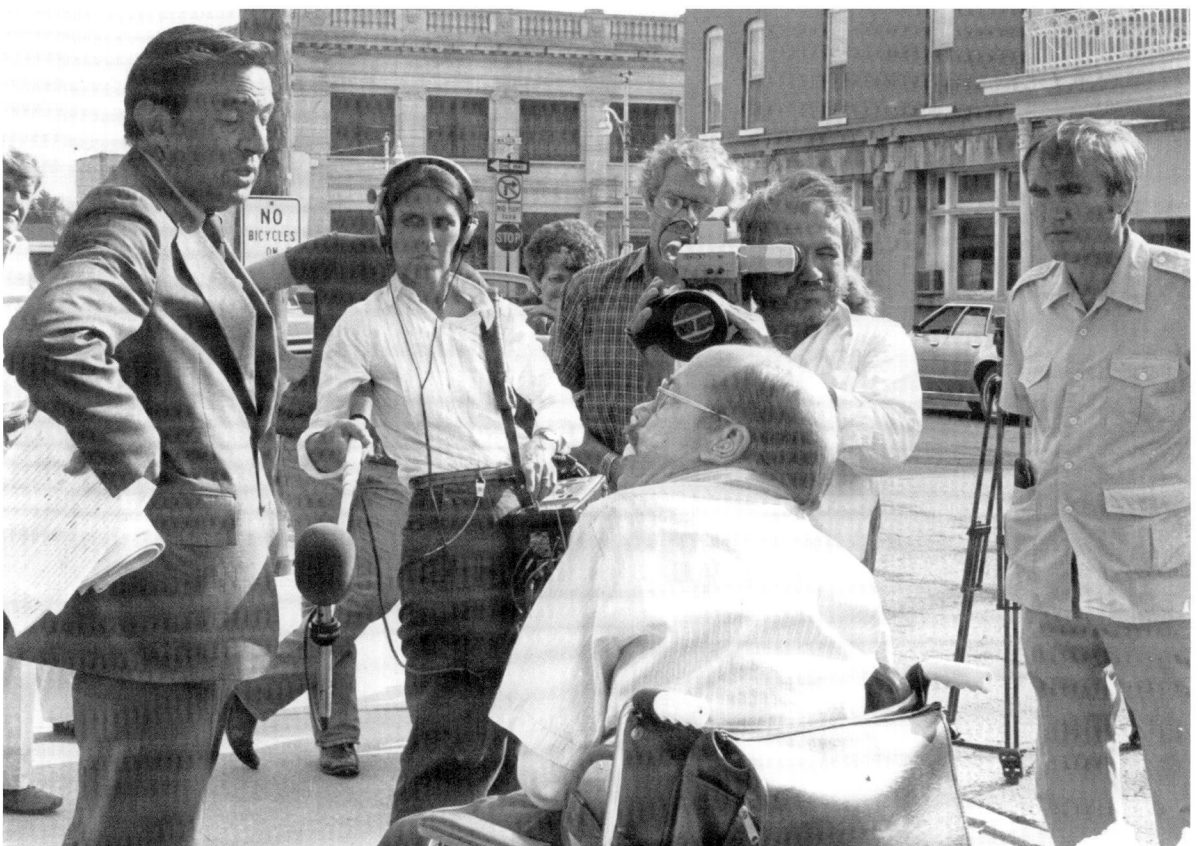

Del shoots a *60 Minutes* interview with Ed Bradley. *Photo by CBS/Dell Hall Collection.*

Mike Wallace challenges peeved locals in this *60 Minutes* interview. *Photo by CBS/Dell Hall Collection.*

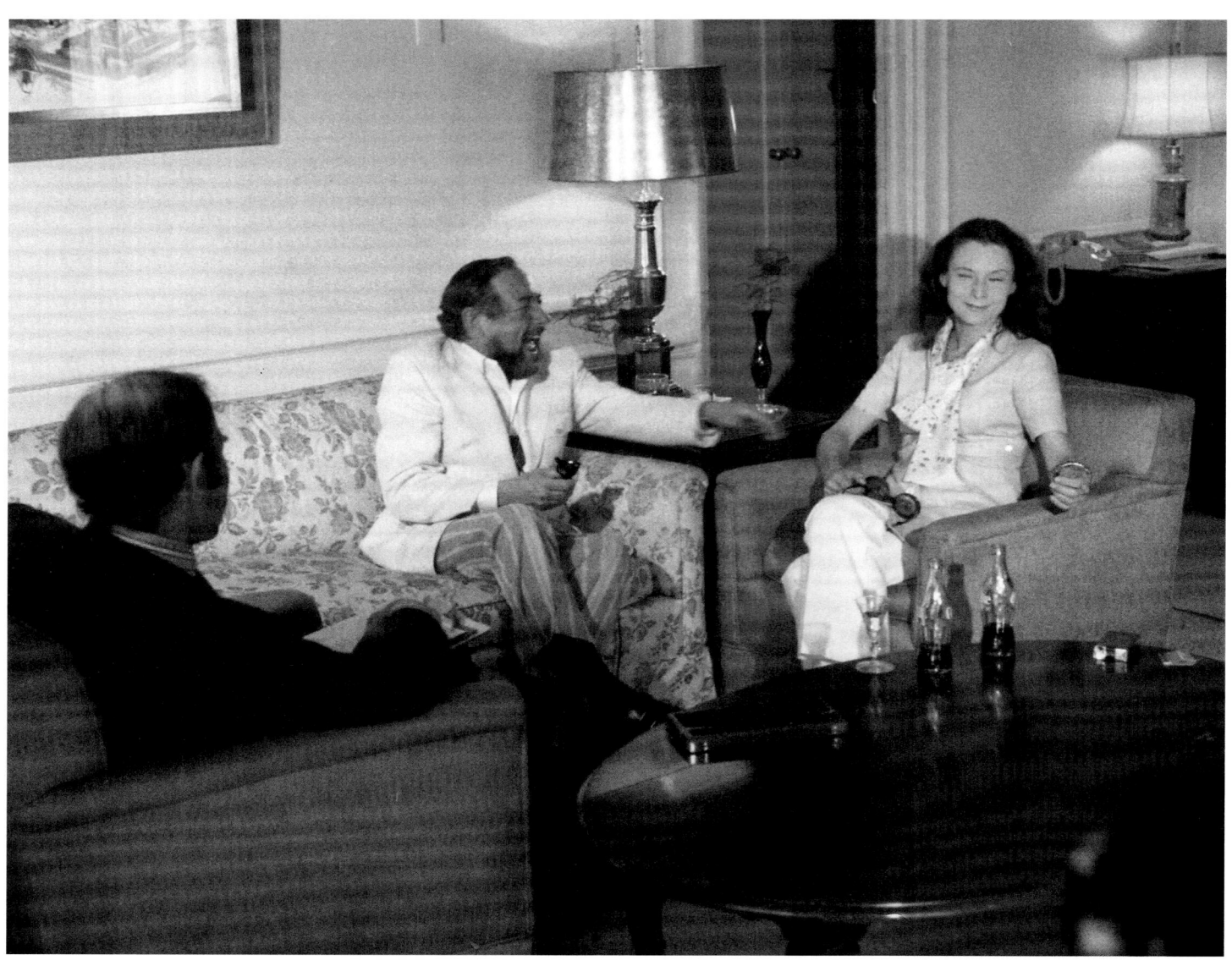

CBS correspondent Murray Fromson interviews a jovial Tennessee Williams and
friend. *Photo by Del Hall/CBS.*

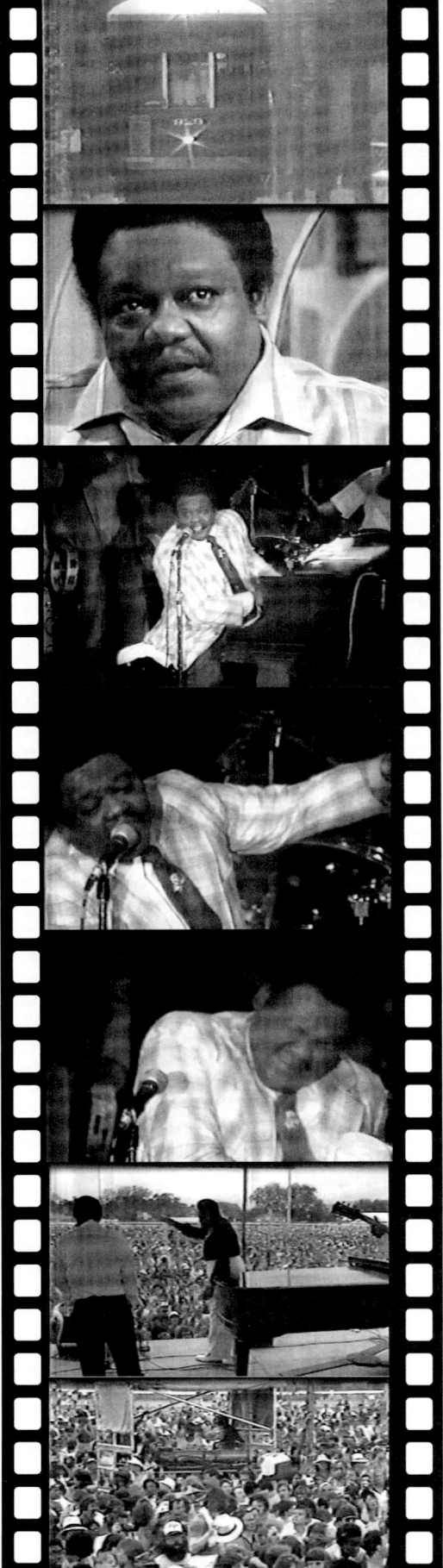

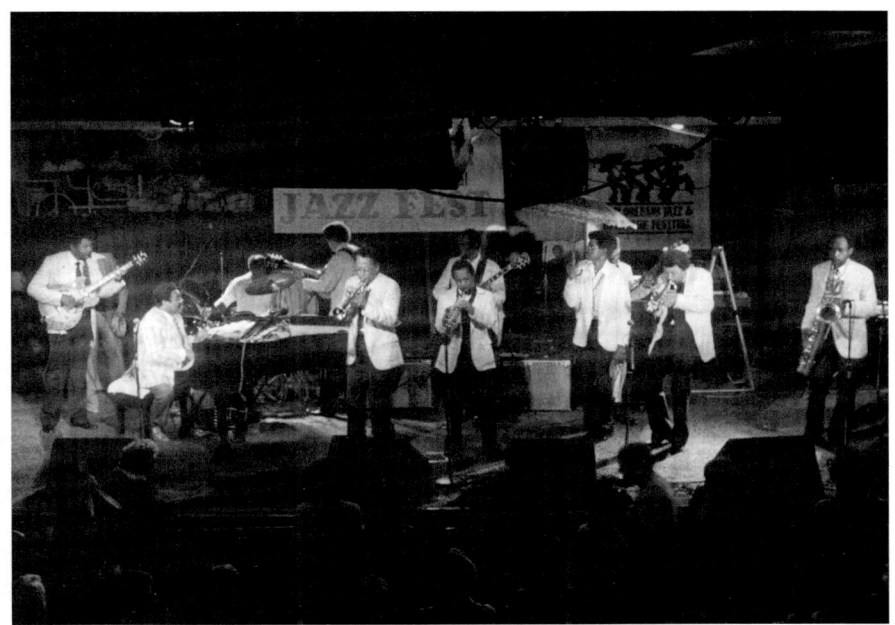

As good as it gets: covering Fats Domino on the steamboat *President* and throughout New Orleans for *CBS Sunday Morning*. *Del Hall Collection/Del Hall Video.*

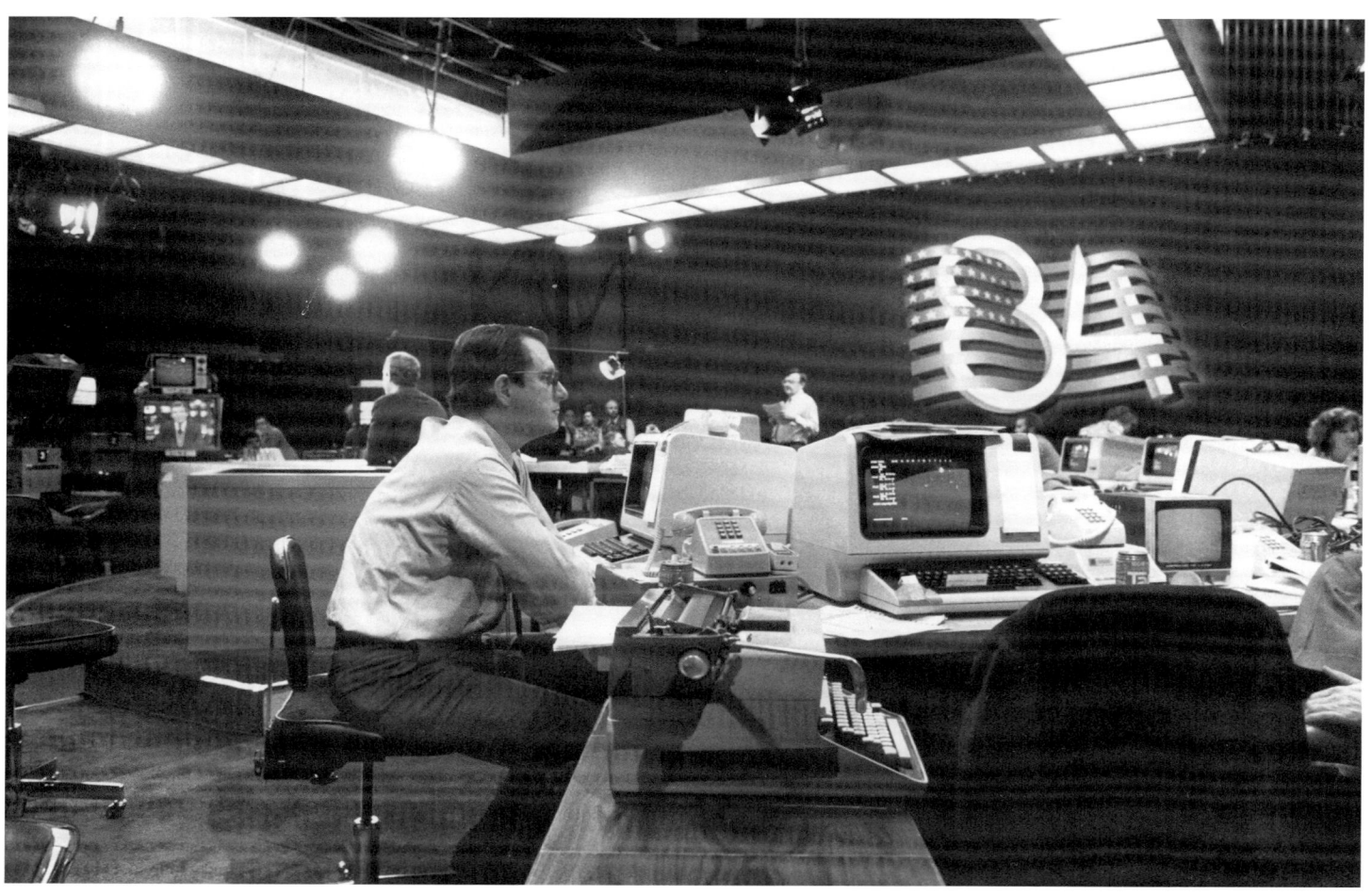

The CBS newsroom during the 1984 presidential election. *Del Hall Collection/ Del Hall Video.*

TAKE FIVE

Never Let It Rest, 1987–2014

THERE WAS ANOTHER reason why the Halls launched Del Hall Video. Technological advances had democratized both the capture and consumption ends of the videotape industry. That is, video cameras had gone up in quality and down in price—Sony's Betacam SP became the industry standard after 1986—and that opened up the market to more budding videographers, who produced more videography. At the consumption end, the VHS format had pushed Betamax off the shelves and cleared the way for mass-market videotape ubiquity. By the mid-1980s you could buy blank tapes by the dozen at K-Mart, record television programs by specialized codes, borrow tapes freely from the library, and rent movies from any 7–Eleven. You could even rent a VCR if you didn't already have one—or two. The only industry niche that remained specialized was the intermediary editing stage, where raw tape was passed through special machines, and talented eyes and skilled hands turned it into watchable programming. That's where Del Hall Video came in.

For a few sketchy years, DHV operated out of 727 North Hudson near the old Cabrini-Green public housing project, an experiment borne of the same progressive origins as Del's own circa-1940 lberville Projects in New Orleans. By the 1980s, that experiment had degenerated into social dysfunction so notorious that even the burglar alarm technician hesitated to visit the DHV office. But the locale kept the overhead low, and the Halls were able to land new assignments with corporate and entertainment clients. They appeared as a camera crew in the Gene Hackman/Tommy Lee Jones thriller *The Package,* and shot behind-the-scenes coverage of John Hughes's *Uncle Buck* and *Home Alone,* the 1990 comedy about a ten-year-old accidentally left behind as his family leaves for a vacation in Paris. The footage entailed Del's getting special permission from the Federal Aviation Administration to shoot on the tarmac at the nation's busiest airport, with jumbo jets taxiing and taking off all around him—"my wildest shot ever," he calls it, and that's saying a lot.

The Halls developed a competitive advantage in the cutthroat world of big-city production and editing houses. Firms competed fiercely for the lucrative "spot" market—producing high-end television commercials for blue-chip clients, a professional subculture in which both client and producer viewed themselves as exclusive and thought of their work as prestigious. When other, less glamorous work needed to be done—corporate training videos, shareholder meeting overviews, behind-the-scenes documentation—the parties viewed each other as second-class, and approached their task as obligatory drudgery. Needless to say, the programming that resulted was perfectly abysmal.

Drawing from his humble origins, his southern courtesy, and his entrepreneurship, Del thought, "Why not treat all clients as first-class? And that's what we did, and we did it well." This might mean documenting a Sara Lee or IBM shareholders meeting, shooting a motivational seminar by J. D. Power for his global marketing firm, making a Ritz-Carlton training video for chambermaids, or producing Chicago's *Come Out and Play* series for children. Regardless, everyone got A-list treatment, and every video came out more like a PBS documentary than the boring banality typical of such shoots.

The clients were flattered by the attentive customer relations and thrilled with the final products, and paid more for DHV's services. More earnings allowed for higher-quality production, which bolstered DHV's reputation and brought in more clients. More work meant more staff and necessitated a move out of Hudson Street. A savvy real estate agent found them a 12,500-square-foot warehouse in West Loop, less than two miles from the Loop, an area that he correctly predicted would boom in the coming years. In early 1988, the Halls bought 1240 West Jackson Boulevard for a song, and hired Krasnopolski and Weintraub Architects to design what Del describes as "the best, most complete, thought-out place in town" for television production. It featured sound stages and acoustics, editing rooms, intricate wiring, a rack room, and a vault, all separated by distinctive curving interior walls. "Business was so good," Ginger says of the 1990s, "we bought an additional camera and hired a second crew." They later added a second floor with two more editing rooms, as well as a second-floor outdoor deck—"for Friday hot dogs."

One of their first major corporate assignments came from the Hyatt hotel chain. The human resources department had recently hired DeeGee Productions, a new company formed by Deborah Del Prete and Gigi Pritzker, to produce a monthly video newsletter for its worldwide employees. Gigi, the Chicago partner, subcontracted DHV to shoot and edit the videos. Hers was no ordinary midwestern family; the Pritzkers own Hyatt and rank as one of the premier benefactors of civic and social projects in Chicago. No matter: Gigi had to interview competitively with Hyatt to win the job. Gigi today is a major motion picture producer and founder of OddLot Entertainment, and remains a close friend. "Gigi tells me today she learned a lot from me in those days. I think she's pulling my leg, but it feels good," says Del. When Gigi married Michael Pucker in 1997, the Halls volunteered to shoot the outdoor wedding at the family's Libertyville Farm. Upon editing his footage the next day, Del came to realize a remarkable coincidence: one of the wedding guests was none other than Raquel "Rocky" Matus, his childhood playmate from Coliseum Square in the 1930s and his high school date from the 1950s. The moment reminded him of how far they all had come from New Orleans days.

With fifteen employees, Del and Ginger allocated their own talents judiciously. Del oversaw DHV's hardware and deliverables, while Ginger managed human resources, record keeping, and finances, which consistently ranged around $2.5 million per year. Their key piece of equipment—what attracted the best employees and won the biggest contracts—was a pair of state-of-the-art Avid nonlinear computerized editing machines. Avids converted analog media, either film or videotape, to millions of pixelated frames associated with digital sound, and enabled the operator to place pointers at will (hence "nonlinear") at which cuts, pastes, fades, dissolves, slow-motions, and other editing interventions would be made. The Avid would then read this "editing decision list" without actually tampering with the source data—and yield a superior final product in a fraction of the time required for physical videotape or film editing. Introduced in 1987, Avid helped change television and movies from the long scenes and slow pace of prior decades to the MTV-inspired frenetic and spasmodic sequencing of today, in which the editing is nearly as influential to the viewer experience as the acting and content. Having been a pioneer in the transition from still photography to television news, from black-and-white to color, and from film to videotape, Del was now at the forefront of the move from tape-to-tape linear editing to tape-to-digital nonlinear editing. He became an expert in Avid and a leader of its user group, and DHV became a beta test site for new Avid products. Ginger, for her part, became the first-ever woman to head the local branch of the International Teleproduction Society.

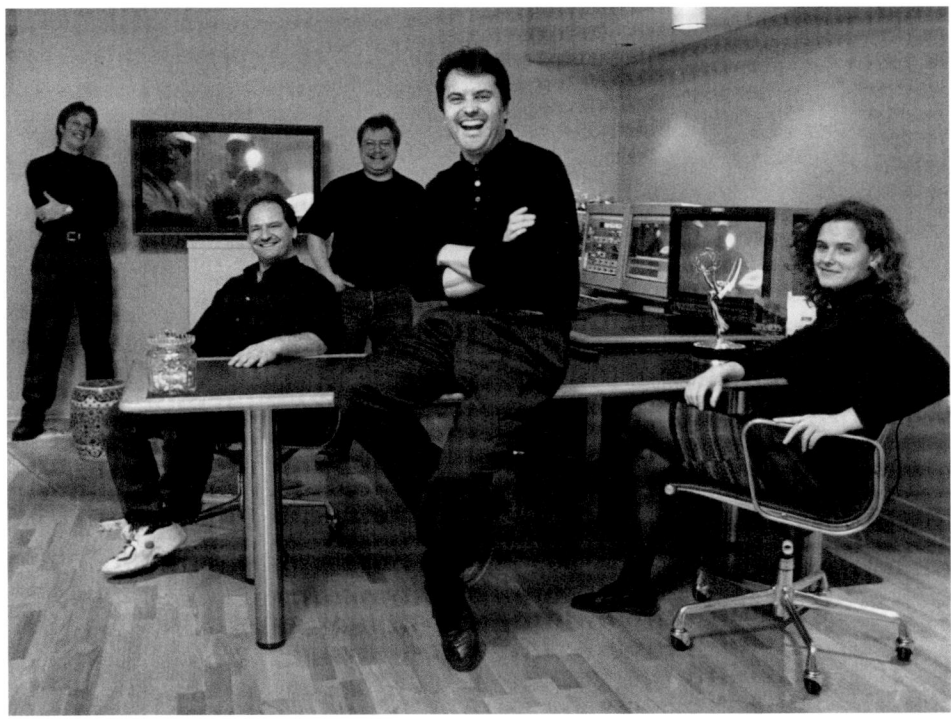

Del Hall Video staff with their Avid nonlinear computer editing tools, which revolutionized video production. *Del Hall Collection/Del Hall Video.*

Chicago's Steppenwolf Theatre Company hired the Halls to shoot film-style scenes of selected plays and rehearsals. They got to know cofounder Gary Sinise and interviewed all the actors, including the enigmatic John Malkovich. (The experience recalled something their longtime friend Bernie Sahlins, founder of the Second City comedy troupe, said in response to a question about what actors thought of you. "You don't," Sahlins replied. "They're actors.") Later work with Steppenwolf, including a commemorative video for the company's twenty-fifth anniversary and a full-cast *Vanity Fair* shoot by Annie Leibovitz, enabled the Halls to collaborate with cofounders Terry Kinney, Jeff Perry, and Sinise, and actors Joan Allen, John Mahoney, and Laurie Metcalf.

With two machines made available to them at wholesale prices before they debuted on the retail marketplace, DHV hardly had to advertise to seek business; it came to them, from the likes of IBM, Ford, the Chicago Board Options Exchange, and Hollywood. When *The Fugitive* came to town in 1993, its makers rented DHV's Avid and used it to transfer the original film reel to digital video and proceeded to edit it into the blockbuster it became. They did the same for Oliver Stone's *Natural Born Killers* in 1994, where at the Jackson Boulevard office a courier would deposit daily packages labeled "NBK," so as not to arouse curiosity. Del also shot footage of the riot scene at the Stateville Correctional Center, including Oliver Stone and Tommy Lee Jones interacting with inmates at the maximum-security prison.

Interest in behind-the-scenes footage, now a standard feature on DVDs, extended to the theatrical world as well.

Del and Ginger made sure they themselves handled as much of the field camera work as possible. When a paying customer asked them to cover an event they fancied in a city they loved—Mardi Gras in New Orleans—they piled their equipment in a van (plus a tuxedo with tails and a ballgown) and drove down the frigid Mississippi Valley to the balmy climes of the midwinter feast. Their customer was the century-old Rex Organization, the most civic-minded (*Pro bono publico* is its motto) of New Orleans's exclusive old-line Mardi Gras krewes. For years Rex had hired a local outfit to record its majestic parade, and rarely was His Majesty pleased with the results. Rex's Official Poet Laureate, the erudite Phil Johnson of WWL-TV, had a better idea: why not hire his old chum, Emmy award–winning cameraman and New Orleans native Del Hall? Thus Del became Rex's Official Documentarian (famed local meteorologist Nash Roberts, incidentally, was Official Weatherman). The Halls hired two additional cameramen to ensure optimal coverage of the parade and affiliated formalities.

One of the most important events was the initial public introduction of the newly selected king of the krewe—that is, Rex himself. While Ginger helped cover that moment, one of the lieutenants pulled her aside and divulged to her, "Young woman, do you realize the significance? In the entire history of the Rex Organization, we have never had a woman present at the Meet the King event." Ginger asked him if women would ever be allowed into Rex. He pondered a moment. "We'd probably let in blacks before women."

Then there was the parade. One year, Del and Ginger set up their cameras early on Fat Tuesday morning at Carnival's ground zero: the Pickwick Club at Canal and St. Charles, where vast throngs anticipated a full day's worth of the Greatest Free Show on Earth. First came Pete Fountain's Half-Fast Walking Club, following by other bands and walking clubs. Finally, the Krewe of Zulu arrived, its African American members decked out in outlandish Afro wigs, grass skirts, and blackface—the sort of thing that could end a career elsewhere, but make a career in New Orleans. As one particular float paused for its members to throw beads to the thousands of revelers, Ginger heard a distant call above the din: "DEL HALLLLLLLLL! DEL HALLLLLLLLL!" They squinted through the morning light to make out a disguised face. "IT'S ED BRAAAADLEY!" Ed Bradley? From *60 Minutes?* In blackface and grass skirt? Del and Ginger wanted proof. "SHOW US YOUR EARRING!" they shouted back, laughing in disbelief. Bradley lifted his raincloud Afro wig and showed his famous earring, a rarity on network news at that time. "HAPPY MARDI GRAS!" It was one of those precious moments, and better yet, the Halls had something to mark it—a golden Zulu coconut, which any New Orleanian will tell you is the most treasured of Carnival throws. The throwing of coconuts had in recent years incurred injuries in the crowd, so Bradley handed it to a policeman and it worked its way to Del and Ginger. New Orleans is the one place on earth where someone like Ed Bradley could dress in vaudevillian blackface, with neither professional nor social consequences—and where the phrase "Zulu coconut lawsuit" not only makes perfect sense, but

comes up in everyday conversation. A few weeks later, Del left a message with Bradley's secretary in the CBS New York office and mentioned seeing him at the Zulu parade in New Orleans. "Oh my God," the secretary sighed, as if she had been needing to tell her story but could not find a trusted ear. "You know, it was ME who had to go out and buy Ed his panty hose! Black panty hose! What exactly are you people doing down there?!"

After Zulu came the Rex and Comus parades, followed by the elegant evening balls and the culminating "Meeting of the Courts of Rex and Comus," an only-in-New-Orleans ritual that is a living relic of nineteenth-century patrician pageantry. The extra cameraman whom they had contracted to help cover the late-night regal rendezvous apparently had a little too much pageantry himself because he never showed up, forcing Del to hire at the last minute an eager if awkward young videographer. They outfitted the hapless commoner in comically oversized tails and sent him out among the aristocracy as they danced to "If Ever I Cease to Love"—played dozens and dozens of times. New Orleanians never tire of that zany old chestnut, but apparently Oversized Tails did, because after thirty or forty minutes, he seemed to have wandered out of the Rex Ball and into the neighboring Comus Ball, whose membership is publically unidentified and whose masked King of Comus is the best-kept secret of Carnival. An attentive captain of Comus spotted Oversized Tails and hustled the young rogue out of the exclusive gathering. Del, meanwhile, came searching for his wayward underling, only to find himself accidentally invading the rarified kingdom. The beleaguered Comus captain intercepted Del and ejected him as well. Rex and Comus treat each other with the utmost of protocol and deference, so the specter of a Rex affiliate invading the sanctity of Comus territory before the Meeting of the Courts represented something of a monarchical crisis. To atone for his transgression, Del had to write a formal apology to the King of Comus, a literary act of contrition in which he was fortunately assisted by his old friend, Rex poet laureate Phil Johnson. New Orleans is a world unto itself: not even in lands with real kings would someone be forced to scribe an apology for an accidental invasion.

The Halls produced movie-quality multicamera coverage for Rex throughout the late 1980s to early 1990s, an era that proved to be tumultuous in the history of New Orleans Mardi Gras. An anti-discrimination ordinance for krewes that paraded, passed by a majority-black City Council and aimed explicitly at the old-line organizations, divided public sentiment along racial lines and brought animus to the midwinter feast. Comus insisted on principle it was a private organization with a right of association beyond government interference, and withdrew in protest permanently after the 1991 Mardi Gras. Rex, meanwhile, agreed to admit members regardless of race or creed and continued to parade, while all krewes retained the ability to segregate by gender. The lieutenant who had confided in Ginger turned out to be right: the Krewe of Rex would admit blacks before it would women.

Imaginary kings and queens reign in New Orleans; in the rest of America, celebrities are royalty, and the Halls covered them as well. One time they interviewed Michael Jordan when he was at the brink of his fame, and found him to be modest and gentlemanly but also guarded and savvy. (Del chuckles that they might have burned down Jordan's Chicago mansion had they not realized, to their horror, that their intense lighting had melted a plastic doorframe. "Aw, don't worry about it," Jordan assured them.) Another time they did a feature on the Dalai Lama, who was as charming and warm in person as his public persona suggests. At one point Ginger suggested they move a piano to set up the shot, and when she and Del struggled with it, the Nobel Peace Prize–winning head of state of Central Tibet did not hesitate to come over and help, laughing heartily as he pushed. Del was also delighted to see that His Holiness shared his penchant for camera equipment, and even peered through the lens to approve the shot.

In another assignment, the Halls did an interview with Oprah Winfrey at her nearby Harpo Productions studio. Already among the most powerful women in the nation, Winfrey shared with them a humbling but ultimately droll story of her longtime friendship with broadcaster Gayle

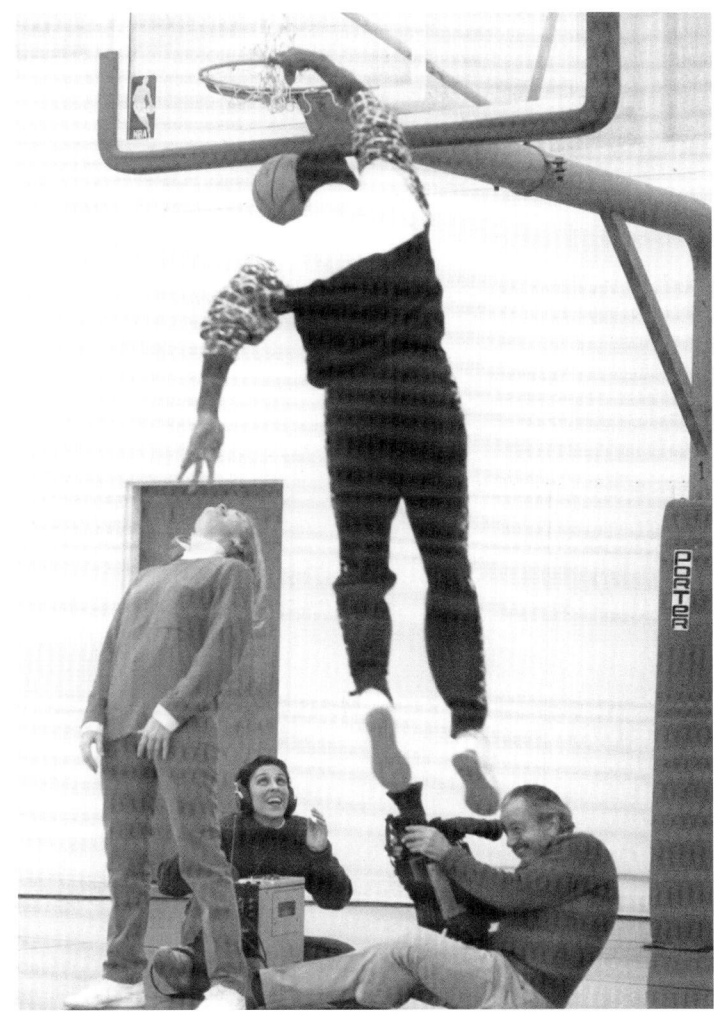

Michael Jordan demonstrating a slam dunk for *60 Minutes*'s Diane Sawyer. *Del Hall Collection/Del Hall Video.*

King. When Winfrey first became famous and her income skyrocketed, she sensed her invitations to King to join her on various outings were becoming disproportionately onerous on King's budget. With the best of intentions, Winfrey decided to Fed-Ex her friend a surprise check for a million dollars, figuring this would neutralize any fiscal imbalances. Instead, Winfrey heard back nothing from King, day after day, and came to fear that her well-intended offering might have been more offensive than munificent. She finally decided to call King and discreetly inquire if she had received the package. "Oh yes," King replied cheerfully. "But I've been so busy I haven't opened it yet!"

Opportunities begot opportunities. One came when the Halls filmed a documentary for Kurtis Productions about McDonald's restaurants, which had them roaming around America, Kuralt-style, tracking down old McDonald's, odd McDonald's, even an Amish McDonald's with a horse-and-buggy drive-through. Owner Bill Kurtis loved the results, and hired DHV to edit his well-known A&E *Investigative Reports* series, which became steady high-profile work for years. It also became grounds for a long-standing friendship with Kurtis and his partner Donna LaPietra, whom they also knew vis-à-vis her board of directors activity with Steppenwolf Theater. Del and Bill have much in common, with careers dating back to the early days of television and similar experiences at, among other moments, the 1968 Chicago convention. In a recent conversation, the two contemplated the history they witnessed across half a century. "We always had the best seat in the house," Bill summed up.

The Internet abetted DHV's business, and the Halls made use of it for promotion, communications, and data moving, as the World Wide Web emerged from its circa-1992 infancy to "Web 1.0" later in the 1990s and "Web 2.0" in the 2000s. The introduction of the digital video camera also helped, as it eliminated the need to digitize magnetic videotape before nonlinearly editing it in Avid. What troubled DHV's waters, however, was the rise of popular off-the-shelf nonlinear editing software packages undercutting Avid's advantage. Del had sensed as far back as 1990 that Avid, which ran on an Apple Macintosh II integrated into its own dedicated hardware and proprietary editing software, might be sowing the seeds for its own decline. "Aren't you guys worried that Apple might steal it?" Del asked the makers at a user-group meeting. Nah, came the response; Apple just sees it as a way to sell more Macs.

In fact, other companies were keenly vying for the editing market, particularly since digital video cameras had rendered unnecessary the clunky hardware to convert tape to pixels. In the late 1990s, Macromedia, Inc., released a program called Final Cut, which Apple acquired a few years later and has upgraded ever since. Running on a desktop Mac, with a digital video camera on one side and an external hard drive on the other, Final Cut Pro decentralized and democratized nonlinear editing, and radically reduced the cost of entry into the production marketplace. By the mid-2000s, just about any ambitious techie with a creative flair, who in the past might have knocked on DHV's door seeking a job, was instead buying his or her own equipment, setting up space in a garage, and competing with the likes of DHV. Willing to work cheap and with practically no overhead, the young entrepreneurs were able to charge one-third to one-sixth of what a firm like DHV might have bid. The firm still won the high-end contracts, and benefited additionally from its artist skills and reputation, as evidenced by a slew of local Emmy and Clio awards. But Del's prescience told him that the industry as he and Ginger knew it had peaked, and it was becoming harder to find good employees.

One August, Del took a brief trip down to New Orleans to visit friends and family. He stayed at the Royal Sonesta, across Bourbon Street from his old hangout, Larry Lamarca's long-gone Gunga Den, and caught up with old friends Phil Johnson from WWL and Mike Lala at his meticulously renovated Olde N'Awlins Cookery. Del's mother Ella had died in 2000, and all the aunts, uncles, and grandparents were now deceased, but there were children and grandchildren to visit, as well as his sister Sharon and her family. As the week wore on, a minor news item—the formation of a tropical storm in the Atlantic—came increasingly into focus. The system earned the name Katrina, struck near Miami, and gathered strength from a loop current of warm water as it entered the Gulf of Mexico. Forecast models at first had it striking the Florida panhandle, well east of New Orleans. But Del, who experienced firsthand the 1947 hurricane and Betsy in 1965, had a bad feeling about this one. "I was surprised at how seriously I took it," he recalls. Each subsequent prediction validated his concern, as the cone of uncertainty nudged westward—to Mobile, Biloxi, and finally New Orleans itself, where the cone tightened and the certainty increased. It was now Saturday, August 27, 2005, and the city was about to get mandatory evacuation orders. "There was a part of me," Del confides, "that was half-way tempted to stay." He crossed paths with Anderson Cooper in the French Quarter, saw the film crews doing stories, and wanted to get to work. The desire to bear witness and document remained strong, even at age 70. What changed his mind was reports of body bags being shipped in. Reluctantly he made arrangements to leave, checking in with family members in Metairie to ensure their safety. He departed on Sunday on one of the last planes out of pre-Katrina New Orleans. Lofting into the air, he was stunned to see every lane of every highway, both outgoing and incoming, packed bumper to bumper with vehicles: a million people, including his own blood, fleeing a metropolis on what some were predicting might be its last day. "As I looked out the window," he says, "I remember thinking, New Orleans will never be the same again. Just like in Washington during the King riots, the smoke rising. Never again the same."

At first, New Orleans appeared to withstand Katrina's wind and surge. What went all but undetected by the national news media, however, was a series of levee breaches, each of which allowed the swollen tide to pour into the city's sunken basins. What had started as a windy disaster turned into a watery catastrophe. Most of Del's hometown, and all his childhood spaces—Na-Ma's flat, Dominique You's tomb, Iberville, Jesuit, Pops's grave—were deeply inundated with filthy sea water. By week's end, Del and Ginger had seventeen New Orleans evacuees plus a dog staying in their Chicago apartment.

The Katrina tragedy reconnected Del with his New Orleans family and gave him a renewed sense of appreciation of how much he owed his birth city. Sadly, it also claimed the life of a beloved friend: Mike Lala, the endearingly eccentric polymath who rescued the famous Oswald footage, died of a heart attack while struggling to clean up his French Quarter restaurant in the storm's sweltering aftermath. Del served as executor of Lala's estate, and attending to that obligation over the next year, as New Orleans began its slow

path to recovery, gave him a chance to renew old friendships, including the one with the city itself.

One day in 2006, one of DHV's best editors announced he was leaving to start off on his own. Who could blame him: Chicago's big production houses were downsizing left and right, while microenterprises were multiplying by the score. In days past, Del and Ginger were always able to replace good employees with better ones; now they struggled to replace them at all. DHV was still getting contracts, but the terrain ahead, Del realized, was not promising. It was time to close. "Del was the first to see it," says Ginger, "and the first one out, while there was still something to salvage." DHV would remain open until each employee found another job. One by one they did, and when the last bid farewell, the Halls hired an auctioneer to sell off their equipment and an agent to sell the building.

Their timing was impeccable: firms overseas paid top dollar for their $1.5 million worth of equipment—the benefit of quitting at the right time—and their 18,750-square-foot lot in West Loop sold for a princely sum to an eager townhouse developer. The rationality and certainty of the decision made closing anything but a bittersweet moment; Ginger calls it a "joyous occasion. . . . We never looked back."

An active and productive semi-retirement helped soften the transition. Among other projects, the Halls documented the creation of the Pritzker-funded Millennium Park, including interviews with Frank Gehry and other designers and artists, and turned the video into a documentary that was projected on a giant screen on opening night and continues to play in the visitors' center today. They are also patrons of civic affairs and the arts, and remain involved with institutions such as the Lyric Opera, where they make behind-the-scenes documentaries to enlighten the board of directors. They travel whenever possible, nowhere with such relish as to New Orleans, which, largely recovered from and in many ways improved since the 2005 deluge, has become a second home of sorts.

Their first home, a tasteful townhouse near Lincoln Park in Chicago, is replete with artifacts of Del's life. Along the walls are his photographs of John F. Kennedy in New Orleans and villagers in Vietnam, of Bourbon Street burlesque and Rex aristocracy, of stoop-sitters and second-liners on the streets of his youth. On the shelves are autographs from Sony president Akio Morita, Walter Cronkite, and all of the Chicago Seven, along with a bust of Lenin and a Red Army belt buckle, pottery from Wounded Knee, and crafts from Hong Kong, Thailand, Laos, and the Philippines. His gleaming 1974 Emmy Award stands near the Vatican II plaque hand-chiseled out of a Roman quarry, and a wooden tag of the ill-fated number 22, which also appears on the Halls' license plate. Perhaps most cherished of all is the original address number "129" taken from the now-demolished antebellum building on South Rampart—his first home and the home of Na-Ma, his cheerful and farsighted grandmother, who bought him the two cameras that would launch him on a career in which he would pioneer a new profession and witness American history.

Whereas the past is commemorated in the parlor, upstairs is all about the future. Not one to stew in sentiment or be left behind by technology, Del now works on three iMac desktop workstations with widescreen monitors plus all the latest digital accouterments, documenting his latest photographs, preparing for gallery shows and lectures, and using the latest version of Final Cut Pro.

Never let it rest, the nuns at St. Joseph drilled him seventy years ago. *'Til your good is better, and your better's best.*

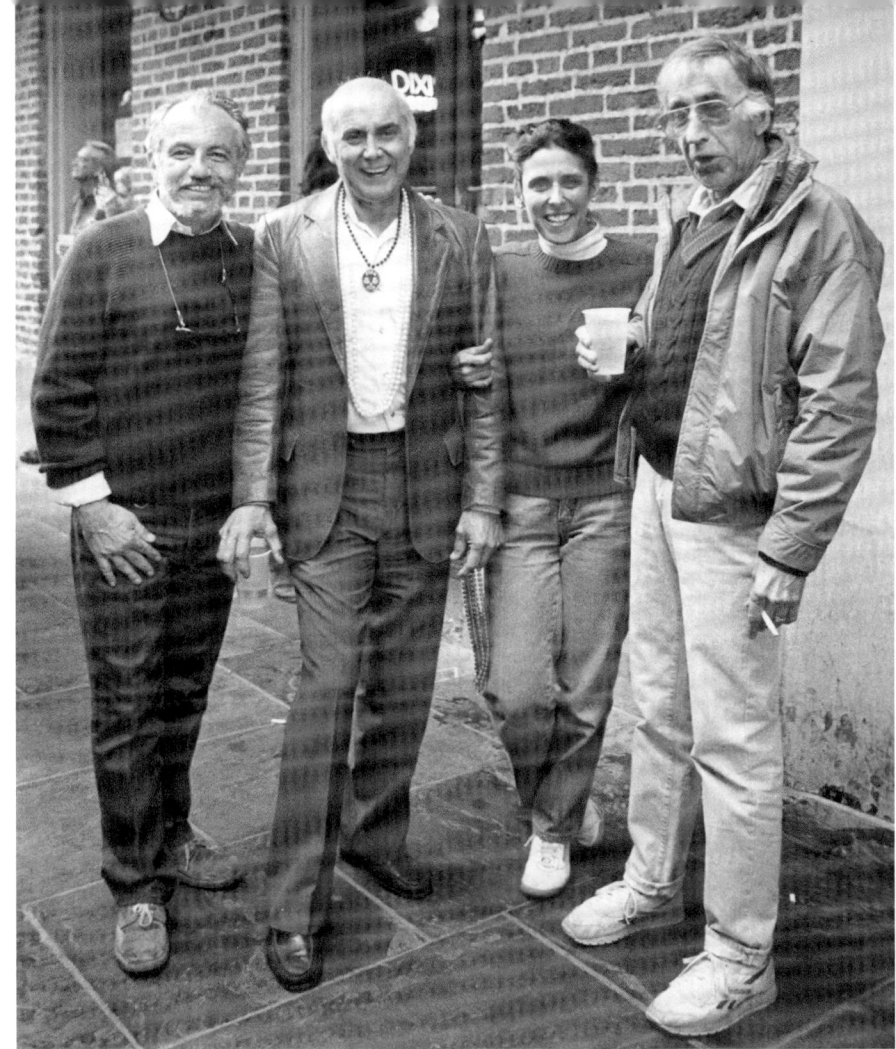

Del and Ginger with friends Mike Lala (second from left) and Jim Tolhurst (right). *Del Hall Collection/Del Hall Video.*

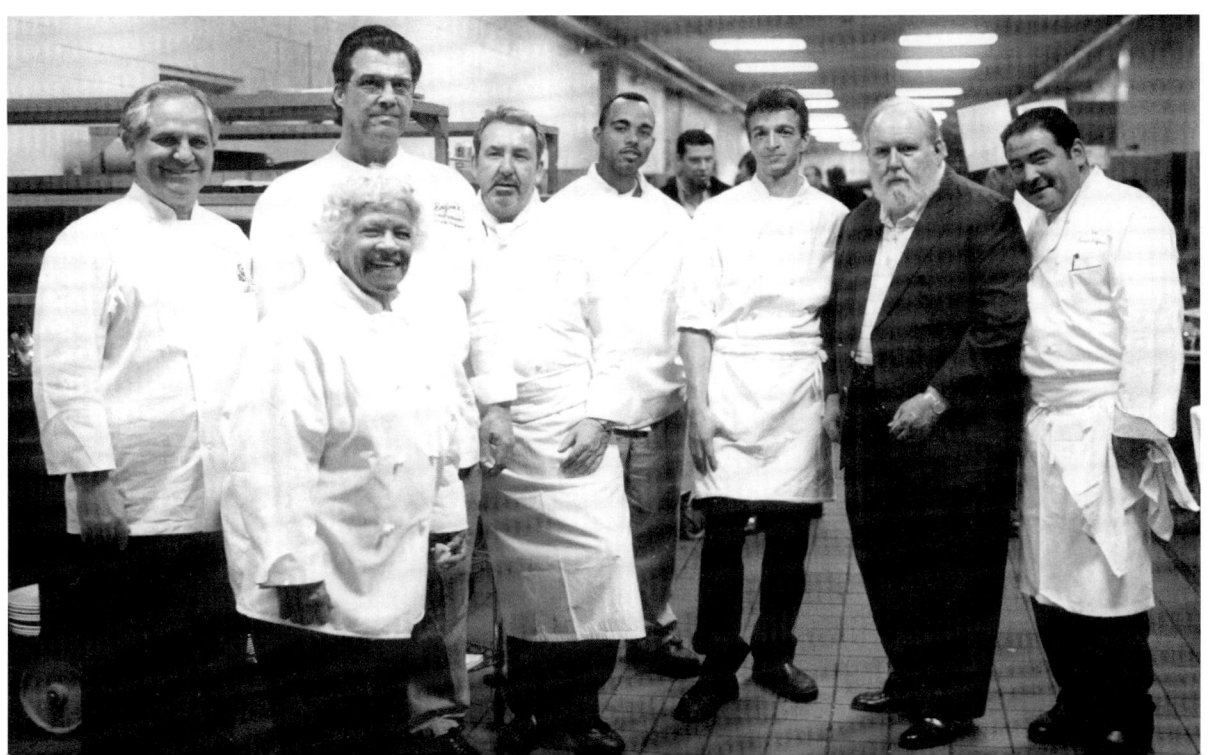

A retired Phil Johnson (in suit) poses with New Orleans chefs John Folse, Leah Chase, Emeril Lagasse, and others at the Chefs' Charity for Children. *Del Hall Collection/Del Hall Video.*

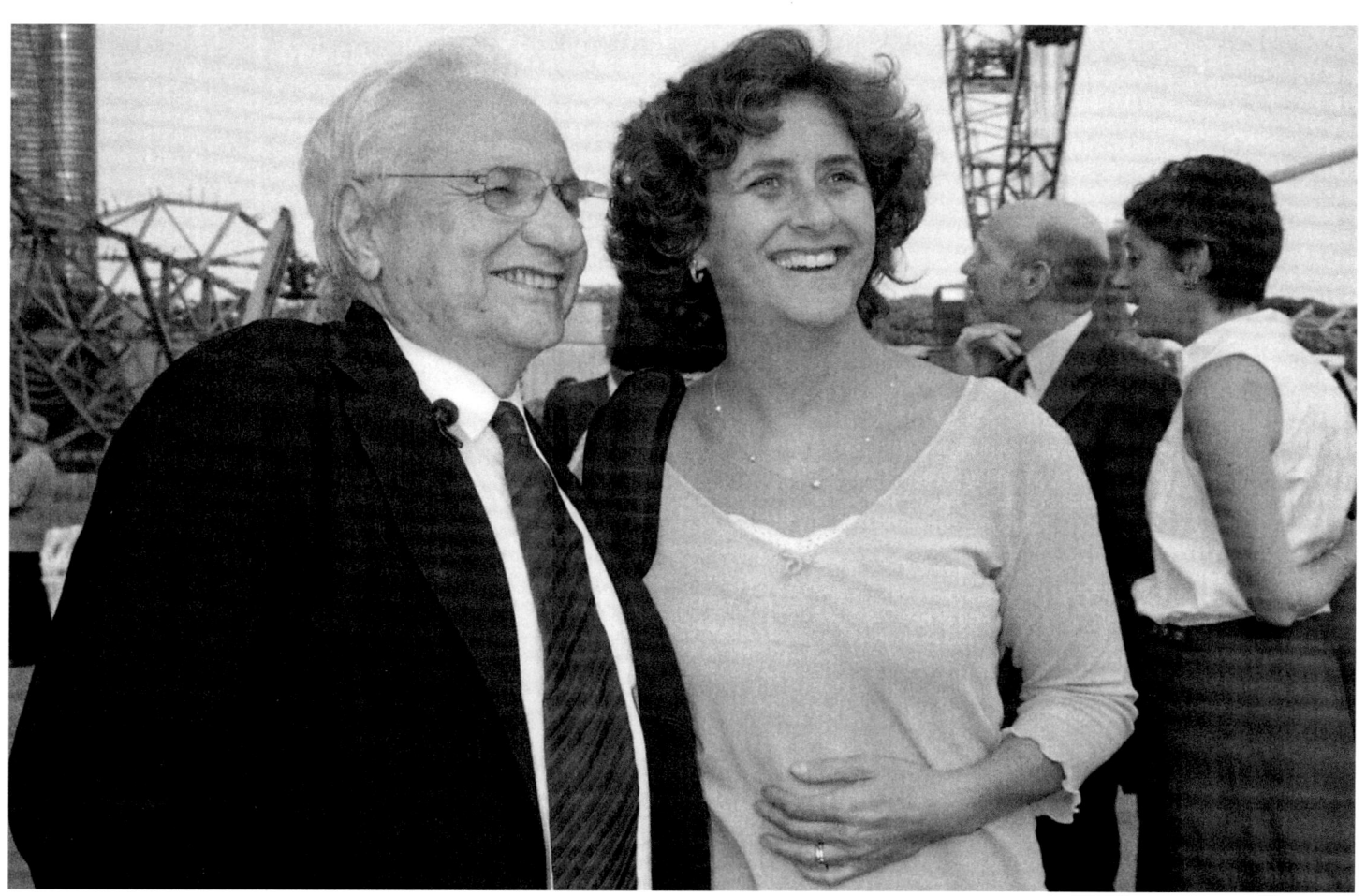

Millennium Park architect Frank Gehry
and producer Gigi Pritzker. *Del Hall Col-
lection/Del Hall Video.*

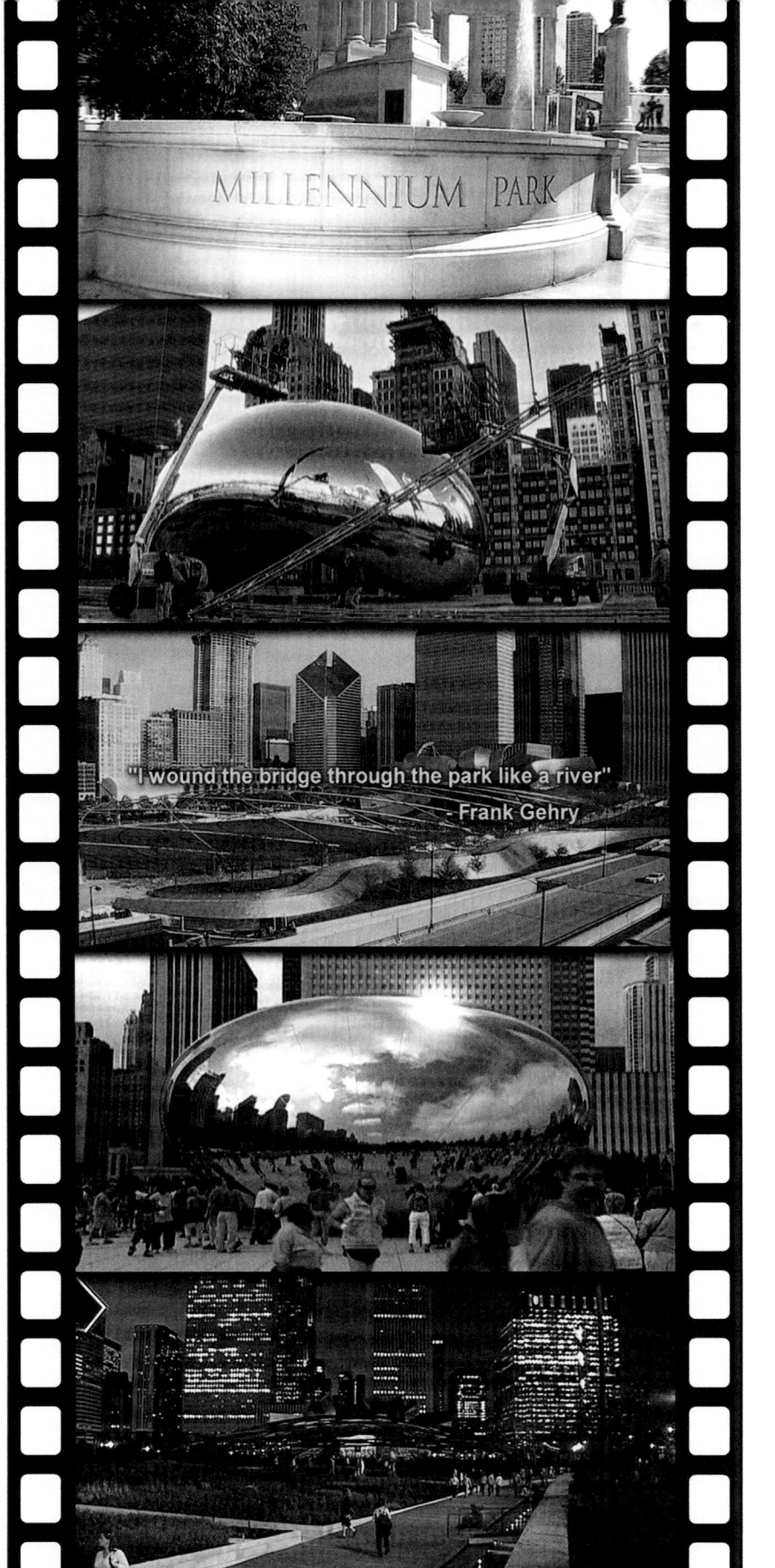

Frames from Del Hall Video's *Millennium Park* production, which was shown at the Chicago park's opening night. *Del Hall Collection/Del Hall Video.*

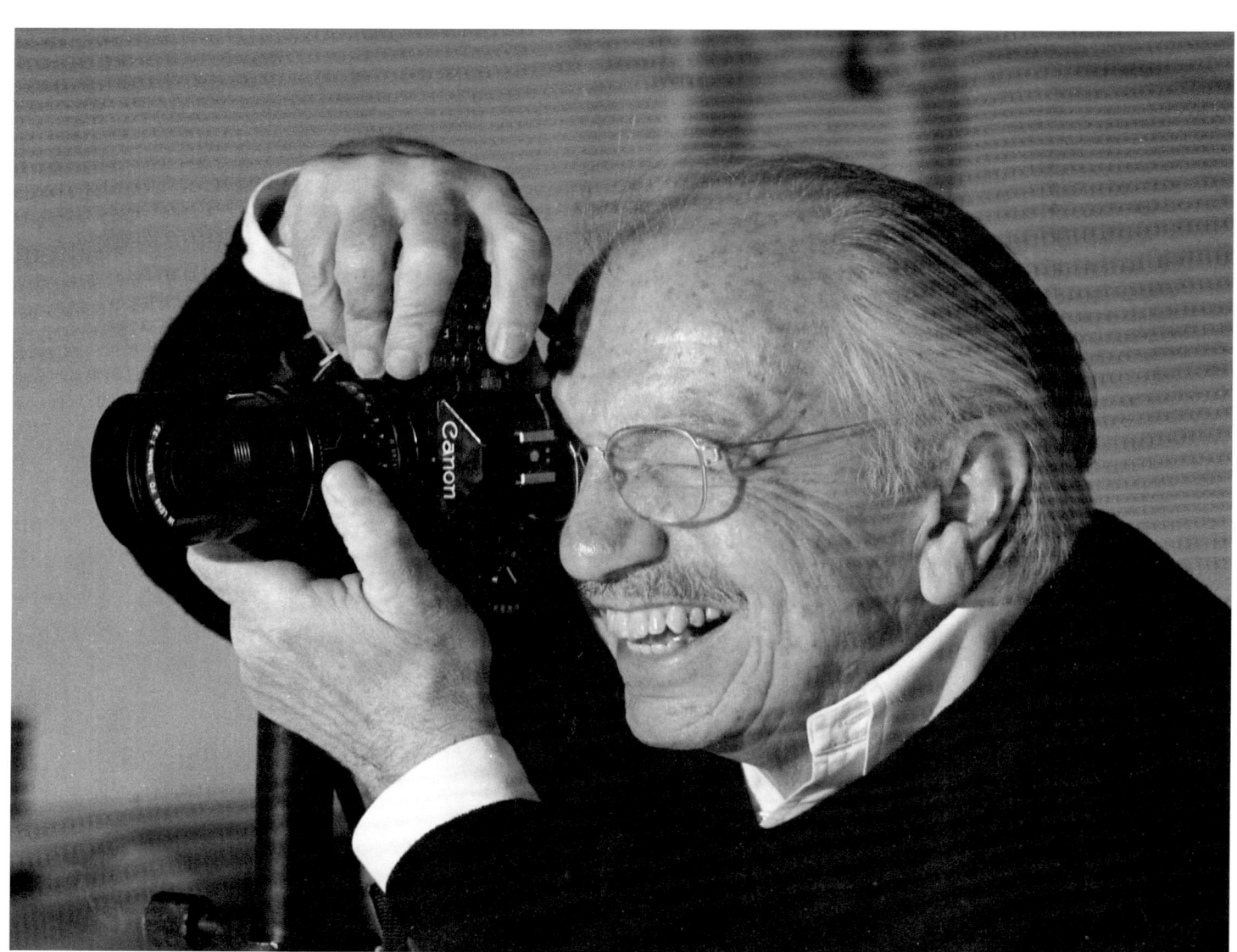

NOTES

TAKE ONE: *South Rampart Street Blues, 1935–1959*

1. These neighborhood vignettes are drawn from various sources in the author's previous research, as well as the memories of Lawrence Batiste, who was born at 1226 Gravier in the late 1930s, as told to Fred Kasten, 2013 Satchmo Summerfest Seminars, August 3, 2013, Old U.S. Mint, New Orleans, attended by author.

2. This was the chaotic hearing at the St. Tammany Parish Courthouse in Covington on Friday, June 26, 1959, at which Governor Long won his release from the mental institution by firing the two hospital administrators who oversaw his confinement. "I'll bet from now on heads will be falling like the French Revolution," crowed one jubilant Long supporter on the forthcoming reprisals. "All he needs is a Napoleon hat." Podine Schoenberger, "Crowd Hails Long's Release; Chairs Leaped in Rush to Felicitate Governor," and Gordon B. Gsell, "Hospital Firings Precede Releasing of Gov. Long," *New Orleans Times-Picayune,* June 27, 1959, p. 18.

TAKE TWO: *Popes, Protests, and War, 1959–1966*

1. Bob Jones, email communication with Del, shared with author, July 31, 2013.

2. Unidentified document, probably a UPI wire report, describing arrests immediately after they occurred, provided to author by Del Hall.

3. John Steinbeck, *Travels with Charley in Search of America,* in *John Steinbeck: Travels with Charley and Later Novels, 1947–1962* (New York: Library of America, 2007), 935–37.

4. "Davis, Session Hailed by Group," *New Orleans Times-Picayune,* November 9, 1960, sec. 3, p. 21; ad, "In Answer to the Sisters of the Blessed Sacrament," ibid., February 15, 1961, sec. 1, p. 13; "Segregation Figures Are Excommunicated," ibid., April 17, 1962, p. 1; Save Our Nation—Christian Caucasian ad, *Times-Picayune/States-Item,* July 22, 1980, sec. 5, p. 5.

5. Bob Jones, email communication with Del, shared with author, July 31, 2013.

6. Ibid.

7. "Police Employ Tear Gas, Make Plaquemine Arrests," *New Orleans Times-Picayune,* August 20, 1963, sec. 1, p. 4; "News of the Week in Review," ibid., August 25, 1963, sec. 2, p. 4; "Farmer Vows Further Action; Prepare for Jail, He Tells Negroes," ibid., August 31, 1963, sec. 3, p. 18; "March Halted in Plaquemine; Mounted, Helmeted Police Chase Crowd," ibid., September 1, 1963, sec. 1, p. 4; "Mayor Wires RFK for Help," ibid., September 3, 1963, sec. 2, p. 2; "CORE's Acts of Violence in Plaquemine Reported," ibid., September 8, 1963, sec. 2, p. 2.

8. Lecture by James L. Farmer, recorded in 1983 by WNVT-TV Channel 53 and posted in 2012 by University of Mary Washington's Adventures in Digital History program, as Lecture 8 of "The James Farmer Lectures: A Civil Rights Leader's Reflections."

9. Bob Jones, email communication with Del, shared with author, July 31, 2013.

10. Ibid.

11. Bob Jones, email communication with Del, shared with author, August 7, 2013.

12. Mike Early, as quoted in "Bulletin Asks Your Views: Exchange of Opinions to Help All," *Radio-Television News Directors Association Bulletin,* December 1962, 10–11. Del's maneuver became something of a minor controversy among his peers. This trade bulletin framed the story as a question to its readers. "Would you—or your cameraman—hide a camera? Would they air photos under such circumstances? Would you put out a 2-page release on such 'fantastic' coverage utilizing such 'ingenuity?'" It is not known how readers responded.

13. "Sights and Sounds: WWL Films Pope Paul," newspaper clipping from Del Hall's personal files, likely from *New Orleans Times-Picayune,* September 1963.

14. "WWL-TV Special Projects Department, 1965–66," file copy 2, internal memo describing station's investment, provided to author by Del Hall.

15. Warren Commission, *Report of the President's Commission on the Assassination of President Kennedy,* chap. 7: "Lee Harvey Oswald: Background and Possible Motives," p. 407.

16. Pops did not rest in peace. He was buried in the plot where his wife's side of the family (the Cadys) entombed their dead, much to the displeasure of Del's aunts, who didn't want to be with the happy-go-lucky rascal in death any more than in life. So Del's mother later paid for Pops to be reburied in the Hall family plot in Cypress Grove Cemetery, next to his mother Minnie. In an only-in-New-Orleans moment, Del recalls that they "went to the cemetery for the exhumation, but it must have been lunchtime for the grave diggers, because we found his casket leaning on the edge of the grave to allow water to drain from it. And it was."

17. "Five Decades Later, Some JFK Files Still Sealed," *New Orleans Times-Picayune,* August 18, 2013, p. A-10.

18. Bob Jones, email communication with Del, shared with author, July 31, 2013.

19. "WWL Team Sent to Viet Nam for La. and Miss. Coverage," late 1965 newspaper clipping, sans date or name of paper.

20. Quoted from WWL-TV pamphlet, *This Season the People of New Orleans Received a Very Special Christmas Gift,* December 1965.

TAKE THREE: *King, Cronkite, and Kuralt, 1966–1974*

1. "Dr. Martin Luther King's Presentation," January 11, 1968, transcribed by Paul M. Logsdon, 1997, Ohio Northern University, Ada, Ohio, http://www.onu.edu/node/28509.

2. Their address at the time was 1960 Lincoln Park West—a high-rise apartment with a perfect view of the action.

3. City of Chicago report, *The Strategy of Confrontation: Chicago and the Democratic National Convention—1968* (1968), 40, 72.

4. Ibid., 29.

5. Official documentation of the riots, including Del's role in them, may be found in *The Walker Report, Rights in Conflict: The Violent Confrontation of Demonstrators and Police in the Parks and Streets of Chicago during the Week of the Democratic National Convention of 1968* (New York: Bantam, 1968), 171, 235–82, 311.

6. U.S. District Court, *Subpoena Duces Tecum* for Delos Hall, Case No. 69 CR 180, September 17, 1969, signed by all seven defendants; typewritten transcript of testimony of Del Hall in *United States of America versus David T. Dellinger et al.*; both provided to author by Del Hall.

7. In fact, a little too much cinematography went into the peddler piece. CBS wanted a more even balance between images and words. "So, I believe CBS killed the piece," Del says. "Then we went to Texas to film a swimming pig."

8. Eddie swore up and down that he once ran into Martin Luther King at a hotel "one morning, coming out of someone else's room—a woman's." True or not, no one believed him.

9. "Del Hall in Moscow . . . On Assignment for CBS News," *Cinema Perspectives,* ed. Charles Lipow, Summer 1973, Los Angeles, California; cover story.

10. Del Hall, "Notes: "Mexico—Drugs," confidential report plus documentation prepared for CBS News, January–February 1972; original provided by Del Hall to author.

11. "Vet Investigative Reporter Jay McMullen Dies," CBS News, March 10, 2012, http://www.cbsnews.com/news/vet-investigative-reporter-jay-mcmullen-dies/, visited September 23, 2014.

12. "United States District Court—District of Rhode Island, Delos Hall, Plaintiff, vs. Bell Helicopter, Textron et al., Defendants, CA NO. 76-0119," Deposition of Charles Kuralt, April 28, 1978, pp. 6–9.

TAKE FOUR: *Near Death and New Life, 1974–1987*

1. Letter, Del Hall to Verne Lawyer, December 5, 1977, filed in legal binder, "Del Hall: From Stardom to Boredom—A Shattered Career," Verne Lawyer, Attorney, Fleming Building, Des Moines, Iowa, 1978, provided to author by Del Hal. Other materials cited include the introduction to this binder, and a letter by Philip K. McCullough, M.D.

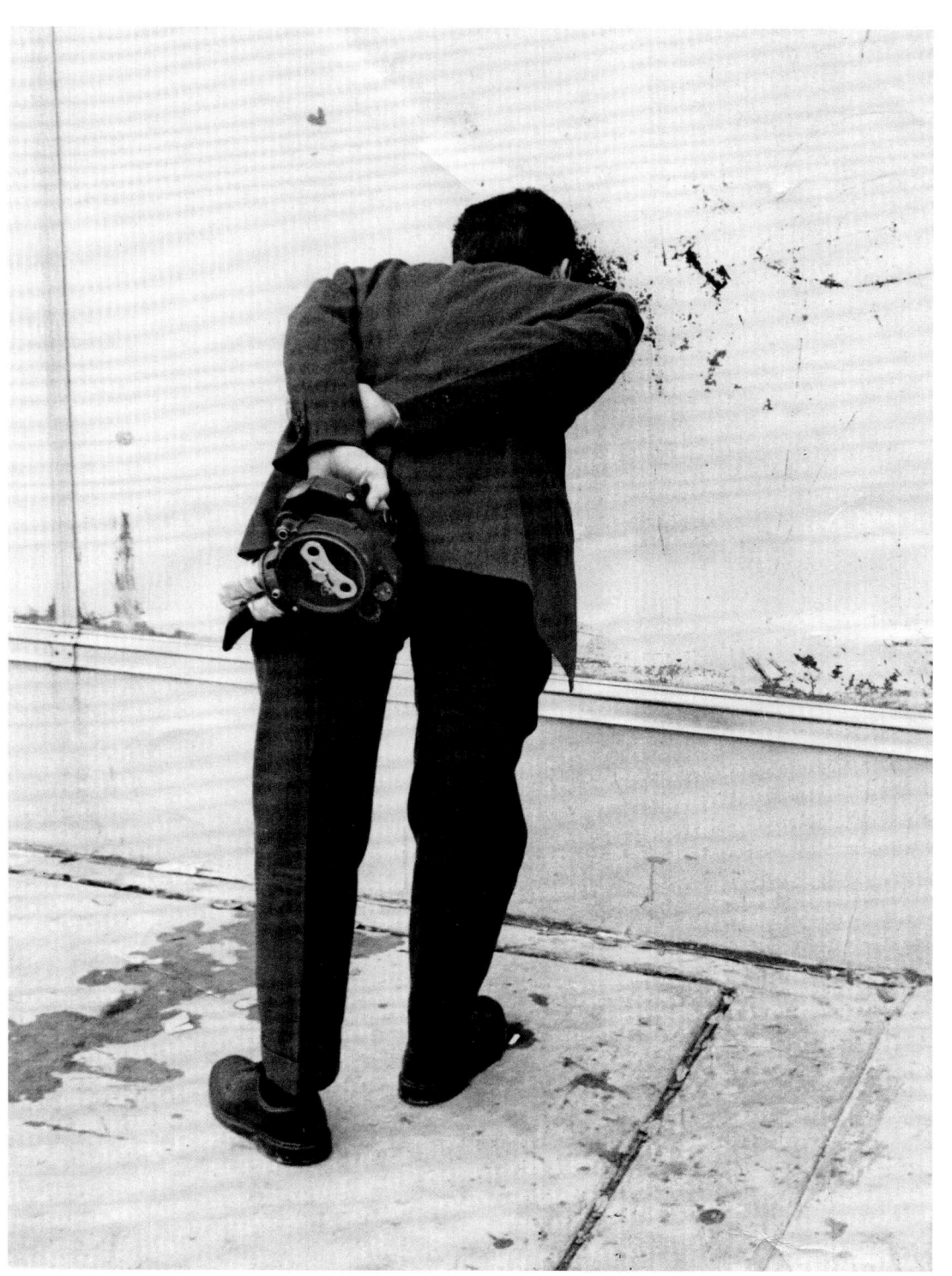